Remnants of Refusal

SUNY series in Feminist Criticism and Theory

Michelle A. Massé, editor

Remnants of Refusal

Feminist Affect, National Trauma

ERIN SHEVAUGN SCHLUMPF

SUNY PRESS

Cover Credit: *Fragment* (1933) designed by Dorothy M. Larcher. Courtesy of the Cleveland Museum of Art.

Published by State University of New York Press, Albany

EU GPSR Authorised Representative:
Logos Europe, 9 rue Nicolas Poussin, 17000, La Rochelle, France
contact@logoseurope.eu

For information, contact State University of New York Press, Albany, NY
www.sunypress.edu

Library of Congress Cataloging-in-Publication Data

Name: Schlumpf, Erin Shevaugn, author.
Title: Remnants of refusal : feminist affect, national trauma / Erin
    Shevaugn Schlumpf.
Description: Albany : State University of New York Press, [2025]. | Series:
    SUNY series in feminist criticism and theory | Includes bibliographical
    references and index.
Identifiers: LCCN 2024042772 | ISBN 9798855802146 (hardcover : alk. paper) |
    ISBN 9798855802160 (ebook)
Subjects: LCSH: Women in literature. | Collective trauma in literature. | Affect
    (Psychology) in literature. | French literature—History and criticism. | Chinese
    literature—History and criticism. | Women in motion pictures. | Collective
    trauma in motion pictures. | Affect (Psychology) in motion pictures. | Motion
    pictures—France—History. | Motion pictures—China—History. | Feminist
    theory. | LCGFT: Literary criticism. | Film criticism.
Classification: LCC PQ145.8.W6 S35 2025 | DDC 791.43/6522—dc23/eng/20241214
LC record available at https://lccn.loc.gov/2024042772

Contents

Acknowledgments

It's difficult to point to the exact moment when I began this book. I suspect this is common with first books, which so often—and as is true in my case—grow out of one's dissertation. But even before the dissertation, perhaps as early as choosing an undergraduate major in comparative literature with a focus on French and Chinese, the first seeds of this project were sown. It's daunting and humbling to account for all of those who have helped my book and me reach this stage.

I'll begin with my teachers and advisers. I'd like to thank Katharine Conley, my undergraduate thesis adviser, who imparted an important piece of advice that I now pass on to my students. As a scholar of Surrealism, Kate encouraged me to dream about my research. Of course, one must read and write, but also let the ideas percolate. See what your unconscious generates when you believe you have put the work aside and are engaged in something else entirely. To me this has meant that ideas sometimes turn up in surprising sources and that—even when I'm not thinking about it—my research is constantly alive in my body and engaged with the world. Having focused entirely on literature in college, it was not until my first year of graduate school that my interests grew to encompass cinema. My first term as a graduate student, I took a French seminar with Tom Conley in cartographic theory. My final paper was about Godard. Since that time, Tom has been a source of encouragement, support, and inventiveness. His emails always contain good-humored puns and well-chosen quotes from Rabelais or Montaigne. He helped me brainstorm the current title of this book. I am lucky to have benefited from the generous and rigorous guidance of my dissertation adviser, Susan Rubin Suleiman, who read each draft of my dissertation with extreme care and pushed me to imagine it as a book. Her writing on French literature and history has been an important influence on my project. David Wang's deep interest in Chinese literature and history has also served as an inspiration. His wonderful graduate seminars in Chinese literature introduced me to Wang Anyi and so much more. Finally, Karen Thornber provided invaluable guidance as a member of my dissertation committee.

After graduate school, my book went through various stages of necessary metamorphosis thanks to the suggestions and comments I received from other scholars. Talks at Penn State and the American University of Paris provided helpful feedback. I'd like to thank the editors at *differences: A Journal of Feminist Cultural Studies* for printing an earlier version of the first chapter: "Historical Melancholy, Feminine Allegory," *differences* 27, no. 3 (2016): 20–44. I appreciate the invitation from Catherine Clark to present on a panel about Sino-French Cinema with Ling Zhang and moderated by Dudley Andrew. My work also benefited after I presented an earlier form of my third chapter on a panel about reversibility organized by Julia Ng and Jan Mieszkowski. After that panel, I decided to completely reimagine the third chapter with women authors, so I'm grateful that Julia and Jan included my essay about exhaustion in Samuel Beckett and Ge Fei in a special issue on reversibility for the *CR: The New Centennial Review*: "Exhaustion: In Defiance of Homogeneous Empty Time," *CR: The New Centennial Review* 21, no. 1 (2021): 237–69. Erica Stein and Jennifer Cazenave suggested useful revisions to my book proposal. Finally, Yomi Braester, Hollis Griffin, Julia Alekseyeva, and Jen Hui Bon Hoa graciously agreed to come all the way to Athens, Ohio, to participate in my book workshop. The feedback they provided helped me to reconceptualize key ideas in the manuscript.

Fellow classmates, colleagues, and friends have helped me hone my ideas and lifted my spirits over the years. I'd like to thank Satoru Hashimoto, Jie Li, Ying Qian, Andy Rodekohr, and Brian Skerrett who included me in their East Asian Languages and Civilizations dissertation writing group even though I was from Comparative Literature. I also appreciated being welcomed by Romance Language and Literatures' graduate students Stefanie Goyette, François Proulx, Lauren Ravalico, and Tali Zechory with whom I taught language courses, served on literature committees, and indulged in choruses of Celine Dion. My compatriots in Harvard Comp Lit, especially Jen Hui Bon Hoa, Stephanie Frampton, Jamey Graham, Christine Lee, and Anita Nikkanen, have continued to offer endless council and friendship. It took until my fellowship year in Paris to become close with Ian Fleishman and he made that year and my life infinitely richer. After graduate school,

I learned so much from Azadeh Yamini-Hamedani and Melek Ortabasi at Simon Fraser University and Catherine Clepper at Seattle University. My colleagues at Ohio University have been incredibly supportive and cheered me on as I secured a final contract for this book and was promoted to associate professor with tenure.

This book wouldn't be seeing the light of day without my SUNY Press editor, Rebecca Colesworthy, and series editor, Michelle Massé. I cannot thank them enough for embracing my project. I am also grateful to the readers of my manuscript, whose advice enriched and enlarged my book's scholarly archive and helped me to better shape the structure. This publication was subsidized in part by Harvard Studies in Comparative Literature.

Family support has meant so much to me. My parents, Jacob Schlumpf and Pamela McMahan, and my sister Brightin Rose have always been sources of encouragement and love. I never thought I'd meet my intellectual soulmate until I fell in love with Ofer Eliaz. Ofer's words are all over this book and they make it even dearer to me. This book is for Ofer and our baby, Francesca Josephine.

Introduction

Emily Xiaobai Tang's (唐晓白) 2001 film *Conjugation* (動詞變位; *Dongci bianwei*) is the earliest film by a mainland Chinese director to reference the June 4, 1989, Massacre at Tiananmen Square.[1] However, this reference to national trauma and its immediate erasure is largely implicit. The first three titles in *Conjugation*—each followed by a black screen—locate the events and set the tone for what follows in the diegesis: the year 1989, winter, Beijing. The score accompanies these titles, reed instruments and a human voice calling to each other as if from the bottom of distant wells. Instead of showing the violence at Tiananmen, the film takes place half a year later and alludes to the trauma through symptoms manifested in the characters' behavior: their resistance to optimism, their adherence to the dead—in a word, their melancholy.

Conjugation's melancholic tarrying between past and present exemplifies a discourse of feminist refusal that I will chart across a series of works of film and literature over the course of this book. This feminist refusal takes its form in affective responses to historical mourning in France and China in the aftermath of two national traumas: the 1940–44 German Occupation and the 1989 Tiananmen Square Massacre. In each case, the events associated with the trauma were either initially or completely erased from the historical record by the official discourses of the countries' governments and an unwritten code of public secrecy adopted by much of the citizenry.[2] And, in each case, these three affects—melancholy, ambivalence, and exhaustion—allow the films and literary texts to express mourning without breaking the taboo of direct representation. This mourning, as I will show, is most frequently borne by and through the bodies of women and illustrates a broader feminist counter-narrative to national progress.

1

To make sense of the multilayered history of silence and refusal in Tang's *Conjugation* and other works of film and literature from France and China, I plunge into melancholy in order to reveal a new theory of affective historiography. Melancholia, Sigmund Freud tells us, "behaves like an open wound."[3] If left untreated, an open wound—a physical or psychic trauma—does not heal. Instead, the wound worsens, spreading infection throughout the body, and producing new symptoms. When a historical situation remains unresolved across generations, history also leaves such open wounds in its wake. According to trauma theory, these open wounds can appear not only in the lives of individuals but also in the histories of nations where they function as historical traumas: unsettled conflicts that shatter the sense of a coherent narrative of history.[4] Moreover, historical traumas are prolonged when nations resist mourning by looking too stridently toward the future: adopting policies promoting aggressive economic expansion, speeding stubbornly forward on an express train that loses sight of the past.

Such is the case following of the uneven spread of neoliberal globalization—West to East, North to South—across the globe up to the present. Although, as David Harvey explains, what is today termed neoliberalism—that "theory of political economic practices that proposes that human well-being can best be advanced by liberating individual entrepreneurial freedom and skills within an institutional framework characterized by strong private property rights, free markets, and free trade"—has only been widely adopted since the 1970s, the beginning of the "neoliberal turn" can be cited following the end of the Second World War.[5] Immanuel Wallerstein's world-system theory offers an explanation of the geographic movement of capital, and stresses its disproportionate and inequitable nature: "The key factor to note is that within a capitalist world-system, all states cannot 'develop' simultaneously *by definition*, since the system functions by virtue of having unequal core and peripheral regions."[6] From "core" to "periphery," the effects and products of globalization pile up and conceal recent national traumas while simultaneously generating new anxieties: the widening gap between rich and poor, the dramatic transformation of urban space that displaces some residents and ghettoizes others, and the allure of new consumer goods that demand an ever higher wage (or, more frequently a double wage). Whereas the architects of the global economy work to bury the past in order to pave the ground for highways, airports, and office towers that will service the new era of intensified accumulation, some works of film and literature register a resistance to these changes by giving form to the affective scars that such "productive" silencing leaves on the bodies of the populace. This book argues that film and literature can thus reveal remnants of refusal, echoes and afterimages of the past that have been left in suspension between the rhetoric of constant progress and the affective persistence of the unmourned past.

The word remnant has a longer history in the scholarship of historical trauma. In his writings on Auschwitz, Giorgio Agamben famously describes the witness who survives to give testimony as all that remains (*quel resto*), or the remnant, of the human: "The paradox here is that if the only one bearing witness to the human is the one whose humanity has been wholly destroyed, this means that the identity between human and inhuman is never perfect and that it is not truly possible to destroy the human, that something always *remains. The witness is this remnant*."[7] Those who did not survive Auschwitz—the dead, but also those desubjectified witnesses who saw "the Gorgon" and "touched the bottom"—have passed outside of language.[8] The survivor who attempts to bear witness for the dead or the desubjectified cannot make up for the gap in speech left by their silence: "The trace of that to which no one has borne witness, which language believes itself to transcribe, is not the speech of language. The speech of language is born where language is no longer in the beginning, where language falls away from it simply to bear witness: 'It was not light, but was sent to bear witness to light.'"[9] Agamben's text theorizes the impossible task facing Nazi death camp survivors like Primo Levi who lived to bear witness to their experience and who attempt to speak for those left behind. While the works of literature and film under examination in this book do not concentrate on narrating the experiences of historical trauma, they resist forgetting by confronting official silence with a speech broken between past and present.[10] Such remnants solidify into aesthetic acts of refusal and create a new historical space: that which is *between* the past and the future, without being a present tense, a "time out of joint" in the words of Jacques Derrida's hauntology.[11] The feelings of melancholy and its vicissitudes of ambivalence and exhaustion appear as such remnants of refusal registered in film and literature: enunciations of protest to the demand to forget the past and bow to the dollar-green god of "progress." If we read the form that melancholy takes in texts of different national origin, we begin to see it as a way of feeling together and structuring a wider refusal to historical forgetting.

Remnants of Refusal: Feminist Affect, National Trauma argues for a theory of such forms of feeling and refusing together. It analyzes a set of shared affective responses to national trauma and the rise of neoliberal globalization from France in the thirty years following the German Occupation (1940–1944) and the conclusion of the Second World War, and from China in the years since the June 4, 1989, Tiananmen Square Massacre.[12] After the Second World War, the French government immediately repudiated the country's collaboration with the German enemy and engaged in a rhetoric of constant progress. The dominant social discourse centered on economic growth, consumerism, and urban development, fostering a concern with the new and a distaste for the past, as well as distracting the people from the violent, contemporary fallout of French imperialism. After the Tiananmen Square Massacre, the Chinese government immediately condemned the student and worker protesters as hooligans and promoted a rhetoric of constant progress. The dominant social discourse, likewise, privileged economic growth, consumerism, and urban development, and discouraged backward glances at the recent national violence or sideways glances at the victims of the contemporary capitalist buildup. In the aftermath of national trauma, therefore, many of the mistakes made by the French were revisited on the Chinese. It is in France and China that we find examples of the explicit work of historical erasure after historical trauma, as well as the affective responses to this erasure. However, this is not a case of straightforward repetition: in the French texts I examine, the affects are tinged with a certain ratio of hope and a utopian longing for a radically different future, whereas in the Chinese texts, the affects give voice to ghosts of the living past and the continuing burden of history. Though the authors of these works lived through the periods of the Occupation and the Tiananmen protests, respectively, as I've previously suggested, their work does not present a conventional account of bearing witness. Instead of locating national trauma in narratives describing historical "traumatic" events, I take melancholy, ambivalence, and exhaustion as the traces of traumas that seem to evade any single source or direct representation.

Trauma, in these cases, makes its presence known by an absence of explicit reference to any specific event. Emerging during the Trente Glorieuses in France (1945–1975) and what is sometimes called the post-New Era (後新時期; *hou xinshiqi*) in China (1990–the present), novels by Marguerite Duras and Wang Anyi (王安憶), Nathalie Sarraute and Chen Ran (陈染), and films by Emily Xiaobai Tang, Jean-Luc Godard, Agnès Varda, Jia Zhangke (賈樟柯), Guo Xiaolu (郭小櫓), and Cao Fei (曹斐) reveal remnants of refusal in the tension between present national circumstances and the past.[13] These affective expressions are necessarily both national and global and offer up multiple visions of the contemporary world. In fact, by bringing together France after 1945 and China after 1989, I argue for an understanding of historical trauma that entails the relation between different periods and contexts, and thus is not locatable in any single event. Affective responses emerge out of a longer period and a series of rhyming events: not just the Occupation, but the years of economic growth during the Trente Glorieuses, as well as the Algerian War and the fallout of May '68; not just the Tiananmen protests, but the introduction of a free-market system and the consequences of China's emergence as a global economic superpower, as well as the handover of Hong Kong. Extending geographically from West to East and historically from the end of the Second World War to the present, trauma transpires durationally and transnationally. However, by resisting any leveling of the linguistic and historical differences between nations, my hope is that this book upholds a practice of comparativism that is sensitive to, in the words of Emily Apter, "the importance of non-translation, mistranslation, incomparability and untranslatability."[14] With Emily Tang's *Conjugation*, and throughout this book, I disentangle the way that languages and images misspeak in order to speak otherwise about the past and present, the national and transnational.

Emily Tang's *Conjugation*: A Case Study of Chinese and French Coupling

Within the context of Chinese film history, Emily Tang, like many of the other Chinese filmmakers addressed in this book, is considered part of the so-called urban generation: independent mainland filmmakers emerging in the 1990s who employ a combination of melodrama, critical realism, and documentary form to capture stories of Chinese cities undergoing rapid transformation.[15] These filmmakers experienced both Maoist and post-Maoist China, the opening up of China to the rest of the world and the Tiananmen Massacre; their work often reckons with these aspects of Chinese history in the context of China's more recent transformations. Tang's *Conjugation* follows a cohort of young people—four men and one woman—all university students or recent graduates, all struggling to make their way financially and professionally in the oppressive atmosphere of

Beijing under martial law in the winter of 1989. One former member of the group is missing: a young man known by his nickname Foot Finger, who disappeared amidst the violence at Tiananmen Square.

In China, the word "conjugation" (*dongci bianwei*) occurs in foreign language classes and textbooks. After all, Chinese, unlike, say, French, does not require verbs to correspond to different subjects or tenses. The Chinese *dongci bianwei* doesn't have the double meaning of "cohabitation" found in its English or French (*conjugaison*) translations; although, the film makes use of this double meaning, making it an implicitly multilingual piece, a piece aware of its own translations. "Conjugation," as the title of Emily Tang's film, works as a stamp of foreignness and triggers an estrangement from the Sinophone. Tang's film makes use of the foreign in order to suggest the alienation of its characters from their local reality.

The film primarily engages with the affective relationship these Chinese university students or recent university graduates have to their city, while also suggesting the impact of government policy changes in the aftermath of the June Fourth Massacre. We learn that the young couple at the center of the film, Xiao Qing (Zhao Hong) and Guo Song (Qian Yu), met during the Tiananmen protests, a time characterized as full of passion and romantic potential. Six months later, they have rented a room in a traditional Beijing *hutong*. However, the daily patterns of their lives make it difficult to sustain the zeal they experienced at the beginning of their relationship. Guo Song has been forced to abandon his burgeoning career as a scientist to work at a factory. Over the course of the film, he quits this job, and—faced with the monthly obligation to pay rent—is compelled to improvise: peddling inexpensive scarves in the street or helping a friend convert his café into a hot pot restaurant. Xiao Qing—still a college student with an interest in French—starts working at a café and occasionally prostituting herself in order to contribute to the household income. In the evening, Guo and Xiao must tread the line between absenting themselves from their room when police drop by to inspect their residence cards (since it is illegal for the unmarried to cohabitate) and avoiding getting caught breaking curfew (one of the features of martial law). Tang's use of long takes provides a map of the city structured by presence and absence. We are shown an empty street, a wall in the *hutong*, before characters enter and then exit the frame. This technique allows the city to emerge as its own subject, while its present inhabitants mingle with those—like Foot Finger—who've departed, whose

invisibility the pauses in pregnant space make legible. The long takes create a city of ghosts, a kind of historical palimpsest where the absences of
the (here, recent) past displace the obviousness or finality of the image.

A sequence occurring at the halfway point, the temporal heart, of
the film brings us to a French class at a Beijing university. This scene,
months removed from the events of Tiananmen, demonstrates further
what I mean by a discourse of feminist refusal. In the classroom, the
voice of the French teacher labels, from off-screen, a series of slides
that are shown to the students. "C'est la cité de Paris," she begins. "L'arc
de Triomphe," she continues. In an earlier classroom sequence, we have
seen this teacher, played by the film's director, Emily Tang, seated in
front of a blackboard filled with the past perfect form of the verb *parler*
(figures I.1, I.2, and I.3). When we see Tang as language instructor, the
film underlines the role of both film director and language instructor as
guides; both directors and language instructors indicate how to understand
and communicate, employing different forms of "speaking," linguistic
and cinematic, while demonstrating that for Tang the two can overlap
in both purpose and form. Placing herself within the frame, underlining
her position at the head of the class and as director of the film, Tang
signals that the mode of address in *Conjugation* will be inflected by her
positionality as a woman, mediated between languages, and—given the
tense in which *parler* is conjugated—in dialogue with the past. In the
classroom sequence beginning with slides of Paris, the film also comments on the role of director Tang as master of narrative: juxtaposing
images in order to form a plot, making the plot the topography of narrative meaning. Likewise, through her slides, language instructor Tang
designates sites in the national landscape in which the French linguistic
vehicle operates and constructs sense.[16] In the first two slides of the "city
of Paris," the fact that Tang uses the word *la cité*—which usually designates either a medieval citadel or a modern day housing project, the
so-called ghetto—instead of the word more commonly employed, *la ville*,
reminds us that both language and image can be imprecise, mislead, or
sometimes contain a partial, broken truth. These two scenes thus allude
to the fact that something has "slipped between the cracks" of language
and image: instead of the straightforward relationship between signifier
and signified we confront something awry, something leading away from
the light and back into the shadows, away from expression and to the
realm of allusion and the unspoken.

Figure I.1. Slide accompanying teacher Tang's explanation, "C'est la cité de Paris."
Source: Tang, Emily Xiaobai, dir. *Conjugation* (動詞變位; *Dongci bianwei*). 2001;
Hong Kong, People's Republic of China: Tang Films, 2001. Digital file.

Figure I.2. Second slide showing "La cité de Paris." *Source*: Tang, Emily Xiaobai,
dir. *Conjugation* (動詞變位; *Dongci bianwei*). 2001; Hong Kong, People's Republic
of China: Tang Films. Digital file.

Figure I.3. Director Emily Xiaobai Tang as teacher Tang in front of a blackboard with the past perfect conjugation of the French verb *parler* (to speak). *Source*: Tang, Emily Xiaobai, dir. *Conjugation* (動詞變位; Dongci bianwei). 2001; Hong Kong, People's Republic of China: Tang Films, 2001. Digital file.

For Xiao Qing, France and French images signify objects of fantasy and romantic longing. However, the overall effect of these francophone refractions in Tang's Chinese film (*la cité* as opposed to *la ville*, so to speak) is not nostalgic. Instead, Tang emphasizes the impossibility of these French fragments cohering into a perfect image of the present or past. Paris offers itself as a tourist destination, a playground for many of its rich and middle class, and an obstacle course for many of its poor, and as such Beijing can only be layered over it, traces of history written between the lines of China's emerging role in the global world order. Think of one of Beijing's own *cités*, the Forbidden City, the walled palace of the final two dynasties of Chinese emperors. The Northern gate, *Tian'anmen* (天安門), literally "The Gate of Heavenly Peace," is the Southern end of Tiananmen Square, a site of shifting national spectacles for over 360 years. When teacher Tang explains to the students that they have work to make up since "our semester was disturbed," she, too, indirectly references the site of Tiananmen Square and the early termination of the spring semester as a result of six weeks of student and worker demonstrations culminating on the morning of June 4, 1989. As Dai Jinhua writes of this date, known around the world variously as June Fourth, the Tiananmen Square Incident, or the Tiananmen Square Massacre, "the Chinese finally came face to face with the secret of the modern governing order—peaceful demonstrations crushed by tanks and troops."[17] Teacher Tang's choice of verbiage, "disturbed" (打亂; *daluan*), however, mimics the language Chinese officials used to erase the events and to shift the blame, the "turmoil" (動亂; *dongluan*). By revealing gaps in French language, location, and history, *Conjugation* makes use of the foreign to speak about the recent, repressed national trauma as well as the impossibilities that are made visible by an increasingly globalized world. A key interest of the theory of historiography I am proposing in this book is that historical traumas are repressed in one language but often appear clandestinely through the embedding of a foreign language, image, or text.

Tang's film has no need to make use of flashbacks of the protest or Massacre; what the past has obliterated is hiding in plain sight. What is more, by referring to the past trauma through shards of dialogue but never through direct visual representation, Tang points to its official silencing. Both Xiao Qing's study of French and a passing reference to the bicentennially of the French Revolution allow *Conjugation* to develop a parallel history, gesturing further back temporally and wider geographically. The spiritual conjugation of China and France in the summer of 1989 when the protesters took up the *Internationale* as their anthem has weakened in the months following the Massacre. In one sequence, Xiao Qing sits on her bed and looks through binoculars at the ceiling, which is plastered with colored cards covered in French verbs. These images render visible the gap between the idealism in the conversation Xiao Qing and her fellow protesters at Tiananmen attempted and the government's response: this language is out of reach, unspeakable, to be admired rather than used, consigned to the status of colorful decor (figure I.4).

In its melancholic wandering in and between languages—a form of positivist refusal shared by all the works of film and literature under discussion in this book—Tang's film allows layers of historical meaning and contradiction to surface. Furthermore, behind this official "translation" of the events of Tiananmen when traced over images of Paris, we can hear echoes of France's own acts of historical erasure following national trauma: the initial repression of the French collaboration with Germany as a result of the German Occupation during the Second World War; the long silence and delayed apology about its deportation of tens of thousands of French Jews. This book presents a reading of these two moments to

Figure I.4. French verb conjugations as seen through Xiao Qing's binoculars. *Source*: Tang, Emily Xiaobai, dir. *Conjugation* (動詞變位; Dongci bianwei). 2001; Hong Kong, People's Republic of China: Tang Films, 2001. Digital file.

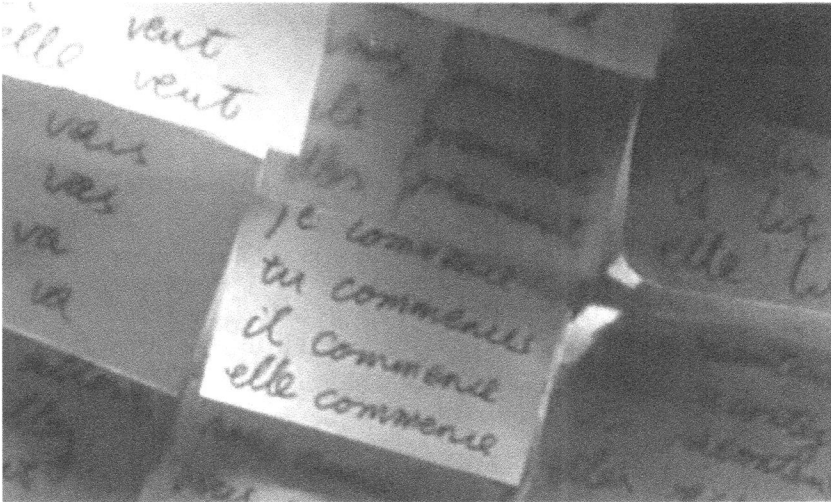

perform a history of the backward glance: looking *from China to France* in order to see how silenced histories become visible when they are made to speak and translate one another.

Sino-French Intervention

The argument that this book presents through its juxtaposition of French and Chinese texts, its layering of French and Chinese language, and its historical and geographical movement between midcentury France and turn of the twenty-first-century China, belongs alongside scholarship in the growing field of Sino-French studies. While much Sino-French scholarship works to question the binary and hierarchal constitution of France and China, I hope to further push the boundaries of the field by uniting French and Chinese texts that speak together about history in a shared language of affect rather than relying on more traditional modes of comparison.

A survey of the current work in this field helps to clarify my unique intervention. In Michelle Bloom's book, *Contemporary Sino-French Cinemas: Absent Fathers, Banned Books, and Red Balloons* she investigates what she classifies as hybrid works by filmmakers originally from Taiwan (Tsai Ming-liang, Cheng Yu-chieh, and Hou Hsiao-hsien) and Mainland China (Dai Sijie, Jia Zhangke, and Emily Xiaobai Tang) that reveal a relationship to the French via funding, personnel, intertextuality, bilingual dialogue, setting, themes, characters, or some combination of these elements.[18] Bloom's chapter on Emily Tang's *Conjugation* and Jia Zhangke's *The World* (a film treated in chapter 2 of this book) describes their connection to the French as one of imitation. "In both films," she writes, "imitation imports Frenchness into China in ways that are neither original nor fruitful within the diegetic worlds because they rely on icons and stereotypes . . . the location, culture, language, and people remain mythic, unattainable others for mainlanders trapped in exploitative, stifling conditions."[19] Bloom's approach to *Conjugation* aligns with one of the larger projects of her book: calling for the Sino-French to be included as an expansion and enrichment of francophone studies. As my book focuses on the relationship between feminist affective forms in film and literature and historical trauma, my reading emphasizes different aspects of Tang's film; I draw attention to how *Conjugation*'s French refractions give voice to the recent repressed history of the June Fourth Massacre as well as the characters' melancholic alienation from their present circumstances in post-Tiananmen Beijing.

The genealogy of Sino-French film and literature provides a framework within which to situate and contrast this book's historiographic engagement. A highlight of Bloom's work is her succinct history of Sino-French cinema, beginning with Georges Méliès's 1904 orientalist *Le Thaumaturge chinois* (*Tchin-Chao: The Chinese Conjurer*), surveying a number of French Maoist films (including Jean-Luc Godard's 1967 *La Chinoise* and Jean Yanne's 1974 *Les Chinois à Paris*), providing an illuminating analysis of the first China-France co-production, Wang Kia-Yi and Roger Pigat's *Le Cerf-volant du bout du monde* (*Kite at the End of the World*, 1958), and concluding with a model of how to further broaden the category of the Sino-French. Here, Bloom draws from the popular 2006 omnibus film *Paris, je t'aime*, concentrating on a short film about one of Paris's Chinatowns in its thirteenth arrondissement, "Porte de Choisy," by Christopher Doyle, an Australian better known for his cinematography for Wong Kar-Wai's most celebrated films. Bloom explains: "The relative insignificance of a director's nationality explains the Sino-Frenchness of the 'Porte de Choisy,' but the same would apply even more interestingly to a film in which another major element, such as the setting, were either [*sic*] Francophone nor Sinophone. The 'Porte de Choisy' vignette underscores the non-binarity of the Sino-French."[20] This book shares Bloom's goal of eliminating a binary or hierarchical relationship in its discussion of the Chinese and French. Though all the films and literature under consideration in this book are by Chinese or French authors, I argue that we might extrapolate from their affective responses to the suppression of national trauma broader claims about the effects of feminist refusal on a global scale.

The lineage of Sino-French literary relations benefits from careful treatment in Rosalind Silvester and Guillaume Thouroude's edited volume, *Traits chinois/lignes francophones: Écritures, Images, Cultures*. Yingde Zhang's essay, "La Francophonie chinoise d'aujourd'hui et l'héritage du général Tcheng Ki-Tong," for example, provides a useful history of the first Chinese writer in French. General Tcheng Ki-Tong (Chen Jitong), whom Zhang describes as a "pure product of Western affairs reform movements begun following the Opium Wars (1840–1860)," served as a Chinese emissary in Paris and published eight works in French between 1884 and 1904.[21] Of note is Tcheng's 1891 novel *Le Roman de l'homme jaune* (*The Novel of the Yellow Man*), which Zhang cites as the first modern Chinese novel despite its being written in French.[22] Zhang's essay, like Bloom's book, underscores the non-binarity of the Sino-French, noting that Tcheng's written reflections were "nourished by the dream of the 'great unity' of the world (*datong*), or of 'one family united under heaven' (*tianxia yi jia*)."[23] However, Silvester and Thouroude's volume departs from Bloom's book in its choice of terminology, privileging "la francophonie chinoise," or the Franco-Chinese, over the Sino-French. This narrows their scope to French-language works (literature, film) by authors of Chinese origin. The Sino-French, by contrast, encompasses a potentially larger group of works whose authors' homelands are either Sinophone (which includes the many Chinese-speaking countries and regions beyond Mainland China) or French (not simply the *métropole*, but former and current French colonies). Bloom focuses on Chinese and Taiwanese films with French connections, but other Sino-French research emphasizes French works inspired by the Chinese.[24] This book departs from previous Sino-French studies in that the connections I develop between Chinese and French texts infrequently rely on an influence story (how a Chinese work, say, derives from or references an earlier French work, or vice versa). Rather, as I will clarify in more specificity in my chapter summaries at the close of this introduction, my process of uniting Chinese and French texts relies on points of correspondence in their feminist, affective responses to historical trauma and the rise of neoliberal globalization.

Existing Sino-French and Franco-Chinese scholarship, of course, offers far more than illustrations of French or Chinese originals and Franco-Chinese, Chinese, or French derivatives. In Shuangyi Li's first monograph, *Proust, China and Intertextual Engagement: Translation and Transcultural Dialogue*, for example, he engages with the relationship of Proust's *La Recherche* (*In Search of Lost Time*) to works by Chinese (Wang Xiaobo, Yu Hua, and Wei Hui) and Franco-Chinese (François Cheng) writers by engaging the theoretical questions of translation, intertextuality, and transcultural dialogue. He asserts, "The analytical focus is on the cross-cultural dialogue between Proust's *La Recherche*—the *hypotext*—and its multiple Chinese translations and novelistic *hypertexts* (written in either Chinese or French), a dialogue underpinned by a wealth of ideologically inflected textual relations: mistranslation, appropriation, adaptation, citation, parody, pastiche, and rewriting."[25] Li's work thus differs from much of the scholarship on "influence," in that he focuses on the Chinese and Franco-Chinese authors' engagement with Proust in their *hypertexts*, rather than beginning with the *hypotext* (*La Recherche*). He considers his method to be one of lateral thinking as it encompasses the variety of unpredictable results of cross-cultural interconnection with a canonical text, rather than prioritizing the vertical impact of *hypotext* to *hypertext*. To offer a specific example, in his book's chapter on François Cheng's *Le Dit de Tianyi*, Li illuminates how the use of Daoist vocabulary in the novel in concert with structuralist and post-structuralist readings of Proust allow for both Chinese and French readers to reconsider their own cultural productions. He explains that this "bilateral process results in an initiation of an intercultural dialogue, in which readers from both cultures are compelled to participate, activating the knowledge of their own cultures while learning about the other."[26] I hope that my reading of French and Chinese texts will also generate intercultural dialogue about the way that affective form gives utterance to feminist refusal when confronting the silencing of historical trauma in different national contexts.

Li's next book, *Travel, Translation and Transmedia Aesthetics: Franco-Chinese Literature and Visual Arts in a Global Age*, continues to investigate François Cheng, and includes new analysis of the work of Gao Xingjian, Dai Sijie, and Shan Sa. Though these writers were all born in China and immigrated to France, Li emphasizes that the geographic scope of Franco-Chinese artistry now extends beyond these two nations and can be considered a global phenomenon, drawing them into broader discussions of world literature.[27] All four of these authors share an uneasy relationship to the Chinese state: Cheng left China during the Chinese Civil War, while Gao, Dai, and Shan fled following Tiananmen. All four create both literary and visual artwork, and Li's book explores their work across three themes: translation, which he began in his first book, as well as travel, and transmedia aesthetics.[28] Translation and intermediality (of which transmediality is a subcategory) are also central to my methodology, though Li's theorization of these areas differs from mine.

My book constitutes a significant intervention into the field of Sino-French studies by foregrounding the impact of historical trauma in France and China: simultaneously specifying the unique circumstances in these two countries and indicating a series of shared feminist, affective responses in cultural production.[29] While I hope to persuade the reader that my analysis of French and Chinese texts offers a new model of speaking together across culture, I do not lose sight of the singular national positions from which these works of film and literature emerge.

National Enunciations

The story of this book begins in France in June 1940, when the nation bowed with the Second Armistice at Compiègne. Thus began the German Occupation of France, the first national trauma of vital concern to this book. After the Fall of France, the German occupiers dominated politically, while Pétain's Vichy government administered locally. Though the Resistance, both at home in France and from the headquarters of Charles de Gaulle in England, continued to try to undermine the Vichy government and fight for French liberation, most citizens acquiesced, some even reluctantly or willingly collaborating with the new regime. Vichy and its collaborators were responsible for the imprisonment of 135,000 people and the internment of 70,000, the dismissal of 35,000 civil servants, and the deportation of 76,000 Jews, of which only 3 percent survived.[30] The blame for this rests on the shoulders of the French, as well as on those of the German invader.

De Gaulle's famous speech on August 25, 1944, set the tone for the dogma of *résistancialisme*, which dominated for many years following Liberation: "Paris! Paris outraged! Paris shattered! Paris martyred! But

Paris freed! Freed by itself, freed by its people with the help of the French armies, with the support and assistant of all of France, the fighting France, the only France, true France, eternal France."[31] Not only does de Gaulle neglect to mention the fundamental part that the Allies played in the Liberation of Paris, he also exaggerates the role played by the majority of Frenchmen. By claiming that "all of France" struggled to achieve freedom from the German occupier, de Gaulle dismisses the efforts of those who actively resisted the invader, while simultaneously rectifying the national image. This discourse of *résistancialisme* bolstered nationalism and encouraged active forgetting until de Gaulle left office in 1969.[32] Susan Rubin Suleiman, too, reads de Gaulle's post-Liberation speeches as a clever and effective manipulation of historical fact: "de Gaulle not only called for unity in his speeches, he rhetorically *presupposed* it. When he spoke of 'true France, eternal France,' unanimous in its resistance to the occupant, he was expressing a wish, not describing an actual state of affairs. In rhetoric, presupposition is a means of persuading your interlocutor that something exists, without empirical verification."[33] Gaullist official discourse amounted to a rewriting of the recent past in order to foster an imagined image of the present in service of the future.

The French texts analyzed in this book date from the thirty years of massive economic expansions, known as the Trente Glorieuses, immediately following the Occupation. Developments in industry, mechanization, and exportation, along with mammoth rebuilding projects leading to the growth of the Parisian suburbs, an exodus of rural inhabitants to cities, and an overall elevated standard of living, all created a rupture with the *années noires*. Kristin Ross's book on this period, *Fast Cars, Clean Bodies: Decolonialization and the Reordering of French Culture*, describes the nationalism during these years as a massive sanitization effort: wipe away the shame of the Occupation and sweep away the difficulties posed by the Algerian War (1954–1962) and decolonialization. She writes: "Certainly the immediate postwar purges (called *épurations* or 'purifications') and attempts to rid the nation of the traces of German Occupation and Pétainiste compromise and complicity set the tone for a new emphasis on French national purity."[34] And later: "If Algeria is becoming an independent nation, then France must become a *modern* nation: some distinction between the two must still prevail. France must, so to speak, clean house; reinventing the home is reinventing the nation."[35] This period, the Trente Glorieuses, was thus one of both outward traumatic repression and careening globalization, a starting point of a period of economic development that will travel unevenly and asynchronously across the globe.

In his 1978–79 lectures at the Collège de France, entitled *The Birth of Biopolitics*, Michel Foucault chronicles the adoption of forms of liberalism and neoliberalism by Western states since the end of the Second World War. His lectures primarily concern those practices of neoliberalism conceived in Germany and the United States and first implemented in the 1940s.[36] While he explains that the loosening of government control over the market seemed to offer a fail-safe to totalitarianism and to be grounded in an ethic of freedom, such that "only a state that recognizes economic freedom and thus makes way for freedom and responsibility of individuals can speak in the name of the people," Foucault emphasizes that neoliberalism hardly decreases the power of the state.[37] Instead, he argues that "the production of well-being by economic growth will produce a circuit going from the economic institution to the population's overall adherence to its regime and system."[38] Hardly a vessel of freedom, then, Foucault also demonstrates that neoliberalism enables the obliteration of history. Foucault untangles how neoliberalism helped to obscure Germany's role as bad actor in the twentieth century:

> History had said no to the German state, but now the economy will allow it to assert itself. Continuous economic growth will take over from a malfunctioning history. It will thus be possible to live and accept the breach of history as a breach in memory, inasmuch as a new dimension of temporality will be established in Germany that will no longer be a temporality of history, but one of economic growth. A reversal of the axis of time, permission to forget, and economic growth are all, I think, at the very heart of the way in which the German economic-political system functions. Economic freedom is jointly produced through growth, well-being, the state, and the forgetting of history.[39]

Although Foucault argues that France's true embrace of neoliberalism would not come until the early 1970s, he, like David Harvey, locates the beginning of the neoliberal turn in France in the "embedded liberalism" used to prompt economic growth after Liberation.[40] Central to my argument is that in post–Second World War France (as in Germany), the intensified focus on economic prosperity allowed for the initial forgetting of recent traumatic history.

The response to economic development across the globe is uneven, asynchronous, and diverse. Though both the French and the Chinese works under discussion in this book communicate the affective symptoms of national trauma and expanded capitalist globalization, they don't do so in precisely the same way. In contrast to the situation in France, as the years have passed, neither state censorship nor the euphemistic discourse of "amnesia" fully account for the lack of national reckoning with the violence at Tiananmen. Margaret Hillenbrand explains, "Mass forgetfulness is a misnomer because rather than being a nation of amnesiacs, China is divided between those who cannot fully forget but stay mostly silent, and those who have never, or barely, learned about the events that are seared across the cortices of their elders and so have nothing to unremember."[41] Importantly, Hillenbrand contends, "those who cannot fully forget but stay mostly silent" have willingly contributed to a culture of public secrecy on taboo topics; the imperative of " 'knowing what not to know' . . . is not shuttered in closed archives but dwells in the interstices of the everyday and the everywhere . . . a form of control in which we are all enforcers."[42] Of course, public secrecy is not unique to China. Hillenbrand quips, "We all live in cryptocracies now," and yet, she argues that "secrecy in China stands out because both the chokehold on information and the deployment of secrecy as spectacular power play operate at full tilt."[43]

The trauma of June Fourth at Tiananmen—by far the largest collective protest in post-Mao China, with demonstrations in twenty-nine provinces and eighty-four cities—represents a pivotal betrayal of the Chinese youth by their own government.[44] I say "pivotal," because the massacre at Tiananmen Square, conceived of within the frame of its rise (since the death of Mao in 1976), fall (in 1989), and repression, dramatizes a *revisitation* of the betrayal of Chinese youth, which had earlier taken place during the Cultural Revolution. During the Cultural Revolution, urban youth were sent to the countryside to receive "reeducation" from rural peasants. These "sent-down youth" were removed from their homes and families and deprived of years of traditional schooling. Cleverly manipulating the memory of the Cultural Revolution to combat the student protesters, Beijing Secretary Li Ximing compared the demonstrations at Tiananmen in 1989 to the mayhem generated during the Cultural Revolution, and accused this new generation of urban youth of taking part in a conspiracy to subvert the state.[45] Taking his cue from Secretary Li's reports, Deng Xiaoping stressed the turmoil, unrest, and chaos caused by the demonstrations; Deng replaced the term "student protest" (學潮; *xuechao*) with "turmoil" (動亂; *dongluan*), the same term used to describe the Cultural Revolution.[46] The Beijing leaders took up further hyperbolic discourse, suggesting that the "turmoil" incurred by the protesters threatened to dismantle the state, and that the achievements won by the "blood and lives of revolutionary martyrs" could be destroyed overnight.[47] In this way, Deng's government conscripted earlier national traumas in order to designate itself "the last defender[s] of socialism and the PRC [People's Republic of China]," thereby justifying the subsequent violent suppression of the protesters.[48] The students were wildly miscast as enemies of socialism and the PRC; the government's crackdown definitively vanquished their hope that the collective voice of China's idealistic youth might affect reform.[49]

The crackdown at Tiananmen also repositioned China globally. In Erin Y. Huang's examination of Chinese neoliberal post-socialism, she reflects on the unique politico-economic trajectory presented by the Chinese case:

> Decades have passed since China entered the era of economic reform [post-1978]. The events that followed signaled for many the beginning of a new era when the globalization of capitalism was conflated with the promise of individual freedom and democracy. However, amid the familiar narrative describing China's liberation from a Cold War totalitarian socialist regime, the Tiananmen Square massacre of 1989 broadcast to the world that the post- in Chinese post-socialism has distinct meanings in the economic and political realms. The "freedom" associated with the "free" market economy is only a flexible façade, subject to infinite redefinition.[50]

This book argues, slightly to the contrary, that the "freedom" seemingly offered by the "free" market is not a false promise in China alone. The rise of neoliberalism in both France and China undermined a collective reckoning with national trauma. However, Huang underlines some specific complications that render Chinese neoliberalism of a different form from that in the West, as "a regime alternately called authoritarian socialist, post-socialist, and post-capitalist—that operates according to the logic of the post-X."[51] The international implications of the June Fourth Massacre for China is reiterated by Dai Jinhua, who claims that after Tiananmen, China fell into the post–Cold War cold war wherein "China Time became disjointed from world historical time once again. And it was misrecognized from both sides. On the one side, the party line insisted on Chinese characteristics to strategically emphasize China's historical time. The other side saw China as a socialist totalitarian nation. Neither view took into account the degree to which China was implicated in globalization."[52] In the years following the crackdown at Tiananmen, China focused on economic reform, especially after Deng Xiaoping's Southern Tour (南巡; *nan xun*) in early 1992, during which Deng "argued that socialism could efficaciously adopt some elements of capitalism, and that capitalism could have socialist elements."[53] The pivotal betrayal of 1989, in conjunction with China's increasing economic reforms in the early 1990s, marked the end of a utopian vision that had persevered since 1949. Although "market reforms, widely acknowledged as having generated impressive growth in Chinese gross domestic product (GDP) over the last three decades, have also revealed a darker side, contributing to economic insecurity, rising prices, and growing socioeconomic disparities," there has yet to be another collective show of dissent of the magnitude of 1989.[54] The ongoing protests in Hong Kong beginning in 2014 show that popular discord may well again be on the rise. The PRC's imposition of the Hong Kong national security law in June 2020, however, threatens to curtail the right to peaceful civil disobedience previously tolerated in the Hong Kong Special Administrative Region.

Translating the Unspeakable

The French and Chinese film and literature under discussion in this book reveal the peculiar demand made on scholars who investigate the aesthetics of texts dealing with national trauma: the need to translate not just across languages but also between the sayable and the unspeakable, the visible and the invisible. In their attention to the unspeakable, the felt and expressed rather than clearly spelled out, psychoanalysis and affect theory act as methods of translation that travel across these domains. *Remnants of Refusal: Feminist Affect, National Trauma* translates the form of affects in French and Chinese texts as traces of an unmourned, impossible traumatic origin.

The work of mourning, according to Sigmund Freud's essay "Mourning and Melancholia" (1917), consists of a painful, piecemeal detachment of libido from the lost object—a beloved person, or "some *abstraction* . . . such as one's country, liberty, an ideal, and so on" (my emphasis).[55] Mourning thus requires the symbolization, through what Freud calls "word-presentations," but which can also appear as images, of the lost object and its relationship to the self. A refusal or failure to mourn, which produces melancholia, occurs when this process of symbolization is blocked through repression. This book begins in the wake of national traumas as governing authorities turned the dead into unmournable bodies by refusing to acknowledge their loss and denying their place in the nation's symbolic sense of self. In its haste to cover over the loss of such *abstractions* in order to reassert a strong, virtuous national image, French and Chinese official discourse thus gave rise to a history of ghosts, the echoes of those lost in the periods of trauma who, denied entry into history, had to linger as fragments or affective specters in the hopes that their names would one day be spoken and their deaths mourned. Here, then, is where we stand at this book's outset: in melancholia, as "the shadow of the object fell upon the ego," the ego becomes identified with the "forsaken object" such that the subject turns on herself.[56] But melancholia is not the only symptom that surfaces when mourning stalls. From the self-censure in melancholia we can observe the subject's ambivalence toward the loved object, when—as the ego comes to substitute itself for the absent object—"the hate comes into operation, on this substitutive object, abusing it, debasing it, making it suffer and deriving sadistic satisfaction from its suffering."[57] Ambivalence and melancholy, in other words, operate symbiotically, each feeding off the other. This picture of distress is completed by "an impoverishment of [the subject's] ego on a grand scale"; sleepless, the subject is exhausted by "an overcoming of the instinct which compels every living thing to cling to life."[58] Melancholy, ambivalence, and exhaustion, therefore, serve each other: a living, "open wound" bequeathed by the traumatic wound. Though I am building this symptomatic lexicon from Freud's seminal essay, I will be making more of melancholy's bedfellows than Freud. Indeed, melancholy, ambivalence, and exhaustion provide the structure for this book.

Freud himself proposes that historical trauma can be transmitted across generations in repressed and repudiated memories. In *Totem and Taboo* (1913), he argues that the collective inheritance of neuroses determines the shape of civilization. This early history treats modern ambivalence and anxiety as an inheritance of totems erected by prehistoric peoples; the Oedipus complex deriving from the trauma of the murder of an ancient patriarch. Freud's last book, *Moses and Monotheism* (1939), like *Totem and Taboo*, centers on the murder of a father figure. Freud rewrites the history of Judaism, suggesting that Moses, an Egyptian, adhered to the earlier monotheistic religion founded by the Pharaoh Akhenaten.[59] Moses transmitted Akhenaten's Egyptian monotheism to his followers and led them to freedom; but these liberated people rebelled, murdering the prophet. Monotheism was seemingly abandoned for a period of latency following Moses's murder, but later reemerged, giving birth to Jewish monotheism.[60] *Moses and Monotheism* is a narrative of departure and return, a repetition compulsion, but one that belongs to an entire people rather than to a singular neurotic subject. It is also a text written at a different time of traumatic departure, between 1934 and 1938 while Freud was fleeing the threat of Nazi persecution in his native Vienna for London. The book's first two chapters were published in Austria in 1937, but Freud had to wait until arriving in England to publish the third chapter in 1938.[61] The history of the text thus replays, in different registers, the fractures that trauma produces within thought and history. Putting these issues another way, Cathy Caruth asks: "Centering his story in the nature of the leaving, and returning, constituted by trauma, Freud resituates the very possibility of history in the nature of a traumatic departure. We might say, then, that the central question, by which Freud finally inquires into the relation between history and its political outcome, is: What does it mean, precisely, for history to be the history of trauma?"[62] Applying the quintessentially modernist example of the train collision that he used in his original theorization of the traumatic neurosis in *Beyond the Pleasure Principle* (1920), Freud leaps centuries backward and draws a connection to Jewish monotheism.[63] What I'm taking from Freud's historiographic exploration of the neuroses structuring civilization—from the ancient tribes in *Totem and Taboo*, to the Jewish ancestors in *Moses and Monotheism*, to the twentieth-century train travelers in *Beyond the Pleasure Principle*—is an idea common to trauma theorists: that we can read human history as a series of traumatic breaks and collective symptomatic responses. The Chinese and French texts in this book reveal these symptoms in the form of shared affective modes. They speak through their symptoms without naming their source. In the place of the Tiananmen Square Massacre or the German Occupation, they give other words and images.

Translation, Transnationalism, and Intermediality

Thinking affectively allows me to work across the usual divisions of media as form. The model of history and historical inheritance that I develop in this book, therefore, requires a revaluation of three key terms in comparative literature and film theory: translation, transnationalism, and intermediality. Translation is a key concept for all three of these approaches, and its importance speaks to the centrality of the movements *between* France and China in my book, as well as across different historical periods and media.

The first approach—which I have already introduced—is psychoanalytic translation. For psychoanalysis, translation involves not only the shifting of one language to another but, just as importantly, the *persistence* of an old language within the new, what analysts Nicolas Abraham and Maria Torok have called the *encryption* of words within words or of bodies within images.[64] What is past, psychoanalysis claims, is never simply the past, but always the many strategies of return by which our history appears as symptoms within the present.

The second approach is transnational translation as a method of mapping the relationships of repetition, return, and resonance that take place across the histories and images of different places, and at different times. I propose a theory of the transnational that accounts not only for the relationships between different nations at a particular historical moment but also for the ways that national histories and experiences are spoken of and for by the echoes they produce in other national contexts. This is what will allow my book to speak about China *through* the French experience and about France *through* Chinese history.

The third approach is intermedial translation: recognizing the ways in which cinema borrows from the history of literature and the ways in which modern and contemporary literature draws from and enters into conversation with cinematic forms. It has often been noted that the popularity of cinema has placed a dual pressure on literature. On the one hand, through its ability to reach the masses, cinema has forced literature to seek other audiences and to address itself to other concerns. But, at the same time, modern literature has constantly borrowed cinematic devices such as cross-cutting, superimposition, and fragmentation for its own purposes.[65] I argue that this formal borrowing speaks not only to an aesthetic project but to a desire for both film and literature to give proper, reimagined form to the disjointed experience of the present when it is shattered by unspoken historical traumas.

In each of these approaches, translation indicates not just a shift from one linguistic system to another, but also an account of the underlying historical and social conditions that make these moves possible, and of their effects on readers and viewers. Regarding "translational transnationalism," Emily Apter writes, "Languages are inherently transnational and time sensitive. Their plurilingual composition embodies histories of language travel that do not necessarily reproduce imperial trajectories. . . . Language worlds that bleed out of dichotomized generic categories afford a planetary approach to literary history that responds to the dynamics of geopolitics without shying away from fractious border zones."[66] Therefore, by applying a comparative approach in accord with translational transnationalism, one that is in constant flux as languages travel, one sensitive to new constructions and chronologies, Apter contends that "comparative literature takes shape as a field in which the *Realpolitik* of language conflict draws on and transforms the philological heritage of humanistic transference, displacement and exile."[67] In other words, the promise of translational transnationalism is that a politics outside of (or in opposition to) systems of Western imperial ideology might be exercised in comparative work, even as comparativism remains aware of the continuing place of the languages and images of the core in the texts of emerging or peripheral nations. Reading echoes of language, history, and image, this book aims for such a politics as it maps out a multi-decade, multi-directional journey of capital, language, and affect. Both implicitly and explicitly, then, I argue that the histories of these two nations' traumas and erasures cannot be understood independently from one another or outside of the broader context of the forms of urban and national development that they serve.[68]

By making use of Nicolas Abraham and Maria Torok's theory of cryptonomy in their study of incurable mourning, *The Wolf Man's Magic Word: A Cryptonomy* (1976; trans. 1986), the texts included in this book can be read as an encrypted dialogue about the melancholy, ambivalence, and exhaustion of global trauma. In the 1970s, Nicolas Abraham and Maria Torok spent five years on the Wolf Man's case, publishing their joint rebuttal of Freud's findings in 1976 in *Cryptonymie: Le verbier de L'Homme aux loups*, translated in 1986 by Nicholas Rand as *The Wolf Man's Magic Word: A Cryptonymy*. Abraham and Torok argue that the secret to the Wolf Man case lies in portions of his dreams and the symptoms that Freud was unable to hear due to his own repressions, and they undertake a multilingual translation in Russian, German, and English (the languages spoken by the Wolf Man or to him by his family or governess), slipping between homonyms and near homonyms or rhymes. Abraham and Torok theorize that the secret to the Wolf Man's suffering is an unspeakable word, which is only utterable "provided it is disguised in the synonym of an alloseme, that is, as a *cryptonym*."[69] The unspeakable is lodged in the patient's psychic crypt, or "the Fractured Symbol, the Rift in the Ego, or to use another image, the Tear in the Ego."[70] A clear example of this encryption within cultural texts appears in *Conjugation*. In this film, foreign (in particular, French) images and words appear as fragments embedded within the scenes of Chinese cultural life. I read these fragments of the foreign as cryptonyms for the trauma of Tiananmen. Unable to speak this trauma directly, the film indicates the presence of the "unsayable" by marking its presence with a *cryptonym* or displaced image of the absent term. With its release in the same year as the 9/11 attacks, *Conjugation*'s cryptic strategy also allows an extra-diegetic third national history to creep into the margins of the viewer's experience. The film thereby depicts the difficulty of shifting from the past to the present to the future, and the delicacy of forming conscious and unconscious links between what once appeared divided and specific. In other words, the central question of the state of the nation in *Conjugation* is asked of China through France and in the shadows of American imperialism. It's framed as imploring, wallowing, staggering: the film's nondiegetic music featuring a barely audible female voice whispering the occasional pathetic prayer, "Je t'aime."

Attention to the transnational, therefore, specifically applies to the filmic analysis undertaken in this project: the way in which the cinematic spectacle may offer a vision of multiple nations.[71] In 2010, Deborah Shaw, Ruth Doughty, and Armida de la Garza responded to the growing interest in transnational film studies by founding the journal *Transnational Cinemas*. In the journal's first issue, Shaw and Garza explain the new scholarly avenues made available through a transnational approach: "Scholars are embracing the challenges of the opening up of borders within academia and within film-making, and are, at the same time, casting an historical eye back to the transnational practices that have often characterized film-making in both textural and industrial terms."[72] Studies of cinema need no longer be confined to either national cinema or the slightly nebulous global art cinema. Unpacking the complexities of transnational cinema implies tracing the *specific* production and diegetic routes that these films take across borders.

However, writers in *Transnational Cinemas*'s first issue also warn that—as with any scholarly endeavor seeking to break down established disciplinary walls—care and caution should be exercised before swinging the metaphorical sledgehammer in the name of the "transnational." Will Higbee and Song Hwee Lim, for example, alert readers that overuse of the term "transnational" may render it meaningless.[73] Attempting a reparative renaming, they call for a "critical transnationalism" that might open up new non-Eurocentric readings of films and emphasize the productive dialogue of the local and national with the global and transnational.[74] Engaging my own version of critical transnationalism, one that embraces the linguistic rigor and attention to written text native to comparative literature in order to forge a multi-decade, postmodern, transnational intervention into film studies, my project shows how fresh readings of films and literature are opened up by considering new comparative processes and new forms of co-production, while also taking into account the negative impact of global capitalism. In 2019, the editors of *Transnational Cinemas* changed the journal's name to *Transnational Screens* as a response to the shift in the production, distribution, and projection of film over the last decade.[75] This new nomenclature not only embraces the study of streaming sites (Netflix, Hulu, and the like), but also opens up a discussion of images flickering on cellular phones, moving multi-image billboards, internet pop-ups, and other platforms for distributing filmic content in the contemporary world.[76]

Though the chapters that follow include filmic and literary fiction, I argue that both kinds of work are building an intermedial reimagination of history. This dialogue between cinema and literature stresses the cross-pollination of art that differs in form but shares a politics. It also underlines the central place that image and cinematic spectacle occupy in the modern and contemporary world.

I take up the cinematic potential of literature in each chapter devoted primarily to literary fiction. As a result of the blurring of genres occurring in the writing and filmmaking of Marguerite Duras (treated in chapter 1 of this book), her works have often been characterized as *ciné-romans*.[77] Her written dialogues read like screenplays. The character descriptions skate across the surface: sketches leaving a profound emotional resonance. In the opening pages of *Moderato cantabile* (1958), for example, Duras portrays the arrest of a man who has just murdered his lover: "The man walked compliantly to the van. But, once there, he silently struggled with himself, then escaped the inspectors and ran swiftly back to the café. However, just as he was about to reach it, the café went dark. He stopped mid-run, followed the inspectors back to the van, and boarded it. Maybe he cried, but in the darkening dusk only his trembling, bloodstained face, but no falling tears, could be seen."[78] As with all the characters in *Moderato*, the reader is given no definitive access to this man's interior life; we watch his movements and are left to guess, seemingly along with the narrator, at his intentions. However, as in a film, his actions and the gory image of his face leave a striking impression. Duras's *ciné-romans* transmit a melancholic affect in their sparse vocabulary and in the spaces left between succinct lines of dialogue and terse descriptions. This form of imagistic writing not only draws on the form of cinematic portrayal but highlights the ambivalence and uncertain expressions of bodies when they are stripped of their inner lives and presented as cinematic surfaces. What we see in Duras's work is that this technical capability of cinema is in fact also the expression of a historical necessity: how to portray the lives of characters who are haunted by a past that remains unreadable and unknowable, even to themselves.

Remnants of Refusal: Feminist Affect, National Trauma extends the idea of the *ciné-roman* to explore other resonances between film and literary fiction in its affective reading across these media. Duras's contemporary and one of the subjects of chapter 3, Nathalie Sarraute, does away with strict boundaries separating various ranges and depths in narration. Using a form of free-indirect discourse in some ways like that found in the work of Virginia Woolf, whom Sarraute greatly admired, the reader swims in and out of the porous minds of characters so continually that the (frequently unnamed) characters often run together. The resulting literature gives an overall impression of the attitudes of a particular social milieu—its "tropisms"—a term that Sarraute would also lend to the title of her first novel.[79] Though in many ways the opposite of what Duras's work achieves, we might consider the pastiche of psychological portraits in Sarraute's fiction as yielding *ciné-romans*. In its prizing of these anti-portraits of mores over conventional Cartesian characters, Sarraute's *ciné-romans* offer collages of historical time and place, joined together only by the lines of fracture that mark their subterranean traumas.

Both the work of Wang Anyi and Chen Ran, by contrast, reference the cinema by suggesting that the difference between human lives and the movies has become indistinct. In chapter 1, I follow Wang Anyi's characters in *The Song of Everlasting Sorrow* (長恨歌; *Changhenge*) (1995), as they bump against the filmmaking industry and movie halls of Shanghai from the 1940s to the 1980s. Her work smudges the space between "real life" and what happens in the movies, commenting both on the importance of cinema to Shanghai's history and, with an ironic melancholy, on the replacement of spectacular relations for human relations in the late twentieth century. In chapter 3, Chen Ran's fiction, in particular her 1996 novel *A Private Life* (私人生活; *Siren shenghuo*), likewise reveals the contemporary dominance of cinematic spectacle. In the opening pages of *A Private Life*, protagonist and narrator Ni Niuniu compares herself to "the person in the American film *The Looking Glass*, who stands for ages in front of the bathroom mirror, whose bright surface the steam has covered over with a layer of mist."[80] This double mirroring—Niuniu imagining what form of self will appear as the steam evaporates from the mirror in the film—becomes a metaphor for the narrator's imprisonment in the echo chamber of her own memories and her alienation from other people.[81] The fiction of Wang Anyi and Chen Ran, therefore, might also be characterized as *ciné-romans* in that they partially take as their subjects how the cinema has forever infiltrated and shaped human lives.

Remnants of Refusal: Feminist Affect, National Trauma focuses on the multiple reflections of history provided by the cinematic as well as the ways in which the making of cinema can be understood as writing. The place of the literary in the films explored in this book takes a variety of forms. In some films, as we've seen with Emily Tang's *Conjugation*, the importance of language and linguistic difference comes to the fore. In other films, such as those by Jean-Luc Godard, books and works of literature populate the mise-en-scène and the dialogue.[82]

Film theorists have embarked on the discussion of cinema as writing by stressing the materiality of mediated texts: cinema as photographic text and literature as linguistic text.[83] Marie-Claire Ropars-Wuilleumier asserts the heterogeneous matter of both cinema and literature. She points to the various semantic series at work in the cinema: "Thus visual series, textual networks, breath of silences, musical themes, figural marks in a contradictory and simultaneous fashion divide the filmic unreeling."[84] However, just as word and image divide a film, it is paradoxically this heterogeneity that binds the film together. Separating out the homogeneous matter would unmake the film. Garrett Stewart, like Ropars-Wuilleumier, stresses that film, like literature, is a "reading matter."[85] He argues for the term *cinécriture* as pointing to the mechanized production of both film and modernist literature, thereby underlying the way that mechanized modernity unites these two textual forms: "From the private appliance of reading to the public apparatus of screen spectacle, industrial imprint across media is modern, whereas modernism is text."[86] Stated with different emphasis, if we consider the shared twentieth-century history across which works of film and literature emerge, it becomes apparent that the two forms reflect back at each other the impact of this shared history—changes in technology and forms of production, among others. Of chief interest to this book is the way film and literature document transformations in France and China, respectively, over the course of twentieth-century and early-twenty-first-century history and develop a dialogue with national and global events, both past and contemporaneous.

My cinematographic reimagination of history comes not only from a commitment to writing a new narrative—one that crosses and bridges nations and media via affect—of the world since 1945 but also from a feminist history. The theoretical modeling of the materiality of literature and film becomes especially important for feminist authors, filmmakers, and theorists. Feminist filmmaker Agnès Varda, for example, employs *cinécriture*, and in a way unlike Stewart's later appropriation of the term. She uses *cinécriture* to refer to how an *auteur* filmmaker like herself creates a film by assembling each of its various parts (the position of actors, the camera angle, the choice of each cut between each shot, etc.), just as a writer selects each word on her page in order to create a work of literature.[87] She also thinks of the patchwork effort of *cinécriture* as in the tradition of other artforms (quilting, handicrafts, etc.) typically associated with women. It is not by accident, therefore, that these intermedial forms and modes—the *ciné-romans* and *cinécriture*—describe the work of women artists.

Feminist Refusal in the Age of Neoliberal Globalization

Women authors and protagonists stand at the center of this voyage of comparativism because they were central to the broader societal shifts taking place after the Second World War and its crisscrossing journey from West to East. Women claim this place of prominence for two reasons. First, because the texts I consider are all in their own ways grappling with the transformations in women's roles beginning in the second half of the twentieth century. Second, because my structuring affects—melancholy, ambivalence, and exhaustion—arise out of specifically feminist forms of refusal, which to a large extent came out of or at least reflected emerging concepts in feminist theory. It is thus important to separate the idea of feminist refusal, which I will use throughout this book, from the acts and possibilities afforded to women in the texts under consideration and the social world to which they refer.

In Denise Riley's important essay, *"Am I that Name?" Feminism and the Category of "Women" in History*, the author troubles the concept of "women" in her historical study of the status of female personhood and its relationship to feminism. Riley mines the discomfort arising from what the word "women" often assumes in its gathering of diverse groups of humans under a generic net ("all women"). While essentializing language that fails to account for individual expression can only be understood as an anti-feminist gesture, feminism nevertheless demands this group consciousness in its call for solidarity. Riley responds to this paradox by proposing that the reader consider "women" within the "peculiar tempo-ralities of 'women.'"[88] In other words, thinking of "women" as "women" when gendered consciousness is forced to the surface either by a physical sensation unique to the biologically female (menstruation, pregnancy, abortion, etc.) or when she realizes (e.g., after being catcalled) that she is being seen "as a woman."[89] Like Riley, I am wary of the generalized category of "women."[90] However, the women—both authors and protagonists—that I study exist in relation to the two temporalities proposed above: specif-ically, as figures who deal intimately with the "womanly duty" to couple with male partners and reproduce, as mothers, and as objects of the male gaze. Furthermore, the form of refusal, the resistance to historical prog-ress, speaks to notions of feminist historiography that resists the phallic drive of history as a forward-moving process of mastery. However, I will also take up, especially in chapter 2, Elissa Marder's articulation of the maternal function, as a metaphorical rather than biological concept that grapples with the uncanniness of the mother's body. My goal is to reveal how these depictions of women's times and feminine refusal unmask a feminist engagement with history.

Owing to the vast differences in Western and Eastern feminist history, the genealogy of Chinese feminisms warrants further discussion here.[91] In their introduction to the edited volume *Feminisms with Chinese Char-acteristics*, Ping Zhu and Hui Faye Xiao chart the articulation of Chinese feminisms over the course of the twentieth century, beginning with its advocation by male intellectuals amid the disintegration of the Qing Empire (1638–1912) and the humiliation brought about by colonialism. These intellectuals saw the expansion of women's rights as a way of strength-ening the nation and as a "counterdiscourse to the Western gaze."[92] This period of Chinese feminism had various aims and avatars but was part of a larger nationalist project and couched within the existing patriarchal system. During the Yan'an period (1935–1948), feminism was rejected as bourgeois, and the Chinese Communist Party (CCP) instead called for "women's liberation" (婦女解放; *funü jiefang*) and "equality between men and women" (男女平等; *nannüpingdeng*).[93] This period of Chinese feminism operated under the assumption that sexism was no longer an obstacle and strove for the common goal of national socialist liberation in cooperation with men. Yan'an and later Maoist state feminism brought about significant positive changes in women's status in China: from the right to choose their marriage partner and a degree of financial support after divorce to increased literacy, education, and employment rates. From 1949 to 1978, the state-sanctioned organization All-China Women's Federation (ACWF) (中華全國婦女聯合會; *Zhonghua quanguo funü lianhehui*, or 婦聯; *fulian*) was the only official women's organization in China. However, after the death of Mao (1976) in the 1980s, many Chinese feminists began to distance themselves from socialist feminism and nationalist narratives.

Though some women writers who came of age under Maoism, such as Wang Anyi (treated in chapter 1 of this book), have remained interested in class dynamics as well as issues of gendered inequality in domestic and social spheres, younger writers, like Chen Ran (treated in chapter 3), have become part of a vogue beginning in the 1990s for "private writing" (私寫作; *si xiezuo)*, which focuses on women's personal lives, individual problems, and sexual adventures. Some Chinese feminist scholars, such as Dai Jinhua and Wang Gan, worry that this trend suggests that "the only unique contribution women writers can make to Chinese literature is candid descriptions and confessions of their own private lives because women are always positioned as the object of the male gaze."[94] Zhu and Xiao remark that this twenty-first-century concern echoes the words of He-Yin Zhen, one of the first Chinese feminists in the early twentieth century. Zhen argued that women should not solely focus on "female consciousness," "because women's 'consciousness,' 'bodies,' or 'histories' are always already defined by masculinist visions of patriarchal power."[95] While some contemporary Chinese women writers and filmmakers have garnered interest by focusing on exactly these issues, it has led other Chinese writers, filmmakers, and scholars to distance themselves from the title of feminist. My discussion of Wang Anyi—a writer who has distanced herself from feminism—and Chen Ran—a writer whose work focuses heavily on women's consciousness, bodies, and histories—will make a claim for both of these women's work as feminist without sidestepping the complexities and contradictions implied by such a designation.

In order to substantiate how my affective triad of melancholy, ambivalence, and exhaustion incarnates feminist refusal, I turn to Sara Ahmed, who writes:

> A feminist history is affective: we pick up those feelings that
> are not supposed to be felt because they get in the way of an
> expectation of who we are and what life should be. No wonder
> feminism acquires such a negative charge: being against hap-
> piness, being against life. It is not simply that we first become
> feminists and later become killjoys. Rather, to become a feminist
> is to kill other people's joy; to get in the way of other people's
> investments.[96]

What I register in the forms that melancholy, ambivalence, and exhaustion take in the texts examined in this book is precisely such a refusal of
happiness and life: a refusal to move forward without working through
national trauma and with blind acceptance of the new reign of neoliberal globalization. My work with affect is thus influenced by a range of
feminist and queer affect theorists who, along with Ahmed, see negative
affects as one of the central sites for feminist resistance. Particularly
impactful have been Lauren Berlant's readings of affect as a means of
unknotting the relation of women and minority groups to life's precarity.
In her articulation of women's attachment to certain popular genre texts
as a mode of coping with difficulties and disappointments in *The Female
Complaint*, she writes damningly: "Utopianism is in the air, but one of
the main utopias is normativity itself, here a felt condition of general
belonging and an aspirational site of rest and recognition in and by a
social world."[97] Later, in Berlant's *Cruel Optimism*, utopian normativity
is treated with still more stinging critique, as she points to the dangers
lurking in human attachments to such hazardous sites of desire. The
phrase "cruel optimism," she tells us, "is an incitement to inhabit and
to track the affective attachment to what we call 'the good life,' which is
for so many a bad life that wears out the subject who nonetheless, and
at the same time, find their conditions of possibility within it."[98] Taking
Berlant's questioning of societal "success" a step further, Jack Halberstam's
The Queer Art of Failure champions those who eschew the lures of utopian
normativity or the good life, since "under certain circumstances failing,
losing, forgetting, unmaking, undoing, unbecoming, not knowing may
in fact offer more creative, more cooperative, more surprising ways of
being in the world."[99] Ahmed, Berlant, and Halberstam render negativity
as a force of critique; my affective triad—melancholy, ambivalence, and
exhaustion—also measures emotional rejection of the contemporary as a
sign of protest, and perhaps paradoxically, as a sign of hope in new ways
of being or in the possibility of new worlds to be forged.

However, the work in this book differs in that feminist refusal comes to the surface as a result of my translation of a transnational history of affects. These specific affects, which I also refer to in this book as feelings (or, with Sianne Ngai, as "feeling-based judgments") and sometimes emotions, are made legible in the textual forms explored in this book.[100] In other words, they are both sewn into the fabric of narratives but also enunciated in other aspects of form: diction, syntax, shot length, color, and something less palpable, which I would term tone. In this way my triad of affects offer both what Amy Villarejo ascribes to the general sense of the term affect, as that which "is in excess of a rational deliberative scheme and can function as a synonym for desire, insofar as that term involves the feeling of longing, inchoate and propulsive," and what she calls emotion, as that which "carries with it a responsive, intersubjective sense."[101] My affects act both irrationally and responsively. My affects both confuse and refuse positivist discourse.[102]

Melancholy, Ambivalence, Exhaustion

The chapters that follow move through my triad of co-symptoms resulting from failed mourning as they enunciate different modalities of feminist refusal in response to the imperative to forget national trauma and hail the growing influx of neoliberal globalization.

In chapter 1, I begin with the "shadow" cast by melancholia in Marguerite Duras's *Moderato cantabile* and Wang Anyi's *The Song of Everlasting Sorrow*.[103] My reading proposes a feminine melancholy manifested in these authors' writings. In Julia Kristeva's *Soleil noir: Dépression et mélancolie*, she concludes with a portrait of Marguerite Duras, whose "aesthetic of awkwardness" she calls "the discourse of blunted pain."[104] Xiaobing Tang reflects on Kristeva's writings on Duras in order to introduce Wang Anyi and announces "the similar response that both writers choose to mount to the postmodern challenge, namely, a melancholy subjectivity."[105] Tang sees these women as united in their "melancholy against the grain," meaning against the non-melancholic thrust of postmodernity.[106] I take inspiration from Tang's insight but argue, on the contrary, that the melancholy in the writing of Duras and Wang can be read as a feminine counter-discourse befitting the relationship of trauma to history. I will illustrate that Duras's "French" melancholy is revealed in a bourgeois woman character's obsession with an always already lost sublime experience, while Wang's "Chinese" melancholy is almost ironic, a feeling of boredom or embarrassment and tied to the specificity of shifting class relations in socialist and post-socialist China. This chapter argues that the melancholic work of Wang Anyi and Marguerite Duras functions allegorically, illuminating a tension between the globalizing present and the traumatic past. Whereas Walter Benjamin draws his theory of allegory from the male perspective of Charles Baudelaire, this chapter initiates the possibility of a feminine melancholy and a feminine allegory. This melancholic feminine allegory reveals a new conception of time and a new focus on aural perception: the eternal return and the resounding cry of trauma reverberating in the era of globalization. I conclude chapter 1 by inquiring into the ambivalent love attachments that are "among the preconditions of melancholia."[107]

In chapter 2, I explore conflicts due to ambivalence in France and China in the years following the Occupation and the Tiananmen Square Massacre; I argue that for the French these conflicts result in a decision to start over, while for the Chinese they allow for the return of the dead. In Jean-Luc Godard's *2 ou 3 choses que je sais d'elle* (1967) and Jia Zhangke's *The World* (世界; *Shijie*) (2004) the filmmakers follow women subjects on the margins of national capitals as they navigate the contractions and mixed emotions of life in nations in flux. The ambivalence of Godard's and Jia's films is not simply a reaction to the present but also an attitude emerging in response to troubling and repressed pasts. Both films focus on the lives of marginalized inhabitants of national capitals. Both films criticize prevailing social conditions but refrain from offering militant condemnations or clear solutions. In Godard's film, the filmmaker mingles the whispered, unconscious concerns of the Trente Glorieuses with a faux documentary of the Parisian suburbs. Jia's film, meanwhile, carves out a hopeless space in the postmodern dystopia overtaking Beijing.

I conclude chapter 2 by linking ambivalence to exhaustion. In chapter 3, I show how trauma leads to exhaustion, and how exhausting traditional narrative forms, Cartesian characters, and gender and sexual norms may register as a form of refusal, with analysis of anti-portraits by Natalie Sarraute's *Le Planétarium* (1959), Agnès Varda's *Sans toit ni loi* (1985), and Chen Ran's *A Private Life* (1996).

Freud concludes "Mourning and Melancholia" with a caveat: "As we already know, the interdependence of the complicated problems of the mind forces us to break off every enquiry before it is completed—till the outcome of some other enquiry can come to its assistance."[108] He accepts that his process of diagnosis is always a work in progress, and I must admit the same. While I argue that melancholy, ambivalence, and exhaustion serve as the contemporary affects bred in the gap left by failed mourning,

I cannot pinpoint what will take their place, or—indeed—if a transition has already come to pass. I conclude this book with a discussion of two "end" dates, 1968 in France and 2008 in China, after which we might speak about the afterlives of melancholy, ambivalence, and exhaustion, before branching further outward to ponder the future of the modern nation and the transnational world.[109]

Emily Tang's *Conjugation* gives Foot Finger, a character whose absence is felt throughout the film and an implied victim of the Tiananmen Massacre, a voice. His words—spoken in voice-over by the central male protagonist Guo Song—are taken from the writings of the Chinese poet Haizi (海子), who committed suicide by laying down on train tracks in March 1989.[110] Though Haizi's death occurred nine weeks before the crackdown at Tiananmen, his violent end renders his melancholic verses portents of the vanished bodies that would result from the June Fourth Massacre. Near the end of Tang's film, Guo Song spends a night drinking with his friend Tian Yu. He cycles home at dawn. The sun rising behind his body, Guo Song becomes a stark, black form, the low camera angle emphasizing the naked winter trees etched across a vast, pink sky (figure I.5). It's the vision of a world cut out of paper; a shadow puppet world; a screen projecting the shapes of animate ghosts. In voice-over, Guo Song

Figure I.5. Guo Song cycling home at dawn. *Source*: Tang, Emily Xiaobai, dir. *Conjugation* (動詞變位; *Dongci bianwei*). 2001; Hong Kong, People's Republic of China: Tang Films, 2001. Digital file.

recites some lines of Haizi/Foot Finger's poetry: "Sister, there is nothing in the distance except remoteness. Sister, what should I leave you? Sister, I saw the wheat fields. Sister, I am standing on the painful lawn of the sun." By uniting language borrowed from the historical dead (Haizi) with the fictional dead (Foot Finger) and the disembodied voice of the fictional living (Guo Song), Tang's film, like the other works under discussion in this book, gives form to the residue of the past by affixing it to the present, and showing how expressions of melancholy, ambivalence, and exhaustion function as remnants of refusal.

Remnants of Refusal: Feminist Affect, National Trauma, like Tang's film, is born of a desire to give voice to those vanished by history. In order to hear their whispered complaints, this book undertakes a form of listening to the gaps and breaks that occur between languages, between forms of expression, and even between the realms of the living and the dead. It's my hope that unveiling these remnants in film and literature will prompt a reexamination of our collective pasts and encourage refusal as a mode of protesting the atrocities of our present.

Chapter 1

Feminine Melancholy, Feminine Allegory

Nothing in the world belongs to me now except that corpse in a ditch.

—Marguerite Duras, *The War*[1]

Everything I had gone through had erected a wall that isolated me
    from the crowd.
The jostling crowd and I were separated in two different worlds.
Even our suns were different.
We stepped on each other's shadows but that was all.

—Wang Anyi, *Years of Sadness*[2]

After the German Occupation and the Tiananmen Square Massacre the mourning of collective losses and the lingering memories of shame, austerity, anger, and death were obscured by intensive industrial buildup, increasing globalization, and aggressive, nationalist ideology.[3] French writers, surrounded by hordes of *jeunes cadres* zipping around the Place de la Concorde in their newly purchased American cars, and Chinese writers waiting to order burgers in the company of other anonymous city dwellers in a McDonald's near Tiananmen Square, faced the shock and alienation resulting from rising neoliberal globalization. The gap between the recent, repressed past and the accelerating present found expression and form in the writing of the two authors highlighted in this chapter, Marguerite Duras and Wang Anyi. While the government desperately tried to smooth out the fabric of history, the jagged crease appeared in these

37

authors' melancholic allegories of the Trente Glorieuses and China post-1989, presenting simultaneous, incongruous temporalities, and murmuring discontent—remnants of refusal—underneath the whir of progress.

This chapter contends that Wang Anyi's *The Song of Everlasting Sorrow* (長恨歌; *Changhenge*) (1995) and Marguerite Duras's *Moderato cantabile* (1958) function allegorically, revealing a tension between the globalizing present and the traumatic past. Wang Anyi's novel chronicles the life—by turns humdrum, hopeful, and resigned—of Shanghai woman Wang Qiyao from adolescence until her murder in middle age cast against the tumultuous backdrop of twentieth-century Chinese political, social, and economic transformation. Marguerite Duras's novel, by contrast, focuses on a single week in the late 1950s during which French wife and mother Anne Desbaresdes stages an emotional and social revolt against the steady rhythm of her staid bourgeois life. Whereas Walter Benjamin famously draws his theory of allegory from the male perspective of Charles Baudelaire, this chapter argues for a feminine melancholy and a feminine allegory. This melancholic feminine allegory reveals a new conception of time and a new focus on aural perception. Here, literature takes a form approaching the filmic: the eternal return and the resounding cry of trauma reverberating in the flat spectacles crisscrossing eras of increasing globalization. My chapter, too, borrows from film in its structure of argument, cross-cutting between the French and the Chinese, Duras and Wang, history and literature. This back-and-forth motion between the chapter's key subjects simulates how films employ parallel editing to unite narrative lines occurring in disparate places and times. By this approach, I hope to link this chapter's "story" of melancholy from France and China while still granting each nation its own unfolding within the particulars of national history.

Duras and Wang have previously been united in what Xiaobing Tang terms "melancholy against the grain," meaning against the non-melancholic thrust of postmodernity.[4] Tang's phrase evokes another Benjamin text, "Theses on the Philosophy of History," in which the author rallies the materialist historian to dissociate from the treasures of culture ("There is no document of civilization which is not at the same time a document of barbarism") and stalwartly take up "his task to brush history against the grain."[5] It is this task—refusing to replace tragedy with false narratives of heroism and victors, declining to cover the ashes with the bright baubles of expanded global capitalism—that Duras and Wang pursue.[6] Both authors' work can be read as remnants of refusal in that they draw a portrait of the present in which dissatisfaction with daily life arises from a desire for an impossible, always already lost, transcendent experience. Produced in post-traumatic, post-revolutionary eras, their work is haunted by the violent disasters of the recent past while being unable to generate enthusiasm for present national projects. Without faith in the heroism embedded in these movements, and suspecting that past heroic gestures were equally illusory, Duras and Wang give us work infused with melancholy.

This is not a purely tonal category; melancholy is formally constructed in such a way that it operates on more than one level in each author's work. The texts by Duras and Wang under examination in this chapter create melancholy allegories of France in the late 1950s and China in the mid-1990s. In conjoining allegory and melancholy, I am borrowing (and then straying) from Walter Benjamin's extensive study of Charles Baudelaire's poetic chronicle of Paris in the nineteenth century. Benjamin writes, "Baudelaire's genius, which is nourished on melancholy, is an allegorical genius. For the first time, with Baudelaire, Paris becomes the subject of lyric poetry. This poetry is no hymn to the homeland; rather the gaze of the allegorist, as it falls on the city, is the gaze of the alienated man."[7] Allegory is the experience of the past (and occasionally the messianic future) in the present, the recognition and expression of history, what for Benjamin was the "truth of the world."[8] This "truth" does not exist outside of allegory, much as Freud's "*historical* truth" does not achieve an articulation beyond its reemergence in compulsive neurotic symptoms.[9] For Benjamin, an allegorical apprehension of history is possible in any age; his *The Origin of German Tragic Drama* cites the appearance of the death's head in baroque *Trauerspiel* as providing such a flash of multi-temporal recognition for spectators in the sixteenth and seventeenth centuries. No matter the age, allegory voices the apprehension of alienation ("the gaze of the alienated man"). Baudelaire witnessed the vast changes taking place in nineteenth-century Paris and felt already out of step and alone. Intrinsic to Benjamin's conception of what Michael Jennings terms the "falseness of modern experience" is the death of art's *aura*—its connection to the place and time of its creation—enabled by mechanical reproduction.[10] Mechanical reproduction liberates the work of art from its prison of specificity and its mystery; replication allows the distance between the image and the viewer to collapse.

Rey Chow's essay, "Walter Benjamin's Love Affair with Death," links the relationship between a reproduction and its viewer to the idea of allegory: the reproduction allows "a certain uncanny effect of the *conjuring* of reality," a simultaneous convergence of life and death.[11] "Ironically," she writes, "in finally perfecting the resemblance always longed for in artistic reproduction, mechanical reproduction also destroys the ways of perception that led up to it, that are inscribed *in its birth*, so to speak. . . . What is important is the repeatability of an experience in the form of a sensorially apprehensible thing. It is this repeatability which is at once a conjuring of life and a witness to death."[12] For Benjamin this "sensorially apprehensible thing" is the whore, and Chow's intention in this exploration of Benjamin's writings lies in deciphering their intersection with gender politics. She explains that in his work on the melancholic, alienated Baudelaire, "the flâneur's jostlings among the nameless and shapeless city masses are punctuated with one *figure* that emerges from all this amorphousness—the figure of the prostitute or unknown woman."[13] Benjamin's allegorical gaze is impotent: consumed with anxiety over the failure (or death) of a sexual encounter (or life) before it has taken place. If Benjamin pays close attention to the figure of the prostitute in Baudelaire it is because "the prostitute gives to all the amorphous feelings stemming from male impotence, feelings which can only be felt but not grasped, *the concreteness of a human shape*. She is, in other words, 'the decline of the aura' *allegorically personified* in the high capitalist world, where 'the commodity attempts to look itself in the face' and where 'it celebrates its becoming human in the whore.' "[14] Chow protests against this allegory of woman-as-prostitute-as-death in the writings of Benjamin and quotes (with some irony) Benjamin's own recognition that "Baudelaire never wrote a whore-poem from the perspective of a whore."[15] This question of the feminine likewise leads me to break with Benjamin's conception of allegory in my readings of Marguerite Duras and Wang Anyi. Their novels, written by women about "fallen" women (the *femme adultère* in Duras, and the mistress in Wang), offer what approaches the "whore-poem from the perspective of a whore," and what I am terming feminine allegory.

Though both authors rely on melancholy, their feminine allegory is not simply a transmutation of masculine allegory with the addition of women authorship and central women characters. As I will explain below, feminine allegory takes a wholly different form, one particularly suited to enunciating historical melancholy: a subtle protest, a remnant of refusal, in eras given over to economic expansion and optimism. Julia Kristeva begins her essay "Women's Time" (*Le temps des femmes*) by announcing the collapse of the nation in the twentieth century.[16] She then examines the discourse proposed by the women after said collapse. Where history has been described (by men) as moving forward linearly, progressing chronologically through time, Kristeva introduces a feminine time better suited to describe history's relationship to traumatic events: "As for time, feminine subjectivity seems to give it a specific cadence which, in its multiple modalities in the history of civilizations, essentially guards the notions of *repetition* and *eternity*. On one side: cycles, gestation, eternal return of a biological rhythm accorded by nature. . . . On the other: a massive temporality, without break and without escape."[17]

Kristeva's essay, published in 1979, articulates the division between two groups of European feminists: first, those beginning with the first generation (the suffragettes) up until the existentialists (Beauvoir), and next, the second generation's second gasp (emerging after 1968). As Alice Jardine explains in her introduction to "Women's Time," the essay "is, in some ways, Kristeva's most extensive and direct analysis of feminism as an international movement in the 1970s."[18] While Kristeva's first group of feminists strive to position themselves within "masculine," linear time, the second group speaks "in a strange temporality, in a kind of 'future perfect' *(futur antérieur)*, where the most deeply repressed past gives a distinctive character to a logical and sociological distribution of the most modern type."[19] Emily Apter takes up the challenge of this "strange temporality" in her article on Kristeva, using it to describe "the multivalent capacity as an aesthetic function of women's time."[20] In other words, she identifies this temporality both in feminist theory as well as in the formal qualities of work by women artists. In addition, Apter writes not about European women in the 1970s but about Americans around the end of the twentieth century. I, likewise, am untethering the chronological and geographical specificity spelled out by Kristeva: moving slightly earlier to include Duras in the 1950s and both later temporally and laterally spatially to include Wang in Shanghai in the mid-1990s. In the place of the "future perfect," Apter calls women's aesthetic temporality the *démodé*, "with that term understood in its full panoply of significations as the out of fashion, the outmoded, and the untimely. . . . There is a temporal violence to outdating; when it erupts, it loosens periodicity's possessive perimeters around spots of time and releases arrested images into the future."[21] I will argue that the future perfect, or the *démodé*, materializes formally in Duras's work with the incongruous emergence of conflicting verbal tenses (present and future), and at the conclusion of Wang Anyi's novel, in its violent (post) anticipation of national trauma.

The "feminine" articulation of time in both Duras and Wang further distinguishes their unique allegorical glimpses of history from those devised by Benjamin. Their feminine allegories offer new understandings of the relationship between the present and trauma's uncanny return, as well as new aesthetic forms, stamped with melancholy.

This chapter thus will focus on the allegories offered by two novels—Duras's *Moderato cantabile* (1958) and Wang's *The Song of Everlasting Sorrow* (1995)—while emphasizing the intimate relationship between these authors' literary work and the cinema. The cinema can be understood as creating a space for these allegories, and as I've already introduced, this chapter—in its cross-cutting form of argument, a back-and-forth movement between France and China—dramatizes this space. However, the union with the cinema and cinematic form extends further. Elsewhere, Duras (first, in the 1950 novel *Un Barrage contre le Pacifique*) and Wang (in the 1999 autobiographical story "Years of Sadness") narrate their childhoods, and particularly their experiences of puberty, notions of love, and ambivalence toward the figure of the mother against the recurring backdrop of the movie theater. Furthermore, the transition in Duras's written aesthetics, first hinted at in her novel *Le Square* (1955) and reaching a fuller articulation several years later in *Moderato*, presents dialogue and narrative exposition in a stripped-down fashion approaching that of a screenplay.[22] The interior subjectivity of the characters is sketched through direct speech and movements through space, painting a mood with images and a soundscape of words, but leaving inner thoughts and motivations shadowy. Duras's novels, plays (and, later, films), then, morph into—like the work of her contemporary, Alain Robbe-Grillet—hybrid forms that have been termed *ciné-romans*. As Alwin Baum writes in his essay on Duras's filmic writing (*écriture filmique*): "Her novels read like films, her films like novels, and she often explicitly blurs the distinction."[23] In Wang Anyi's *The Song of Everlasting Sorrow*, meanwhile, the history of Shanghai, the novel's setting, as a center of film, in concert with images reminiscent of films from China's second golden age of cinema (in the 1940s) become touchstones and serve as bookends to the story of the life of one unremarkable city dweller spanning the course of four decades. In other words, while the two texts of central importance to this chapter are literary, the boundaries between my work with these texts and the cinema blur and bend without collapsing.

"French" and "Chinese" Melancholy and Feminism

While I claim that both the work of Marguerite Duras and Wang Anyi formally express the affective symptom of melancholy, I consider each author's approach in the light of their different national circumstances and relationships to feminism. Duras's childhood in colonial Indochina served as her introduction to the ruling class and to those others who serve it, but there is a starker binarism in her work between the haves and the have-nots than in that of Wang Anyi. Instead of the multiple and shifting class positions in twentieth-century China and in the writings of Wang, Duras primarily concerns herself with only three: the bourgeois (Anne Desbaresdes and her family), the worker (Chauvin and other factory workers), and, occasionally, the subaltern (the beggar of Calcutta, though this character and category are not included in *Moderato*). *Moderato*'s protagonist, Anne Desbaresdes, is clearly bourgeois, married to a rich man and living in a grand house, and the novel lampoons the lives of the wealthy. For Duras, bourgeois women and children are often agents of refusal and social change.[24] Duras's engagement with women subjects and the feminine thus must be considered alongside her political engagements: her work with the Resistance during the German Occupation, her signature on the 1960 *Manifeste des 121* and the 1971 *Manifeste des 343*.[25] These political acts, furthermore, were inseparable from her commitment to anti-colonialism and socialism, even as her alignment with the French Communist Party (PCF) waxed and waned over the course of her life. In fact, Jane Winston goes as far as to claim, "Duras came to writing and psychoanalysis and (perhaps) feminism, *through* Marx."[26] Her Marxism and broader political profile occasionally grated against her public success as a writer. Winston points out that Duras's *Un Barrage contre le Pacifique* was removed from consideration for the prestigious Prix Goncourt and Alain Resnais's *Hiroshima mon amour*, for which Duras wrote the screenplay, was withdrawn from the 1959 Cannes Film Festival because both works were considered in opposition to the conservative, imperialist, pro-American Gaullist government.[27] Even taking into account Duras's allegiance to Marxism, her *Moderato* has a far less complex depiction of class background than Wang Anyi's *Song*.

Wang Anyi, born during the Mao era, is attuned to the intricate workings of class in socialist and post-socialist China. Her "Chinese" melancholy in *The Song of Everlasting Sorrow* is situated within a particular class, specifically with the young woman protagonist Wang Qiyao, whom the author calls a "petty city dweller" or an "urban petty bourgeois" (both possible translations of *xiaoshimin*).[28] This makes Qiyao a kind of Shanghai "everywoman," neither rich nor poor, without any significant connections, biding her time until marriage to a man of the same class. Duras's *Moderato cantabile* presents a personal, desperate melancholy, self-destructive to the point of self-annihilation. Wang's *Sorrow*, meanwhile, reveals a more diffused melancholy, harbored within each "young lady's bedchamber" in Shanghai's *longtang*, the "vast neighborhoods inside enclosed alleys."[29] Each young lady keeps this space carefully and bides her time until marriage. Wang writes, "The lady's bedchamber in the Shanghai *longtang* is a room where anything might happen, where even the melancholy (愁; *chou*) makes a clamorous noise. When it rains, drops write the word 'melancholy' (*chou*) on the window."[30] In my 2011 interview with Wang Anyi, she claimed that the character *chou* (愁) that I have rendered in the previous passage as "melancholy" lacks the gravity expressed by such a translation.[31] She argued, "It isn't this type of grief, rather it is something lingering. It is not the mourning for a person who has passed away. Therefore, we could say that what I describe is a middling suffering." In other words, this middling suffering is a gnawing, dull pain, a sense of shame, and contrasts with the overwhelming, full-bodied melancholy in *Moderato*. The melancholy in *Song* results from the gap between banal dreams and an even more banal reality. It is precisely the ironic contrast of unexceptional lives and unrealized sublime experiences that renders such an effect.

Qiyao tries to climb the social ladder by entering into an extramarital affair with a wealthy older man attached to the Chinese Nationalist Party (GMD/KMT), but the logic of the novel is such that history and class background absolutely determine one's fate and, therefore, render Qiyao's attempts doomed from the start. As Ping Zhu points out in her essay about gender and labor in Wang Anyi's fiction, the most tranquil (and arguably least melancholic) period of Qiyao's life takes place after the death of her lover and during the first seventeen years of Maoism when she works as a nurse.[32] Zhu explains that Wang Anyi's "deep aversion to the contemporary consumer culture that turns women into objects of desire . . . leads to her nostalgia for the effective feminist practices in socialist China, when men and women worked as equal laborers."[33] Zhu locates this nostalgia for Chinese socialism in particular in Wang's novel *Fu Ping* (富萍) (2000), set in Shanghai during the mid-1960s before the Cultural Revolution, which Wang describes as "a utopia in time and space."[34] In *Fu Ping* the role of women's "unproductive labor" and the affective relationships that such labor fosters is elevated and proposed as an alternative to the capitalist market. "Because affective labor involves the production and reproduction of human relations," Zhu asserts, "it is no longer the same as the compulsory wage-earning labor that is felt as oppressive and alienating."[35] The titular character, Fu Ping, a migrant from rural Yangzhou, and the other subaltern laborers featured in the novel, act as service workers (domestic laborers, trash collectors, and repair people), exemplifying "with utmost directness and spontaneity the unification of production and consumption, need and intention, as well as the bodily and spiritual."[36] Zhu, furthermore, claims that by promoting the positive impact of such labor on the lives of workers, Wang's *Fu Ping* proposes a reevaluation of the hierarchical relationship between masculine "productive labor" and women's "unproductive labor" in canonical historiographies of Chinese socialism.

While Wang Anyi's fiction usually focuses on women protagonists and highlights the positive value of women's work, she has distanced herself from the position of "feminist" writer. In a 2001 interview with Liu Jin-dong, Wang protests the description of her work as "feminist." Instead, she explains, "My finished works don't belong to me anymore; they are open to anyone's criticism . . . I do not want to solve the women's problem in my works. . . . However, I do have one belief that can be related to feminism: I have created so many female characters because I think women are more aesthetic (具有審美性質; *juyou shenmeixingzhi*) than men, probably because men have been more socialized."[37] Wang specifies that women's "aesthetic" qualities distance women from intellectualizing or from abstract lofty ideals and render them fuller of vitality and energy for life; "Knowledge is feeble, life is robust. Who should embody knowledge and who should embody life in stories? I think it is better that women embody life, because men do not have women's aesthetic aura (美感; *meigan*) in life. I've barely seen a man full of power and vitality in real life."[38] Still, Wang depicts women's possibilities for satisfaction and self-sufficiency as largely dependent on historical time and place. In the "utopia in time and space" of Shanghai during the mid-1960s in her novel *Fu Ping*, the subaltern woman might gain fulfillment through the fruits of her labor and the relationships this labor garners to others of the same class. In Shanghai in the post-reform period in the 1980s in *The Song of Everlasting Sorrow*, however, the aging "urban petty bourgeois" woman who no longer measures up as an object of desire is rejected by consumer culture as valueless.

While both Wang Anyi and Marguerite Duras draw from historical, gendered, and class experience to spin affective melancholy into their narrative webs, the "Chinese" melancholy that I chart in this chapter in Wang's *The Song of Everlasting Sorrow* is tinged with irony and firmly attached to the plight of those, like the "urban petty bourgeois" Wang Qiyao, who find themselves cast aside in the emerging era of neoliberal globalization. This corresponds to a degree with Wang Anyi's self-professed belief that "the feminist ideas we learned from the West do not fit squarely with the reality of Chinese women."[39] The "French" melancholy of Duras, by contrast, acts as a sincere, all-encompassing, unstoppable rejection of the status quo on the part of the bourgeois Anne Desbaresdes, which Duras might describe as an expression of an "entirely negative politics" by which "simple inertia, refusal, a passive refusal, in sum the refusal to respond, has a callosal power."[40]

Duras: Vers la sincérité

The desperate, searing melancholy in Marguerite Duras's work emerged in her 1958 novel *Moderato cantabile*. It was here that she began a new stage of writing. Years later, Duras reflected on this development: "I've been thinking about this for two or three years; I think that the turn, the veering toward . . . sincerity (*vers la sincérité*) happened then."[41] This turn toward sincerity can be detected in the first chapter of *Moderato cantabile*, which opens at twilight in a seaside town. As Anne Desbaresdes listens to her son's piano lesson, the sky outside is washed in bursts of pink and red. Suddenly, a cry is heard from the café below. As the chapter continues, an anxious crowd gathers in front of the café. Mademoiselle Girard, the piano teacher, meanwhile, reminds her student to heed the Diabelli Sonatina's tempo: "Don't forget: *moderato cantabile*. Think of a lullaby."[42] The boy eventually succeeds in pleasing, and the lesson ends. Before going home, Anne Desbaresdes slides through the throng blocking the café's entrance and sees a dead woman and a man in the shadows at the rear of the establishment. Anne watches as the man lies down and embraces the corpse. The authorities arrive and load the man into a police van. By now night has fallen and his face is obscured: "Maybe he cried, but the advanced dusk made it impossible to glimpse the bloody grimace and trembling face or to see the tears streaming down it."[43] As mother and child near home, the chapter ends with a reminder of the lullaby with which it began: "All the same," Anne says to her son, "you could remember once and for all. Moderato means moderately, and cantabile means singingly. It's simple."[44] The novel, camouflaged in its tuneful title, uncovers the difficulty lurking beneath the simple rhythm of life in this French town: the red of the sunset uncannily doubled by blood, the fading light in the night's sky a harbinger of darkening desires. Anne casts off the bourgeois morality that has previously administered her choices, becoming fixated on the tragic couple in the café and the intensity of feeling that brought them there. After meeting a man, Chauvin, on a pilgrimage to the café, Anne spirals closer to the violent event by listening to and probing Chauvin's eyewitness account. As Duras biographer Laure Adler has noted, "*Moderato cantabile* is neither moderate (*ni modéré*) nor singing (*ni chantant*)."[45] Duras writes Anne's escalating freedom from the dissimulation of bourgeois life with a sparse, poetic frankness. This thematic and stylistic "veering toward sincerity" infiltrates Duras's *Moderato cantabile* with an emotional violence and imprints it with a melancholy—a refusal to abandon the most desperate obsessions—that comes to define her future work.

In her 1973 interviews with Xavière Gauthier, Duras sketches the shifts in style of her work beginning with *Moderato*: the increasing spareness, the severing of traditional narrative plot, the refusal to provide narrative closure, and the accumulation of "blanks" (*des blancs*). She laments: "Yes, but you see, that's how it's been in my life, too. I think that the life I lead is sometimes, is so . . . hard . . . I think . . . looking from the outside, it's hard to be with writing, the way I am . . . or with film . . . yes, I'll finish my sentence: . . . so hard that I wear myself out."[46] The hardness in Duras's work—that perpetual, resolute return to the scene of self-destruction—comes partially out of her practice of working, the deep relationship that her writing has to her life. The distance between autobiography and literature is always indeterminate, and in Duras's case it is particularly narrow.[47] The landscape of her colonial childhood in French Indochina, the murkiness of her Resistance years in occupied France, and the apparitions of family and lovers flicker in and out, defining her oeuvre. History funnels through her or reverberates inside of her body. As Duras explains to Gauthier, "If I were alone in the world, the story wouldn't have come to me. . . . The transformation that it undergoes may be a little strange, the sound that it makes when it passes through me, but that's all. It's a sound that it makes when it passes through somebody it's given to."[48] In Duras's writing, the strange sound of history is melancholic, feminine, like the scream of the anonymous woman with which *Moderato* begins.

Moderato partakes of larger trends aligned with postmodernism in the mutability of its central protagonist's shattering subjectivity and in the fluidity of its narrative plot.[49] Duras's expression of the feminine goes beyond the novel's depiction of a woman protagonist and her interior and exterior world. Duras's exploration of feminine routine (childcare, housework) in *Moderato* is quickly overshadowed by Anne's obsession with the lovers' history and the woman's murder.[50] Anne circles the event in her conversations with Chauvin and arrives at a complete refusal to move beyond or forward. Anne's embrace of melancholy is mirrored by Duras's text, whose syntax eventually cracks and breaks open. Later in her career, Duras would famously describe this "violent rejection of syntax" in her writing as "blanks."[51] Though the blanks only increase in her future work, *Moderato* introduces them to the reader. These blanks embody—shape formally—the novel's multifold enunciation of the feminine and the melancholic.

I am, of course, not the first to cite the melancholy in Duras's writing. In Julia Kristeva's 1987 *Soleil noir: Dépression et mélancolie*—named after a line from Gérard de Nerval's 1853 poem "El Desdichado"—she explores her own melancholic disposition by unveiling the way in which melancholy operates in patients' case studies, literature (Nerval, Dostoyevsky, Duras), and visual art (Holbein). She ends the book with a portrait of Marguerite Duras, whose "aesthetic of *awkwardness*" she names "the discourse of blunted pain."[52] Kristeva sees Duras's melancholy as a response to history, explaining that traumatic catastrophe unsettles the artist's capacity to represent the world.[53] The traumas cited by Kristeva include Auschwitz and Hiroshima; though, in an earlier chapter on Paul Valéry and the Surrealists, Kristeva also points to World War I. In so doing, Kristeva proposes historical cycles of disaster and human response.

Yet not all writers respond to trauma with melancholy and not all emerge from historical devastation with a new form of writing: an aching terseness. Duras's way of writing, then, comes partially from a national history, but also—as I have already suggested—from her biography. Kristeva points to Duras's difficult relationship with her family ("her hard but courageous mother," "the early encounter with her brother's mental illness"), to which I would add the years of the German Occupation, and particularly the year 1944 when her then husband, Robert Antelme, was arrested by the Gestapo for his participation in the Resistance and deported to Buchenwald, then Gandersheim, before being discovered barely alive at Dachau by family friend François Mitterrand just after the war's end.

Following Antelme's arrest, Duras wrote about the anguish of awaiting word of his life or death in the autobiographical *La Douleur*, which would not be published until 1985, while her journal from the period was compiled in the posthumous book *Cahiers de la guerre et autres textes* (2006). In *La Douleur*, the author explains how she stumbled upon this lost journal: "I rediscovered this Journal in two notebooks from the blue armoires at Neauphle-le-Château. I have no memory of having written it. I know that I did it (*Je sais que je l'ai fait*), that it is I who wrote it (*que c'est moi qui l'ai écrit*)."[54] In this short passage Duras inscribes her past self onto her present self in the movement from "Je sais que *je* l'ai fait" (accepting that in the past "I *did* it") to "c'est *moi* qui l'ai écrit" (asserting that "it *is* I who wrote it"). Even if these repressed memories of the trauma did not reach full expression until 1985, the resulting symptom, *la douleur*, sorrow, entered Duras's literature with *Moderato* and would be impressed on her oeuvre ever after.

Like most of her compatriots, during the Trente Glorieuses Duras outwardly concerned herself with remaking life in the present, but the truth in all its "sincerity" emerges in her writing: the melancholic *Moderato* contends with the return of the violence suffered collectively by the French. *Douleur*, a word denoting both pain and sorrow, the plural form (*les douleurs*) used to speak of the agony of birth, is an apt title for this work and Duras's future melancholic creations, in which Duras, thinking Antelme dead, writes, "Nothing in the world belongs to me now except for that corpse in a ditch." As Kristeva would later say, Duras's work reveals that she has placed "the malady of death at the center of psychic experience."[55] History, biography, but also feminine subjectivity will ground Duras to melancholy, to "the malady of death." Her work shows both an inability and a stubborn refusal to leave the corpse behind. This act of defiance flies in the face of the discourse of *résistancialisme* operative in postwar France. While De Gaulle asked the French to move on, and the country began to embrace neoliberal globalization, Duras and her works, these remnants of feminist refusal, clutched history's corpse.

Wang: Fiction as a Diary

Duras's experience of personal and national history inspired a writing that crawls into the grave, whereas Wang Anyi's trajectory allowed for a literary union of the intimate and the public tinged with an ironic melancholy. At

the beginning of the New Era (following the death of Mao) and increasingly in the post–New Era (following the Tiananmen Square Massacre),
the market for writing by women increased in China. Wang Anyi's 1988
essay "A Woman Writer's Sense of Self" (女作家的自我; *Nüzuojia de ziwo*)
comments on this phenomenon, beginning with her memory of the
Chinese readership's passionate reception of fellow women writer Zhang
Jie's 1979 story, "Love Must Not Be Forgotten" (愛, 是不能忘記的; *Ai, shi
buneng wangjide*).[56] Suddenly, the private emotions and experiences of an
individual replaced the Mao-era imperative to write only in the mode of a
Chinese collective. Wang explains that it was this shift that made it possible
for her to become a writer: "Previously, I had dreaded literature. I was
highly emotional and had strived to connect these feelings to social and
collective consciousness. But every effort failed. At the time, the greatest
portion of my literary output was diary- and letter-writing. Thus, I have
said several times, 'In the past, I wrote my diary as fiction, while today
I write my fiction as diary.' "[57] Wang understands this fiction that springs
from the affective and its narrative that blurs the divide between autobiography and invention as the provenance of women writers: "In fact,
literature's original impulse is emotional revelation; women and literature
share the same natural origin."[58] Like Duras, then, Wang Anyi sees her
work as emerging out of a historical shift (from Mao era to New Era to
post–New Era), feminine affectivity, and biography.

Her 1997 autobiographic story, "Years of Sadness," negotiates all
three of these threads (history, feminine affectivity, and biography) as she
reflects on her preadolescence in 1963, the moment during which Mao
introduced the Socialist Education Movement or "The Four Clean-ups."
As a result of this initiative, intellectuals (like Wang's writer parents) were
sent to villages or factories to be reeducated by peasants and workers. For
Wang, this meant that her parents were largely absent during the crucial
and confusing stage of early puberty.[59] Wang's "Years of Sadness" narrates
her memories of this period—between trips to the cinema and playing
with other children in a back alley—as rife with feelings of injustice,
shame, and isolation. I will show that these personal forms of "sadness,"
this particular brand of melancholy and type of feminist refusal, also
structure her fictional *The Song of Everlasting Sorrow*; we can hear the
echo of the Durassian-cum-Kristevan *black sun*, a melancholic remnant of
feminist refusal, when Wang writes, "Everything I had gone through had
erected a wall that isolated me from the crowd. The jostling crowd and I
were separated in two different worlds. Even our *suns* were different. We

stepped on each other's shadows but that was all."[60] Specifically here—in the doubling of the *black sun*—we have a hint of the uncanny phenomenon I suggest in the introduction of this book: that one historical trauma may evoke another across time and in a different language.

Lingzhen Wang's 2004 study, *Personal Matters: Women's Autobiographical Practice in Twentieth Century China*, undertakes a feminist reappraisal of the autobiographical writing of Chinese women authors from the late Qing martyr Qiu Jin (1875–1907) to the 1990s post-socialist work of Chen Ran, Lin Bai, and Wang Anyi. Her book borrows from American feminist Carol Hanisch's slogan "the personal is political," shaping it to fit the historical and cultural particulars of twentieth-century China. In the final pages of her introduction, Wang argues: "The idea that the personal is political is not only relevant but critical, for it illuminates the functioning of the determining patriarchal structure throughout China's twentieth century and the political character of the private. Modern Chinese women's autobiographical practice, which demonstrates the complexity of being a woman and a writer both in public and in private, has thus made possible a feminist study of the personal with a specific historical and cultural significance."[61] In the case of the 1990s and the work of Wang Anyi, Lingzhen Wang claims that "Years of Sadness" confronts the heightened consumption and materialism of this period with an affective shame. The political thrust of the personal, thus, often functions as a counter-discourse, or a writing that brushes "history against the grain," with—as I am claiming in the case of Wang Anyi and Marguerite Duras—a "melancholy against the grain," or a remnant of feminist refusal. To further delineate the vicissitudes of feminist refusal in Wang and Duras, I will now examine a novel by each author in more detail.

Moderato Cantabile:
Melancholy against the Trente Glorieuses

I will begin with Marguerite Duras's *Moderato cantabile* and its protagonist Anne Desbaresdes, who cannot help but return to a café in which a young woman was murdered by her lover. Like many of Duras's later women characters (Anne-Marie Stretter, Lol V. Stein, Alissa, etc.), Anne is reserved, seemingly aloof or apart. She lives in a state of discontent, incompletion. Heretofore the docile wife of a prominent local businessman, Anne becomes fascinated by the passion that would drive one to murder. She meets a man,

Chauvin, in the café who agrees to join her in a dialogue centered on the violent event. It is a small town, and Chauvin, whose name alludes to his machismo, his *chauvinism*, recognizes her: "You are Madame Desbaresdes, the wife of the director of the Import-Export Company and the Coastal Foundry. You live on the Boulevard de la Mer."[62] This is how Anne has been defined for the ten years of her marriage; her individuality eclipsed by the role she plays in society. Yet, suddenly, she becomes disgusted by the rules that have governed her life. She seeks to understand the unknown woman's murder, at the risk of throwing her own life into chaos. We are given no real history of Anne, no reasoning for her actions; she could be any young bourgeois mother of the Trente Glorieuses. To explain her continual returns to the café, the site of the murder, she says simply: "It would have been impossible for me not to return."[63]

The timid Anne Desbaresdes, living out her days in a repetition of bourgeois obligation, awakens with the scream of the dying woman in the café, and her longing to be consumed by a fire more violent than the quotidian flicker of habit continues to expand over the course of the novel. Formerly a child, a docile foil of her inscrutable, impish son, Anne now inquires into her adult desires. The scream, the founding traumatic event of the novel, spawns Anne's melancholic adult subjectivity. Her nascent recognition of the potential of violence in society induces an investigation into the scream's origin that will dominate *Moderato*'s narrative. However, Anne cannot locate the true origin. The traumatic event remains clouded in mystery, indecipherable; as Anne grows increasingly obsessed with understanding, in compulsively postulating new theories, she sinks further into melancholy.

Unlike Benjamin, whose *gaze* generates an allegoric experience, the feminine allegory in Duras's *Moderato* does not arise from something seen. Anne Desbaresdes does not witness the events that caused the scream. She *hears* the sound, "a long moan," and *feels* its import.[64] In this way, the novel dramatizes an initial allegory via the aural: the realization of ancient human violence coming in a present moment of apparent security, comparable to the resurgence of the trauma of the Occupation in the Trente Glorieuses. Anne experiences this as both a threat and a promise. She obsessively pursues all routes by which she might grasp the "truth" of this experience and becomes immersed in a process of melancholic repetition. Sound, in fact, is privileged over sight throughout the novel. The melodic piano music of Diabelli, repeated imperfectly by Anne's son at his piano lesson, sets the tone of the opening pages of the novel, but is almost immediately complicated by a contrary noise, that of the scream of the dying woman. These opposing sounds repeat throughout the narrative.

Whereas the novel's first allegory is Anne's apprehension of the scream—what I'm terming the sound of trauma—the novel's second allegory is created out of a confrontation between historical space and time. Duras's *Moderato* presents slightly over one week in a desolate, nameless French coastal town, the size of which is determined by industry. Chauvin comments, "It's indeed a small town, barely large enough for three factories."[65] The café's costumers, practically all male employees of a local factory, stream in after the bell signals the end of their shift. We could be in any coastal town in France. The sounds of the sea and the comings and goings of barges reinforce the plodding rhythm of the novel and the monotonous lives of its characters.

The class hierarchy of the nameless town—a bourgeois governing class (living in tomb-like mansions) at the top, and ranks of nameless factory workers (who are native to the place, known to each other, and communicate the inner workings of their world off-stage) below—reminds one of the demarcation of colonial spaces exposed in Duras's earlier work (*Un Barrage contre le Pacifique*) and foretells her later fascination with these landscapes after the collapse of French colonialism in Southeast Asia. The decaying estate in her film *India Song* (1975), where ghostly figures dance to endlessly circling gramophone records, presents a world after its obliteration. These places are imagined, culled from the unconscious; although they are partially drawn from the recesses of her childhood memories in French Indochina, Duras transforms these spaces into mythic archetypes. The Durassian archetypes take on such dominance in her literature and film that their presence becomes presupposed; a work seems atypical without them. The nameless town in *Moderato* introduces the myth and its archetypes, sharing the class distinctions and haunted quarters that incessantly reemerge over the course of Duras's oeuvre. In *Moderato*, Duras evokes the specter of declining French colonialism, as well as the shadows of the solid national identity that passed away under the Occupation. Her insistent reliance on archetypes discloses Duras's project, beginning with *Moderato*, as an allegorical one: the compression of multiple French spaces and national periods only fully comes to light by following the itinerary of her oeuvre; we encounter over and over the paralyzed remnants of a past (which is also the present and the future).

Both Duras's first and second forms of allegory in *Moderato* are unlike those of her contemporaries.[66] Anne Desbaresdes also departs from

previous models of the melancholic heroine. The clearest influence is
Gustave Flaubert's 1856 novel *Madame Bovary*, a fact that did not escape
the attention of critics at the time of *Moderato*'s publication.[67] Flaubert
describes the progression of Emma Bovary's melancholy subjectivity over
the course of her tragic life. Emma Bovary and Anne Desbaresdes are
similar melancholic heroines in some important regards: both feel stifled
by bourgeois married life, try to satisfy their desires elsewhere, commit
adultery (in fact or in fantasy), and finally wish only to die.

The different aesthetic approaches the authors take in constructing
these women in language, however, mark them as radically dissimilar.
Flaubert devotes pages to describing Emma's death. Duras indicates
Anne's ultimate death wish in two sentences. Displaying his mastery of
nineteenth-century realism, Flaubert accounts for all the facts governing
provincial, bourgeois life in France under King Louis-Philippe I. Emma's
characterization is grounded in these details: the books she reads, the
clothing she dons, the habits and opinions of everyone she knows. Her
subjectivity appears complete. Anne, on the contrary, does not achieve full
subjectivity; we know nothing of her past nor of her interests. Duras does
not even give Anne's son a name. If this lack of detail fractures Anne's
subjectivity, Duras fragments it further by the particularly sparse style
she debuts in *Moderato* and would be loyal to ever after. Duras writes
Anne in gestures and dialogue, never by disclosing her inner thoughts.
The holes in Anne's subjectivity and the sparse, unadorned language used
throughout *Moderato* breaks with Duras's earlier realism, creating a form
unique to her. Brimming with the "unsaid," suffused with melancholy,
Duras's *Moderato* conveys an unconscious relationship to trauma: giving
new, feminine voice to this shared French heritage, and breaking her bond
with earlier forms of modernism.

However, like Emma Bovary, Anne becomes less and less capable of
fulfilling her maternal and domestic duties as she grows more beholden
to her traumatic neurosis, and her investment in the stories she and
Chauvin are inventing intensifies. One evening, Anne serves as hostess
to a society dinner. She arrives late and drunk. Duras demarcates this
scene—the penultimate chapter in the novel—by curiously beginning in
the present tense and concluding in the future tense. This striking break
with the prevailing narrative time in the novel, heretofore written in the
conventional *passé simple*, dramatizes Anne's revolt. Anne's heightened
level of experience (and of intoxication) in this chapter is out of joint
with that in the rest of *Moderato*. Duras propels this scene out of the

past and into the present, coloring it with vivid descriptions otherwise absent in the novel:

> The women are at their most radiant. The men covered them in jewels (*bijoux*) in proportion to their balance sheets (*leurs bilans*). . . . The salmon makes another round in its diminished form. The women will completely devour it. Their naked shoulders have the luster and the solidity (*la fermeté*) of a society founded on the basis of the certainty of its entitlement, and these women were chosen at its convenience. The rigor of their upbringing demands that their excesses be tempered in the greater interest of their position.[68]

These nameless men and women share a certain set of bourgeois values. Duras shows us here how the men have purchased the women, and how these couples both constitute and reinforce the ideals of a society whose excesses (the women's "jewels") and deprivations (determined by the husbands' "balance sheets") must be controlled and consistent ("the solidity" of bourgeois society). They only indulge certain appetites. Anne has begun to explore other, taboo hungers; there are probably already whispers circulating in her milieu about her fall from respectability, her new status as a *femme adultère*. The use of present tense and the heightened visual detail makes the scene resemble a tableau, frozen in time or excised from history, rather than an episode contributing to the chronological trajectory of the novel's narrative. At the dinner party, Anne finalizes her social suicide. She drinks past the point of drunkenness. She wants to self-destruct with feeling, a passionate outrage absent from her controlled life. So, as everyone at the table savors the duck dish, we learn that "Anne Desbaresdes has just refused to be served."[69]

After the meal, she retreats upstairs to her son's room in physical and emotional revolt: "And to the sacred rhythm of her child's breathing, she will vomit (*vomira*) at length the strange nourishment that she was forced to take that evening."[70] The arrival of the future tense in this sentence (*vomira*) further destabilizes the scene's position within the narrative development of the novel. Beyond its destruction of conventional narrative structure, this movement likewise scoffs at linear monumental history. As I will describe below, Duras's literary intervention (zigzagging chronologically forward, backward, no-ward) acts as an historiographical mediation. "She will vomit" sounds like a supposition, a prediction, rather than a fact. It reminds the reader of the hypotheses Chauvin and Anne have been making about the motives of the dead lovers. These are often posed in the conditional or introduced with structures such as "I think that" (*je crois que*) and "it seems to me" (*il me semble que*), both of which unhinge objective certainty. The future tense also resembles a command. Perhaps Anne's experience in the chapter is filtered through a continual, imaginative dialogue with the absent (though conceivably peeping from the bushes) Chauvin, revealing how the supremacy of his desire filters her experience. Perhaps she allows Chauvin's words in her head to direct her awareness and actions in the scene.

With such an excess of asynchronous possibilities emerging from one scene, Duras, therefore, introduces a third form of allegory. This scene of revolt in the penultimate chapter destabilizes the narrative time of the novel (just as does the *démodé* proposed by Emily Apter) in order to force *the reader* to an allegorical realization. As the chapter defies the logical sequencing of all other events in the novel, the reader must consider the possibility that the scene may not have taken place at all. Or, still more radically, that the rest of the story establishes a false narrative, and only the scene in this chapter truly took place. Does the narrator give us this chapter, or does some other voice (Chauvin's, Anne's) intervene? As the steady diegetic ground crumbles, the reader recognizes that *Moderato*'s reckoning with the impact of trauma on history has penetrated and altered its own basic, grammatical laws.

Moderato cantabile circles death. After her total rejection of life, exemplified by the disastrous dinner party (and complete with a literal elimination of food), Anne arrives at the final state of melancholy: hoping that in death she will achieve the sublime experience, the origin of her traumatic neurosis she has long sought. Chauvin and Anne *become* the tragic couple they have been imagining. They examine the reasons for the woman's murder at the hands of her lover; "I imagine that one day . . . a morning at sunrise, she knew suddenly what she wanted from him. Everything became clear for her to the point that she told him what her wish would be. There is no explanation, I believe, for that kind of discovery."[71] Chauvin and Anne reduce the imaginative distance between themselves and the violent couple by identifying more and more with them. Finally, they finish their circling, and Chauvin utters the phrase Duras has promised us since the original crime of passion that began the novel: "I wish you were dead." Anne replies, "It's done."[72] But, Anne does not die. The stasis of melancholy having installed itself heavily on her; we are left without the catharsis of conclusion or any chance of escape.

The lack of escape or catharsis in *Moderato* manifests the melancholic legacy of trauma on contemporary France. While Duras's very personal relationship to national trauma gave birth to the entirely original occurrences of aesthetics in *Moderato*, her lasting significance and influence indicate the way this novel and her larger oeuvre speak to a collective experience of melancholy.

As trauma theory—from Freud to Abraham and Torok to Caruth and LaCapra and beyond—teaches us, the site of trauma eludes all access and the word of trauma escapes distorted, encrypted.[73] Moving away from the verbal metaphor, the *image* of melancholic paralysis given by *Moderato* refracts rather than replicates France's traumatic history. Like Perseus's shield, evoked in Siegfried Kracauer's repurposing of the Medusa myth, the cinema (and the *ciné-roman*) offers images inflected by real terrors, but not the devastating truth that will turn the spectator-reader into stone. Kracauer writes, "The moral of the myth is, of course, that we do not, and cannot see actual horrors because they paralyze us with blinding fear; and that we shall know what they look like only by watching images of them which reproduce their true appearances."[74] This, for Kracauer, is the *good* of film experience. Even though we may only skim the surface, these images "beckon the spectator to take them in and thus incorporate into his memory the real face of things too dreadful to be beheld in reality."[75] An encrypted mise-en-scène of history, Duras's *ciné-roman* stages an intervention in the Trente Glorieuses. When feminine melancholy and feminine allegory resurface in China post-1989—after the Tiananmen Square Massacre and amid a growing tidal wave of neoliberal globalization—in the writing of Wang Anyi, the result is an uncanny double exposure. Wang's *The Song of Everlasting Sorrow*, a projection in the absence of real moving pictures of the trauma of Tiananmen, reflects China in the 1990s on the one hand, and brings to mind France's Trente Glorieuses on the other. It is not that Wang's melancholic allegory resembles that of Duras; unless we think of resemblance as the flip side of a coin: made of the same metal, the images are different and face opposite directions. To extend this metaphor slightly further, the work of Duras and Wang serves as an alternative global currency of feminine aesthetics cast by disparate national traumas.

The Song of Everlasting Sorrow: Hypotext and Hypertext

Wang Anyi's 1995 *The Song of Everlasting Sorrow* is not the Durassian intimate memoir of traumatic encounter and its melancholic symptom;

rather, Wang's novel positions both the writer and her reader at a distance from the narrative. *Song* takes an ironic stance toward its non-melancholic woman protagonist, but soberly announces the novel's wider characterization of the fate of individuals in China following the national trauma incurred by the 1989 Tiananmen Square Massacre and the onset of neoliberal globalization.

Wang Anyi's novel, more ambitious in chronological scope than Duras's, follows roughly forty years in the life of a Shanghai woman named Wang Qiyao, beginning after the end of the Second Sino-Japanese War in the mid-1940s and concluding in the mid-1980s. The reader meets Qiyao as a teenager and follows her through a succession of failed relationships, the birth of her daughter, and her eventual murder by a casual lover-thief, with the ever-changing landscape of twentieth-century Shanghai in the background. Qiyao represents not just one woman but also a certain kind of woman in twentieth-century Shanghai. Wang speaks of Qiyao as being "the archetypal daughter of the Shanghai *longtang*."[76] The narrator goes on to make the banality of this girl explicit by pluralizing her: "Wang Qiyaos always follow the trends, neither falling behind nor taking the lead: they are the modern crowd. They (*Tamen*) follow trends to the letter with complete faith: without expressing their individuality, and without questioning."[77] In my interview with Wang, she described Qiyao not as a heroine with lofty intellect, beauty, or integrity but as a "petty city dweller" (*xiaoshimin*) whose insignificant clout but representative experience reminds the reader of characters from the work of another celebrated writer from Shanghai: Eileen Chang (*Zhang Ailing*). Therefore, from the beginning of the novel, the reader understands Qiyao to be not only a specific character but also a member of a class of prosaic women. Wang's chronicle of this "petty city dweller" reveals history, not on a grand scale but through the small footprints left by a trivial person. Of her work's relationship to history, Wang told me: "I have never suggested that I have written a national epic. Yet, each and every person has his or her own conception of history. Everyone's method, angle, and material for looking at history differ. When I write history, it is with the desire to show its traces in the quotidian."

One such historical "trace" comes unmistakably to the surface in the title of Wang's novel (*Changhenge*), which clearly echoes Bai Ju-yi's (772–846) famous Tang dynasty poem, also titled "The Song of Everlasting Sorrow" (*Changhenge*). Drawing from Gérard Genette's useful terminology to address this unambiguously intertextual association, we can label Wang's *The Song of Everlasting Sorrow* the hypertext and Bai's the hypotext.[78] Each version charts a broad narrative arc: taking the reader from the promising youth to the violent death of its heroine. Each heroine is, furthermore, an attractive, even beautiful young woman, whose tenure as mistress to a powerful man alters the course of her life.

Wang's novel transforms the ethos of Bai's poem by depriving its heroine of enduring romance and of transhistorical import. Of course, Bai's *Song* treats real historical personages. Yang Yuhuan (719–756), better known as the beloved Noble Consort (*Guifei*) of the popular Tang emperor Xuanzong (685–762), is said to have dominated the great man's heart from the first day of their involvement. Yang Guifei captivated Xuanzong to such an extent that he began neglecting his duties as emperor. During the An Lushan Rebellion (*An Shi Zhiluan*) (755–763), Yang Guifei's cousin, Yang Guozhong, became a powerful and contentious leader within the Tang government. His perpetual conflict with An Lushan largely prompted the gory rebellion. Yang Guozhong's blood connection to Yang Guifei placed her under suspicion; many high officials deemed her a liability, perhaps even a traitor. Under pressure from these officials, Xuanzong had Yang Guifei strangled to death. However, the legend does not end there. Bai Ju-yi's poem tells of Xuanzong's long quest to be reunited with his beloved; the emperor finally consults a Daoist priest who is able to track down Yang Guifei in the Mountains of the Undying (*Xianshan*) and return with a token of her love. The legacy of the story of Yang Guifei and Xuanzong proves contradictory: both a parable of the dangers of falling prey to feminine influence and neglecting official duties, as well as a sentimental tribute to romantic love.

Yang Guifei was just a young girl when she first caught the emperor's eye. Bai Ju-yi writes of Yang's protected childhood and radiant beauty:

> The House of Yang had a daughter, just grown to maturity,
> Raised deep in the women's quarters, no men knew her.
> When Heaven births such beauty, it is loath to waste it,
> So one morning she was chosen to be by the ruler's side.[79]

The prose piece written to accompany the poem, "An Account of *The Song of Everlasting Sorrow*" (*Changhenge zhuan*) (829), by Bai Ju-yi's friend Chen Hong, provides more details about Yang: "She was then sixteen years old" (*Ji ji yi*: literally, "She had reached the age of wearing hairpins").[80] At sixteen, Yang Guifei has her whole love story ahead of her.

The first time the narrator of Wang Anyi's *The Song of Everlasting Sorrow* mentions Wang Qiyao's age, this protagonist is also just sixteen.

However, unlike Yang Guifei, the sixteen-year-old Qiyao does not revel in the freshness of her youth: "Wang Qiyao was sixteen at this time . . . but she already felt much older."[81] Wang Anyi's transformation of the hypotext flattens any nascent, monumental relevance that its heroine might bear to history. Bai's poem foreshadows Yang Guifei's destiny to serve a higher calling from the beginning: "When Heaven births (*Tiansheng*) such beauty (*lizhi*), it is loath (*nan*) to waste it (*ziji*)." Wang's novel does not attribute the lot of Qiyao to a loftier fate. In fact, Qiyao arrives at her own gloomy self-assessment—"She felt" (*Ta juede*)—and denies any implication of liberation via self-knowledge. Qiyao neither bears the favor of heaven, nor the May Fourth generation's empowered subjectivity. She is simply a very ordinary Shanghai girl: a type who "never falls behind nor takes the lead" (*Bu luowu yu bu chaoqian*).

Wang's novel not only transforms Bai's poem but also levels a critique. Xuanzong's reign corresponded to the pinnacle of culture during the Tang dynasty. Paul W. Kroll states that the Tang never regained these heights: racked and ousted by the An Lushan Rebellion, the Tang government remained unsteady after it resumed power. As a result, the peace and prosperity before the rebellion, and principally Xuanzong's reign, became subject to an intensely nostalgic discourse in literature: "The drift of history into legend was already underway in the generation immediately following the An Lu-shan rebellion. . . . Scholars made Hsüan-tsung's [Xuanzong's] reign a conservatory for memories and images both radiant and monitory. . . . Indeed, the remembrance and re-creation of the High T'ang's aura of sun-splashed joys extravagance was to become, by the ninth century, a topical subgenre of T'ang poetry."[82] Xuanzong's reign, of course, contains the love story between the emperor and Yang Guifei. In the aftermath of the An Lushan Rebellion, their touching tale was recounted in myriad forms, and the Noble Consort's place in the Chinese imaginary was secured.

Wang calls this nostalgia into question. Her staunchly anti-nostalgic rewriting of Bai's poem stresses the mundane aspects of women's hopeful alliances with men and women's ultimate disposability throughout history. Perhaps, Wang seems to suggest, Xuanzong and Yang Guifei's legend has less to do with these characters and more to do with what later generations needed from them. She refuses to allow Qiyao the meaning that Yang Guifei received out of historical nostalgia; Qiyao's story must remain lackluster, common, and local.

Wang's anti-nostalgia brushes up against the resurgence of nostalgia in China following Tiananmen. During the 1990s, the discourse of nostalgia grew in China as one of the consequences of neoliberal globalization. As Dai Jinhua puts it:

> From a certain point of view, this process of the giddy and aggressively rapid urbanization of the 1990s embodies the most contradictory sentiment of contemporary Chinese people, especially contemporary Chinese intellectual elites. On the one hand, the ideology of progress is undergoing the materializing process of identification and verification, which consequently brings the joy and excitement of discovery; on the other hand, even a 'homegrown' Chinese is suddenly stripped of hometown, homeland, and home country and abandoned to the beautiful new world.[83]

However, Dai claims that Wang Anyi's *Song* offers nostalgia as a reprieve to the new sense of homelessness in the China after 1989: "Wang Anyi's Wang Qiyao slips through historical upheavals in an evasive and illicit manner, like an outdated, forgotten, and therefore clandestinely kept bunch of dry, dead flowers."[84] Ban Wang, too, argues that Wang Anyi's *Song* offers an intervention into the homogeneous, empty time of revolutionary history (in the second part of the novel) and neoliberal globalization (in final section of the novel) through its nostalgic (re)vision of pre-revolutionary Shanghai (where the novel begins). He explains that the novel "depicts the commercial culture in Shanghai in its halcyon days before 1949, which tenaciously persisted in a submerged existence through the Mao era, and finally resurfaced in the post-Mao period. By evoking its prehistory the novel attempts to infuse an aura of authentic experience and lend a historical dimension to the commodity."[85] The commodity is offered a human face in the novel's heroine Qiyao; during the socialist period, she accumulates a following of friends and admirers who gather daily to reminisce about the Shanghai of their childhoods when Qiyao was considered a beauty queen, though only enough to win third place in the 1946 Miss Shanghai pageant. Ban Wang explains, "Against a raging history outside, the characters indulge themselves in trivialities and mundane details. But it is precisely the trifles and details that form the building blocks of a livable life, a tiny strain of temporality that survives the storm."[86] While I agree that the characters' nostalgia for old Shanghai's commercial, material culture allows for real human connections to develop in the novel and acts as a subtle form of individualistic resistance to Chinese socialism's "mythical mirage: the colorless, disembodied ideology of production and efficiency for collective, utopian goals," I judge *Song* as ultimately critical of Qiyao's celebration of herself as commodity.[87] Even given his positive assessment of the role of commodity nostalgia in the novel, Ban Wang also recognizes that the tragic end of Qiyao's story reveals the darker consequences of even gentle forays into commodity fetishism: "The market, endowed with an aura and a human face in nostalgic memory, has a tendency to dwindle into the blind and heartless pursuit of profit and disintegrate into social chaos."[88] This is the vicious world in which *Song* arrives at its conclusion, where Qiyao must confront the fact that her role as commodity has—like other perishable products—a limited shelf life.

While the novel opens with a poetic union of apparent nostalgia and melancholy, the former sours as the novel progresses and finally appears mockingly ironic. When Wang Anyi introduces us to Qiyao, she is a charming (if rather commonplace) young girl, but age leaves her with only inflated memories of her youth. Qiyao's nostalgia does not make the novel nostalgic. Outdated, forgotten, and ultimately murdered by her lover, Qiyao does not inspire a longing for the past. Although Wang Anyi's account of Shanghai begins long before the Cultural Revolution and the Tiananmen Square Massacre, the melancholy that she describes belongs to a writer who has emerged from these traumas and into the post-Mao age of industrializing, globalizing, capitalizing China. Xudong Zhang offers a wonderful summation of the contrast between nostalgia and melancholy in Wang's treatment of Shanghai: "For Wang, the self-sublimation the city seeks can only be found in its ironic, degenerate form of melancholy, that is, in the mourning of the loss, in which a phenomenological restoration of the void, rather than the glorification of a mythological past, proves vital in acquiring an astute sense of time and history for a complacently atemporal city."[89] Shanghai, this "atemporal city," acts as a locus of nostalgia throughout the twentieth century. It has occupied a site of "modernity" since the end of the nineteenth century: first in its early cosmopolitanism, carved into foreign concessions following the Opium Wars (*Yapian zhanzheng*) (1839–1842 and 1856–1860), then in its heyday as the center of Chinese cinema in the 1930s and 1940s, and finally in its distinct global character by the end of the twentieth century, as one of the largest cities in the world. Authors have tried to articulate its special personality, always at the cross section of the old and the new, yielding a portrait of contradiction. We see this in Eileen Chang, with her emphasis on the old-fashioned details at the center of her modern, 1940s Shanghai. We see it in Wang Anyi, with the character of Wang Qiyao growing outdated and out of place over the course of her life, and with the coexistence of places built in the past (the *longtang*) and those dominating the present (the modern high-rise). Xudong Zhang argues, "In this sense, Shanghai may be a privileged site to witness the central dilemma of modernity as it is described by Max Horkheimer and T.W. Adorno in *Dialectic of Enlightenment*: it is a historical process which enlightens by mythologizing; that Enlightenment always creates its own myth that is the mythology of the modern."[90] Wang Anyi, then, can be understood as an allegorical figure of Chinese (post)modernity and as an illustration of the temporal contradictions at the heart of the city of Shanghai.

Chinese writers and intellectuals first appropriated the Benjaminian conception of allegory in the 1980s, attempting to make sense of the world that surfaced after the Cultural Revolution. China emerged from this ten-year traumatic period (climaxing with the death of Mao in 1976) on shaky legs, unsure of where it stood. Ban Wang explains that Benjamin's "account of experience resonated strongly with Chinese intellectuals' understanding in the post-Mao era. 'Experience' entered the vocabulary of Chinese literature, criticism, and aesthetic discourse as a prominent new concept different from the obvious Chinese term *jingyan*. Its altered usages reveal the basic Benjaminian sense: the sense of aesthetic wholeness and affective fulfillment combining present and past, individual and culture, ideal and everyday."[91] In the 1980s, Chinese artists attempted to capture what was lost while in the midst of an ever-changing present by mining the depths of collective memory. The result was the "searching for roots" (*xungen wenxue*) and "scar literature" (*shanghen wenxue*) movements, epitomized by the work of Ah Cheng, Mo Yan, and Han Shaogong, among others. However, after Tiananmen, in the China of the 1990s fixated on economic growth, consumerism, consumption, and nationalism, writers faced these new jarring realities with another kind of allegorical, literary response.

Shanghai, like Wang Qiyao, is given a voice in its allegorical treatment in Wang Anyi's *The Song of Everlasting Sorrow*. Wang begins her novel with a long, lyrical exploration of Shanghai's *longtang*. The *longtang*, like Shanghai, lives and breathes, giving birth to and housing the people of Shanghai, growing and changing. The narrator describes it exactly as such a living organism: "Whispered secrets remain on the roof, the balcony, and the windows. At night, the sound of knocking on doors rises and descends."[92] The lyricism of the novel is most effective in this first chapter, as Wang links the places she describes to sound. The intermittent tapping at *longtang* doors at night becomes a synecdoche for the comings and goings of Shanghai's inhabitants. Gossip and rumors are the language of the *longtang*: "If the *longtang* of Shanghai could speak, they would certainly speak in rumors. . . . If the *longtang* of Shanghai could dream, then that dream would be gossip."[93] This is a language that goes against official discourse ("It can change an official biography into an ambiguous thing"), and it carries within it a certain truth.[94] This language, like the *longtang*, has mundane gloom attached to it.

Wang Qiyao, murdered in the mid-1980s, does not live to see the 1989 Tiananmen Massacre. However, many other Chinese who survived those years were also deprived of the images of June Fourth. I read Wang's *Song* as an encrypted ode to the events of June Fourth in its descriptions of more trivial acts of national violence. Qiyao's visit to a film studio and observation of a murder "on-screen" will be uncannily doubled in the novel's narrative and mimicked by Chinese history.

In the 1980s, international journalists gained more access to China, and the Chinese press liberalized. Stephen R. MacKinnon explains:

> Since Deng Xiaoping initiated reforms in the late 1970s, the Chinese press had been liberalizing rapidly. *Xinwen gaige* (journalism reform) was the catchall phrase for reforms running from technical changes like the introduction of computers to structural changes in press financing, advertising, and censorship. . . . By 1987, 2,578 newspapers of many varieties were being published, in contrast to the low of 46 during the depths of the Cultural Revolution. . . . By spring of 1989 the Chinese press was in the midst of a flowering of free expression the likes of which had not been seen since the 1930s and 1940s.[95]

However, this new freedom did not last through the spring of 1989. The Chinese press was banned from Tiananmen Square in May, denying those outside of Beijing access to the events. The consequences were grave: "Suppression of the Chinese press after May 20 is said to have prefigured the tragic outcome of June 4."[96]

After May 20, international audiences witnessed the escalation of the student protests: the erection of a ten-meter statue called the Goddess of Democracy (*Ziyou nüshen*), the increased number of protesters in the square, and Mao's portrait defaced with spatters of black ink and egg. In many ways, the protests partook of a longer Chinese tradition of street theater in their ability to captivate the attention and sympathy of their audience and in their use of provocative props like the Goddess of Democracy. Locally, nationally (before May 20), and globally, audiences reacted to the rising drama in the streets of Beijing. Theater as a metaphor continued to hold after the Tiananmen incident: "There was significant debate as to whether or not it should be termed a 'tragedy.' But the sense in which Chinese people see all this as performance was most powerfully suggested by a wise old peasant from Northern Shaanxi who, when asked the difference between Mao Zedong and Deng Xiaoping, simply laughed and said, 'They were just singing opposing operas [*chang duitai xi*]!' "[97]

While international spectators watched helplessly as the military crackdown began in the wee hours of June 4—the tanks, batons, and armed soldiers mowing down students—these moving images did not (and still have not) legally circulated in the Chinese press. Of course, the Chinese press was forced to offer an account of that day and those leading up to it, but exclusively at the government's bidding

> On the few occasions that images of violence were employed, it was to heighten the victimization of the PLA [People's Liberation Army]. The way images can be appropriated and radically recontextualized by different media sources can be seen in the example of one of the most violent and disturbing ones from the massacre. On June 3, as violence was escalating, a soldier was beaten to death, burned, and strung up, his body dressed up in a military hat and sunglasses and eventually disemboweled. Photos of this morbid scene were published in several major news outlets.[98]

Only violence directed *against* the government secured mention and memorialization. Michael Berry's study *A History of Pain: Trauma in Modern Chinese Literature and Film* divides its inquiry into twentieth-century Chinese trauma into two categories: those imposed by colonial forces on the Chinese (which Berry terms "centripetal trauma"), and those inflicted by the Chinese upon their own people ("centrifugal trauma"). The Tiananmen Massacre clearly lies in the latter group: "The term 'centrifugal trauma' is used to describe a radical shift in the creation of traumatic narratives, which are introduced from within, generated in the center, and projected outward into a new series of global dreams . . . and, sometimes, nightmares."[99] This indigenous trauma at Tiananmen, though rendered invisible in China (with the exception of those images bolstering the government's aims of inspiring renewed loyalty), evades an official narrative. As a result of the large number of foreign journalists in Beijing in May for Soviet leader Mikhail S. Gorbachev's state visit, the violence at Tiananmen was projected on screens across the world, and the event took on an unwieldy and disproportionate relevance in the heterogeneous responses of global spectators. Within China, I read the invisibility and the unconscious echo of this centrifugal trauma conveyed in two pivotal passages of Wang's *The Song of Everlasting Sorrow.*

The first passage occurs early in the narrative. At the beginning of the novel, Wang Qiyao dreams of standing apart from the crowd, while ironically, she only stands for it. As a young teenager, she visits a film studio where a cousin of her friend Wu Peizhen works. Qiyao admires the lives of the actors and actresses. She watches from the wings as a scene is being shot: "She felt something like déjà vu, but she could not recall where or when she had witnessed this scene. Wang Qiyao moved her gaze to the woman under the lamp, and suddenly realized that this woman was pretending to be dead—but she didn't know if it was a suicide or a homicide. The strange thing was that the situation did not appear tragic, terrifying, or foreboding, only insipidly familiar."[100] This moment foreshadows Wang Qiyao's murder at the end of the novel. As a testament to the melancholy pessimism of the novel, her future death appears simply "insipidly familiar" (*qi ni de shu*). However, are there not traces of another familiar event in this scene? The actress's murder is being filmed; its destination must be the screen; and audiences will respond to the projection of this scene in ways unexplored by and outside the scope of Wang's novel. *Song* does not tell of the impact of the completed film. Perhaps the film did not even make it beyond the walls of the studio. Moving pictures of Tiananmen on June Fourth did not breach the censorship barricades and did not gain access to screens across China. The sense of déjà vu, or flashback (*jiujingchongxian*), Qiyao experiences in the scene results in an allegory she significantly fails to realize. Her own death, described at the end of the novel, takes on a matching form. Qiyao senses this, not as "terrifying or foreboding" (*yin can ke bu*) but as "something with which she is tired of being familiar" (another possible translation of *qi ni de shu*). The murder of the protesters at Tiananmen, filmed but

not nationally broadcast, resembles other acts of official violence that
have transpired at Tiananmen over the course of Chinese history, and so
takes on a corresponding "insipid familiarity." The site of the torture of
prisoners until the fall of the Qing dynasty in 1912 and of beatings and
arrests of citizens mourning the death of Premier Zhou Enlai (1898–1976)
in April of 1976, "the age-old memory of Tiananmen Square as a place
of public abuse and humiliation" has been continually refreshed over the
course of history.[101] In Wang's novel, Qiyao does not connect her sensation
of an uncanny return to any past or future violence, but I read in her
unconscious prescience the future calamity, the traumatic event's return.

Qiyao's own death does not close the circle opened by her unconscious allegorical encounter with history; it simply secures the melancholy
bestowed on China in the last decade of the twentieth century. When
Wang Qiyao is strangled to death by her lover Long Legs (*Chang jiao*),
her mind returns to the scene from the film studio: "Only then did she
realize that the woman on that bed was herself, and she was the one who
had been murdered. After this, the light was extinguished and everything
fell into darkness. . . . The potted oleanders across the way were beginning
to bloom, opening the curtains on another season of blossoming and
withering."[102] Of course, an additional repetition occurs in this scene, that
of the strangulation of Yang Guifei in the legend of the Noble Consort
and the Emperor Xuanzong. Bai Ju-yi writes of the Emperor's sorrowful
response to this politically necessary execution: "The sovereign covered
his face, unable to save her; looking back, he saw tears and blood flowing
together."[103] Over Wang Qiyao's death, no living person weeps; "Only the
pigeons will bear witness."[104] In this statement, too, lies a doubling of
meaning: the character for "pigeon" (*ge*) is a homonym for the character
for "song" (*ge*). Only the commonplace cooing of pigeons (transcribed by
the narrator into a banal "Song of Everlasting Sorrow") spreads the dreary
news of Qiyao's misfortune.

The novel's last lines clarify that the finale of Qiyao's drama simply
allows the "curtains to open" on additional tales of "blossoming and
withering." I interpret these lines written in the future perfect (after the
blossoming will come the withering) as a prediction of the traumatic
event at Tiananmen, which *has already taken place* before the publication
of Wang's *Song* in 1995. The theater in the streets of Beijing, a flowering
and exhaustion of grassroots reform efforts has already been suppressed;
its promise extinguished. The melancholy resulting from the failure at
Tiananmen marks Wang's narrative. Wang Anyi had personally suffered

an initial government betrayal as a sent-down youth during the Cultural Revolution. Her own experience, shared by many Chinese, allowed her to recognize that the decisive betrayal of 1989 marked the end of a utopian vision that had persevered since 1949 and engendered the political apathy that came to define some Chinese citizens in the 1990s.

As the novel returns us to the *longtang* depicted at the story's outset, the potted roses that once sat on windowsills are replaced by the poisonous oleander. The place remains the same; it has merely been stripped of any hint of romance; or perhaps the novel suggests that it the romance was suspect from the outset. Similarly, the description of the actress's death, taking place in a production studio, under bright lights, during the heyday of Shanghai cinema, does not linger on a nostalgic celebration of the glamour of that other age. Rather, when Wang Qiyao remarks something "insipidly familiar" in the scene, the author indicates that this glittering space cannot last; it has, in fact, already disappeared, and when the scene repeats at the novel's end, it does so in order to completely divest the original of any romantic allure. Qiyao's murder mimics the actress's well-lit and expensively produced performance of death in a mode appropriate to the post-Tiananmen age, an age without illusions. Wang Anyi, an allegorist, captures the present, past, and future in her descriptions of Shanghai and in her unconscious recasting of the traumatic event. The end of the novel does not promise a new story, but simply another one. As this scene concludes in darkness, the curtain parts for another. We never go forward, but continually circle back.

Cinema: Mother of Ambivalence

The Song of Everlasting Sorrow thus rewrites Chinese history—especially the trauma of Tiananmen—through the phantasmagoric and hauntological mediation of the cinema. The film studio is both the site of romance and the site of deception. While the resulting film—that cyclical betrayal of women by their male lovers and the Chinese people by their government—is absent except for its encrypted literary form.

Cinema also occupies a central role in Wang's short autobiographical story "Years of Sadness," where "events always occurred in connection with movies."[105] The first third of this story describes Wang Anyi's loneliness during a period of her childhood and her frequent trips to either the luxurious Cathay Cinema (which "boasted a resplendent lobby, a marble floor, and large, framed photographs of well-known stars") or the rather commonplace Huaihai Cinema (which had a "narrow lobby and entrance . . . only one step away from the road so that the clamor of cars and people outside mingled with the film soundtrack").[106] In the second third of the story, Wang explores the back alleys near her home in Shanghai where she suffers an embarrassing accident when she is pricked between the legs by the needles of a caterpillar. In the final third, this injury results in an infection that lands Wang in the hospital, where she first "cried and screamed, and wouldn't let the doctors or nurses near my body. I felt that the sky had fallen. This happened precisely during the period when your body's changes embarrass you to no end, so even you can't directly face your own body."[107] However, by the end of the story, the infection heals, and Wang leaves the hospital with the sensation of a new tranquility and maturity; "The sun shone brightly, and that erstwhile era suddenly receded, submerged in dark shadows."

This coming-of-age story is tied to the cinema both in its conventional three-act narrative structure (ending with the screen fading to black, the past events "submerged in dark shadows") and in its prominence as a setting. The movie theater is a refuge for Wang in her preadolescence. Her mother and father absent as a result of the Socialist Education Movement, she goes by herself, with a neighbor boy, or with her older sister to see the communist films by third-generation Chinese directors like Yu Yanfu and Deng Pu. The Cathy Cinema, in particular, becomes not only a safe place but a figural return to her absent mother's womb; Wang's description suggestive of its colors, textures, and sensation: "I skated to the screening room entrance, colliding into the purple-red velvet curtain. I was unable to resist wrapping myself in its downy smoothness. As I rolled myself in it once and then again, a small corner of the pitch black screening room became visible and I heard a woman's sobs."[108] At the cinema, Wang simultaneously returns to the origins of life, sees other lives played out on-screen, and experiences revelations about her life in the present. It's when she hears the woman crying that she realizes she, too, is unhappy: "In that instant, like a cork popping, sadness burst out and filled my heart."

Marguerite Duras also writes of her childhood sojourns to the cinema and connects the cinema to her difficult mother ("She was hard, the mother. Terrible. Unbearable"), who for ten years, during the final part of the silent era, played the piano at Eden Cinema in Indochina.[109] The cinema—both in its name and in its connection to Duras's early childhood—signals once again a return to origins. In one of her fictionalized accounts of her youth, the novel *Un Barrage contre le Pacifique*, Duras points with irony to the fact that her mother (in the novel called simply "the mother," "*la mère*") played for ten years without ever being able to see a film. The mother explains in conversation with her daughter Suzanne, "Sometimes it seemed as if I slept while playing. When I tried to look at the screen it was horrible, I became dizzy. There was a mush of black and white which danced above my head and made me nauseous."[110] If, for the mother, the cinema is a nightmare, for Suzanne and her brother, "going to the movies every night was, like taking a drive in an automobile, one of the forms which human happiness could take."[111] Suzanne also sees the cinema as a refuge: "It was an oasis, the dark movie hall in the afternoon; it was the night for the solitary, the artificial and democratic night, the great equalizing night of the cinema, truer than the real night, more wonderful, more consoling than all of the real nights, the chosen night, open to all, offered to all, more generous, more of a dispenser of good deeds than all of the institutions of charity and all of the churches, the night where one can comfort oneself of all one's shame, where one goes to be free of all despair, and where youth can wash itself clean of the all the filth of adolescence."[112] However, such a passionate description makes of the cinema more than a simple refuge and foretells the deeper engagement with this "chosen night" Duras will explore in her future *ciné-romans*.

In these remnants of feminist refusal by Marguerite Duras and Wang Anyi, the historical melancholy sutures to a historical ambivalence: the longing for and impossibility of another life in the new eras of neoliberal globalization following national trauma, the love and hatred for the inaccessible lover (or mother). In Duras's *Moderato cantabile*, the blanks (*les blancs*) in her work—articulated both in her movement away from established forms of fiction and in her increasingly radical refusal to give answers or offer closure—suggest that she responded to her melancholic ambivalence by starting afresh, throwing out her old ways of writing for the new. In Wang's *The Song of Everlasting Sorrow*, the ironic rewriting of the Tang myth of the beloved Noble Consort Yang Guifei demonstrates not a new beginning but a summoning of ghosts. Ambivalence, this exhumation and haunting on the part of the Chinese at the end of the twentieth century, and the violent rejection in the place of unprecedented forms of creation on the part of the French in the Trente Glorieuses, will be the subject of my next chapter.

Chapter 2

Capitals of Ambivalence

I forgot everything, except that, since I have been reduced to nothing
(*à zero*), it is from there that I must start again.

—*2 ou 3 choses que je sais d'elle*

—Are we dead?

—No. This is just the beginning.

—*The World*

This chapter begins in the French and Chinese capitals in the years
following their respective national traumas, the 1940–44 German
Occupation and the 1989 Tiananmen Square Massacre. In both cases, these
periods were marked by an advancement of neoliberal globalization that
can be partially accounted for by the recent historical trauma as well as
a furious attempt to erase and forget the past. The films that I analyze in
this chapter, Jean-Luc Godard's *2 ou 3 choses que je sais d'elle* (1967) and
Jia Zhangke's *The World* (世界; *Shijie*) (2004), however, reveal another side
to the affective reality of these post-trauma moments in national history.
Against the positivist logic of modernization and commercial expansion,
these works register a profound ambivalence toward these historical projects, an ambivalence manifested as a passivity, a refusal to rush headlong
into the future. This chapter examines how these films responded to the
swift economic and social transformations following national trauma with
sets of ambivalent affects: fascination and disdain, desire and disgust,

enthusiasm and apathy; questioning the seemingly flourishing present, remembering the recent traumatic past, and stalling at the crossroads of history. As suggested by this chapter's epigraphs, Godardian ambivalence in *2 ou 3 choses* culminates with a desire to take a cue from the historical wreckage and begin again from nothing (*à zero*); whereas the final lines in Jia's *The World* show that his film's ambivalence has unhinged the door separating the past from the present, the living from the dead.

Jean-Luc Godard's *2 ou 3 choses que je sais d'elle* captures a day in the life (from eight o'clock at night until around the same time the following day) of Juliette (Marina Vlady), a thirty-year-old wife and mother of two children who works as a prostitute. Juliette lives with her husband, Robert (Jean Narboni), and their children, Christophe and Solange, in a *grand ensemble*, an HLM (*Habitation à loyer modéré*, the equivalent of an American housing project) in La Courneuve, a postwar *ville nouvelle* to the North of Paris. During the day, Juliette goes to the city, deposits her young daughter with an elderly gentleman, Monsieur Gérard (a sort of benign, male "Madame" who watches the other children of prostitutes), and tries to buy a dress. Not having enough money, she asks the proprietor of the shop to hold the garment for her until evening. Juliette then goes to a café in order to attract clients. She entertains a young, pimpled man in a hotel, earning enough to purchase the dress. She has her hair done and accompanies her friend Marianne (Anny Duperey) to another hotel to service a second client. Robert, Juliette's husband, spends the day working at a Mobil service station. He passes his time after work in a café, talking about sex with a young stranger (Juliet Berto). Finally, Juliette and Robert pick up their children, return home, and go to bed.

Jia Zhangke's *The World* places its protagonist Zhao Xiao Tao (Zhao Tao) as a dancer at the World Park (an amusement park similar to Disney's Epcot Center) in the Beijing Suburbs. At the World Park, Tao is joined by her hometown boyfriend, Chen Taisheng (Cheng Taishen), who works as a security guard. Since their arrival in Beijing, the couple's relationship has been rocky: Tao hopes that Taisheng will propose marriage, while Taisheng seems more focused on convincing her to sleep with him and developing his connections to a small-time crime boss and petty criminal underworld. In addition to the other Chinese dancers at the park, Tao befriends Anna (Alla Shcherbakova), a Russian who hopes to make enough money to visit her sister in Ulan Bator. Even though they speak different languages, their friendship deepens, and Tao discovers with sadness that Anna's desperation for money has led her to prostitution. Taisheng meanwhile has an affair with an older, married woman from Southern China, Qun (Huang Yiqun), a seamstress managing a small sweatshop that fabricates designer knockoffs. Taisheng also shows off the World Park to acquaintances from Shanxi province who seek unofficial employment as laborers in Beijing. One of these newcomers, Chen Zhijun, called Little Sister (*Erguniang*), comes to a tragic end, perishing in a construction accident. Later, at a wedding for two dancers from the World Park, Tao discovers a text message from Qun to Taisheng that leads her to believe he has betrayed her. Finally, while housesitting, Tao and Taisheng die when Tao intentionally allows the gas to leak.

Both films are set in the suburbs of the capital, in many ways sites synonymous with the new social formations brought on by economic renewal projects. The national capital functions both symbolically and politically as a country's center of power and unity. Home to the seat of government, mapped with landmarks of national history, and frequently home to a sizable population, an attack on the capital signifies an assault on the nation. The traumatic periods of the German Occupation of France and the Tiananmen Square Massacre in China shared a metaphorical and literal sullying of the national capital: from the swastika flying above the Arc de Triomphe on the afternoon of June 14, 1940, to the People's Liberation Army (PLA) attacking students on the streets of Beijing late in the evening of June 3 and into the morning of June 4, 1989. As part of an effort to cleanse the national memory of these blemishes, of the familiar and homely now become foreign and uncanny, the French and Chinese capitals became sites of intense modernization.

It is this "French modernization *as* an event" that Kristin Ross spells out in her work on France in the late 1950s–1960s, the peak of the postwar period termed the *Trentes Glorieuses*.[1] She specifies that "in France the state-led modernization drive was extraordinarily concerted, and the desire for a new way of living after the war widespread. The unusual swiftness of French postwar modernization seemed to partake of the qualities of what Braudel has designated as the temporality of the event: it was headlong, dramatic, and breathless."[2] Ross inventories some of the particularities of French midcentury modernization:

> The speed with which French society was transformed after the war from a rural, empire-oriented, Catholic country into a fully industrialized, decolonized, and urban one meant that the things modernization needed—educated middle managers,

for instance, or affordable automobiles and other "mature" consumer durables, or a set of social sciences that followed scientific, functionalist models, or a work force of ex-colonial laborers—burst onto a society that still cherished prewar outlooks with all of the force, excitement, disruption, and horror of the genuinely new.[3]

Following the Occupation during the Trente Glorieuses, this "force, excitement, disruption, and horror of the genuinely new" was particularly concentrated in Paris, the mutating national capital. As the French economy flourished, products unavailable during the war returned to stores and new merchandise appeared for the first time. In the early 1960s, Carrefour, the first megastore (*hypermarché*), opened in the Parisian suburbs. Between 1960 and 1968, the percentage of blue-collar workers in possession of a television rose from 14.1 percent to 67.2 percent. With similarly large increases in television ownership across the spectrum of French classes, the society of consumption reached into homes and targeted viewers with commercials that stimulated their appetite to buy even during leisure time.[4] The population and urbanization of France surged. A baby boom swelled the numbers of potential consumers and migration of rural residents to urban centers—by 1968 two-thirds of the French population were city dwellers—prompted massive construction on the periphery of cities, especially around the edges of the Parisian megalopolis.[5]

China in the 1990s also saw a dramatically expanding economy as well as resettlement in Beijing and other large cities. Dai Jinhua pinpoints the full adoption of neoliberal capitalism and China's new global position in these years as resulting from what could be considered the "headlong, dramatic, and breathless" *event* of the Tiananmen protests:

> Without a doubt, the turning point and event in China with international implications was the 1989 Tiananmen Movement. Threatening the regime for the first time since 1949 and tragically crushed with brutal military force, this citizens' resistance movement nevertheless helped the collapse or implosion of the socialist camp . . . the violent conclusion of the Tiananmen protests totally destroyed and purged socialism's spiritual legacy and mobilization potential that had once hindered the path of Chinese capitalism. The Chinese regime began pushing for capitalism with unprecedented energy.[6]

Thus, Mao's utopian vision for a modern, agrarian China was firmly put to rest at the end of the 1980s. In the years following the 1989 Tiananmen Massacre, China embraced a free-market economy and renewed interest in urban centers. The new Chinese citizen of the 1990s was now expected to metamorphize into a savvy urbanite, and widespread disillusionment with politics in the 1990s inspired fierce individualism: visible in a new generation of young, urban slackers termed "hooligans" (*liumang*), and later in a fervent drive for personal economic success.[7] Meanwhile, low-skilled migrant workers from the country flocked to new jobs in factories, construction sites, and mines, boosting the overall Chinese economy and increasing the chasm of education and the horizon of opportunity dividing rural and urban Chinese.[8]

Dai stresses the irony of post-socialist China's position following Tiananmen as the "last infallible socialist giant" in the eyes of the world, thereby "falling into a post–Cold War cold war."[9] The Chinese government partially collaborated with this positioning on the geopolitical global map, persevering the name Chinese Communist Party (CCP) and wielding "vacuous soliloquies" of socialist discourse in order to justify their crackdown at Tiananmen.[10] This mess of misperceptions and misrepresentations, Dai explains, created gaps in the global understanding of China as well as Chinese lived experiences "as a dynamic zone within the global capitalist map, China remains caught in rather bizarre cultural-political circumstances. In the last decade of the twentieth century, Chinese society and culture were consistently mired within the delirium and aphasia of multiple ideological discourses."[11] The confusion of competing discourses—the swift recasting of the massacre at Tiananmen as a victory of "nationalist martyrs" (soldiers of the PLA) over "anti-socialist turmoil" (nonviolent protests by students and workers), the persistence of Chinese communist branding even as socialist policies perished under capitalism, the increasing focus on developing costal Chinese megacities at the expense of the majority population in the vast, poor, rural interior—contributed to a rumbling of ambivalence audible in the Chinese films I will treat in what follows.

In my previous chapter, I argued that the French and Chinese refusal to move on and embrace the future arose out of a melancholic response to national trauma and rising neoliberal globalization. Here, I begin by establishing that such melancholy is nourished by a fundamental ambivalence. I read the ambivalence in these two nations toward the contemporary in the formal film aesthetics in the work of Godard and Jia. Thus, I analyze the ways in which a historical tarrying is manifest in

the affective structures of film, thereby rendering the films into remnants
of refusal. As in my last chapter, I will concentrate on the experiences of
women. In these films, women—mothers or would-be mothers—come
to stand as allegories for the nation and as figures of ambivalence, bearing in their relationship to the familial the dilemma of an unmournable
national past and future.

Visible Structures of Ambivalence

Before turning to the films, I will theorize ambivalence: an affect that binds
itself to a broad spectrum of objects in the era of neoliberal globalization.
In *Our Aesthetic Categories: Zany, Cute, Interesting* (2012) and *Theory of
the Gimmick: Aesthetic Judgment and Capitalist Form* (2020), Sianne Ngai
analyzes affects and devices aligned with contemporary aesthetics: the zany,
the cute, the interesting, and the gimmick. The zany, cute, and interesting
circulate in both high and low strata of capitalist culture (the museum,
literature, the internet and its marketplace, film, and television). Ngai calls
this triad "subjective, feeling-based judgments," thereby combining and
troubling the relationship between our affective and logical responses.[12]
These categories are ambivalent; both likable and disagreeable, inspiring at
the same time our love and our hate: "The interesting oscillates between
interest and boredom. Aggression is central to our experience of objects
as cute. Zaniness is as much about desperate laboring as playful fun."[13] In
Theory of the Gimmick, Ngai is even more explicit about tying ambivalence
to our experience of capitalism. She explains,

> In a world in which everything is made to be sold for profit
> and engineered to appeal to what a consumer is preshaped to
> desire, how can there not be a philosophical as well as his-
> torically meaningful uncertainty at the heart of the aesthetic
> evaluations through which we process the pleasures we take in.
> This uncertainty does not mean that our aesthetic experiences
> *feel* weak. As we learn from Freud's theory of ambivalence and
> the thinkers who treat it seriously, the copresence of negative
> and positive affects strengthens the overall intensity of our
> attachment to an object.[14]

In my readings of French and Chinese films, I focus on the ambivalence
that marks an affective response to expanded capitalism, while arguing that

what these affects register is not only a personal conflicted response to the shaping of subjectivity but also a cultural refusal to partake in celebrations of capitalist renewal. I am not claiming that the ambivalence in Godard's and Jia's films shows an indifference to the nation; rather, ambivalence is figured in these films by the tension between diegetic images (circulated by television, advertising, packaging, or theme park spectacle) selling a "happy" or "beautiful" life and the unglamorous work sustaining the daily lives of citizen-characters. Just as the ambivalence described by Freud and picked up in the contemporary context by Ngai fuses subjectivity to the objects of our psychosocial experience, so too does national ambivalence arise out of an investment, at times even an overinvestment, in the images of national identity during these historical periods.

In her engagement with Chinese-language cinema, Rey Chow investigates the broader ambivalence of circulating, diegetic images as "an inherent part of a contemporary global problematic of becoming visible."[15] Chow's work shows how the structures of ambivalence and their ability to fuse the subject with the object, the familiar with the strange, work in the discourses of feminist film theory and Chinese cinema. Tracing this problematic to the institutional relationship between Anglo-American feminism and the academic inauguration of the field of film studies in the 1970s, Chow teases out how feminist theory unwittingly coupled the politics of gender and sexuality to that of the commodified spectacle, even as feminist film theory critiqued the fetishized female object of mainstream narrative cinema. She writes, "The ambivalent logics exemplified by feminist film theory from the very beginning may be seen as constitutive, perhaps paradigmatic, of the process of a subordinated group's rise to visibility."[16] Chow uses this logic of visibility to illuminate how Chinese cinema since the 1980s came to be *seen* globally for the first time.[17] She identifies the sentimental, a tonal quality often associated with domestic melodrama, as a persistent affective mode in a selection of global Chinese films from the 1990s to the beginning of the twenty-first century. However, she specifies that the particular quality of Chinese sentimentalism—adopting the term *wenqing zhuyi* (溫情主義), or "warm sentiment-ism"—differs from what Westerners expect as the excesses of melodrama. *Wenqing zhuyi* indicates something else: "Being warm, to be exact, is being in the middle between the extremes of hot and cold, bespeaking a kind of moderation that is, interestingly, not quite the affective outpouring that is the typical definition of sentimentalism."[18] It is precisely its state of in-betweenness, its ambivalence, one could say, that allows the sentimental in Chinese cinema to level a critique using the domestic or the idea of home, refracting "modes of human relationships affectively rooted in this *imagined inside*—an inside whose depths of feeling tend to become intensified with the perceived aggressive challenges posed by modernity."[19] Paradoxically, the culturally specific idealization of the domestic, particularly the value of filial piety, which Chow acknowledges "seems neither timely nor fully communicable," clings stubbornly to Chinese cinema as one of the attributes offering it visibility.[20] Jia Zhangke's *The World* makes this paradox plain: pitting the sentimental weight of the family, the home, and the filial relation between children and parents against the lure (and requisites) of the neoliberal "worldly." I will argue that this is one of the fundamental structures of ambivalence underlying Jia's cinema. However, both the French and Chinese films under discussion in this chapter are caught up in the "problematic of becoming visible," projecting contested, ambivalent versions of an imaginary Frenchness or Chineseness against the funhouse mirrors of the spectacularized world. In the case of both films, images of foreign nations (those of "Frenchness" in Jia's Chinese film, for example) speak about the changing relationship of citizen to nation and sometimes allow for subtle transnational revelations of repressed historical traumas.

Anxious Maternal Function, Ambivalent Mothering Body

In Godard's *2 ou 3 choses* and Jia's *The World*, the collision of contradictory affects attached to the idea of the nation play out on two sites: the suburbs of the national capital and the figure of the woman. However, both films stress the interrelation between these bodies: the woman protagonist as embedded in and exemplifying the uncertainty of life in the transform-ing capital; life in the capital as a tug of war between intangible fantasy images and the constraints of subsistence constituting the ambivalence of this environment. The woman protagonist functions as a vector of homemaking, as either mother or would-be mother, caught in a crosswind pulling toward an unknown future. Crucially, the linked figures of nation and woman are both subject to profound ambivalences, as they point on the one hand to the past, the domestic, and the familiar, and on the other hand to the profound and far-reaching changes in this period. The films ask the viewer to question what strange new nation is being birthed.

The anxiety elicited by these various forms of birth does not solely emerge from the women protagonists, but materializes more broadly across characters and spaces, suggesting the films as engaged in what

Elissa Marder (appropriating before deviating from Julia Kristeva) terms the "maternal function." Marder contends that "the very concept of the 'Mother' (as bearer of human birth) is haunted, from the beginning, by a radical confusion concerning the possibility of discerning between birth and death, and between presence and absence."[21] She describes birth as marked by the uncanny: an event universally experienced and yet never consciously remembered. One is both present and absent at one's own birth, the primary transition between life and nonlife. The mother—though attendant and active in the event of birth—does not function as the child's witness. The mother has her own understanding of the event, separate from that of the child, but also dissociated from her conception of herself as a subject outside of the limit-experiences of labor and delivery. Thus, the child cannot account for either their own birth or clearly identify the mother (because of her radical separateness) as their "original" "home." This is why Freud singles out the womb as paradigmatically uncanny (*Unheimlich*): something frightening exactly because it discloses something familiar, something terrifying yet home-like (*Heimlich*), the return of the repressed. Indeed, Marder affirms that "the figure of the mother becomes associated with many of the most unruly and enigmatic concepts within psychoanalysis: the uncanny, anxiety, the primal scene, 'deferred action' (*Nachträglichkeit*), shame, déjà vu, telepathy, magical thinking, and various forms of failed morning."[22] Marder is explicit in delinking the maternal function from the woman as a flesh and blood mothering body, focusing instead on readings of the womb as tied to the technological (nonbiological) conception of reproduction in contemporary culture. However, my argument here, while desiring like Marder to avoid the pitfalls of essentialism, follows the lead proposed by Godard and Jia and returns the woman's body to the maternal function in order to more explicitly connect ambivalence to the uncanny, anxiety, and failed mourning at work in their films: treating women as figures both in accord and at odds with national (re)birth in the wake of historical trauma and in the growing age of neoliberal globalization.

Few have better argued for the primary role of mother-child ambivalence than Melanie Klein. My chapter, therefore, extends from Marder's anxiety-ridden maternal function to embrace Melanie Klein's theorization of ambivalence in children to examine how cinema's collective affective responses to history function as remnants of refusal. Klein shows that ambivalence emerges in early childhood and is first oriented toward the mother—or, rather the breast as the synecdochic maternal object—an object of both intense need (creating the idealization of the mother's breast as a full plentitude) and primal aggression (leading to fantasies of assaults on and destruction of her body). This "splitting" of the mother's body into good and bad objects, by which the infant defends the "good mother" from its own aggression (and, in turn, defends itself against the mother's projected retaliation), produces anxiety and ambivalence.[23]

The site of this sadism is not simply the partial object (the breast), but also the inside of the mother's body, onto which the baby directs its aggressive fantasies, "scooping it out, devouring the contents, destroying it by every means which sadism can suggest."[24] The baby, in turn, is comforted when, in spite of its aggression toward the mother's body, the mother returns again and again to nurture, care for, and hold it. Here, ambivalence serves a constructive function: "Ambivalence, carried out in the splitting of the imagos, enables the young child to gain more trust and belief in the real objects and thus in its internalized ones—to love them more and to carry out in an increasing degree its phantasies of restoration of the loved object."[25] Klein, however, does not foretell a complete resolution: even in normal development, she reminds us, ambivalence will only "diminish in varying degrees" and is thus always liable to reassert itself throughout our lives. Internal and external objects continue to undergo distortion by the subject's ego, and ambivalence—requiring the splitting of imagos—persists.

The emphasis on the foundational position that violence (or aggression) occupies in the baby's relation to the love object, the priority given to the death-drive over the pleasure principle, renders Melanie Klein a troubling figure. As Jacqueline Rose writes, "Far from offering reassurance . . . Melanie Klein disturbs."[26] She disturbs because she ties the birth of the ego to destruction, revealing "negativity in the process of the emergence of the subject, as the passage through which subjects come to be."[27] In the films under discussion in this chapter, affective ambivalence also acts as a disturbance: opposing historical "progress" and allowing the unmourned past to resurface.

Synecdoche and Simile:
Breast Is to Mother as Capital Is to Nation

This chapter takes one of its cues from Kleinian psychoanalysis in order to argue that ambivalence, shown through the films' formal preference for partial objects, or remnants, registers a refusal to accept the "wholeness" proffered by dominant discourse. I identify the relationship between partial and whole objects as constellations of *synecdoche*: moving from the Kleinian relationship of the mother's breast as signifying the mother to consider the woman's body as metaphor for the nation as well as the national capital as symbol for the nation. I figure Klein's slippage between good and bad objects, real objects and projections, through the tantalizing objects of globalization and the inability to control or possess them, and through the increasing prominence of the spectacle as global organizing structure. Whereas my previous chapter's argument—on the melancholic literature of Marguerite Duras and Wang Anyi—took the cinematic form of cross-cutting, this chapter's argument—on the ambivalent films of Godard and Jia—hinges on a literary device: Klein's synecdoche.

My argument follows synecdoche—how the part stands for the whole—on three levels. First, in these films the capital stands for the nation. Second, the woman protagonists in Godard's and Jia's films stand for the French and Chinese citizenry. Though these fictional women appear in films by male directors, my reading argues for the women characters as central enunciators of ambivalence in the films, and thereby as figures of feminist refusal. These films also hold up to view the struggles of women under capitalism by showcasing working-class women's attempts to stay afloat economically by engaging in sexual alliances (dating or marriage) and/or sex work (prostitution). Third, throughout this chapter I will highlight moments in which these films break the fourth wall and reveal a strategy of puncturing cinematic illusion as strategies of what Richard Neupart terms "dysnarration" in order to consider cinema's responsibility to history.[28] Godard and Jia chop up their films—by inserting photographs, instances of frontality, baring the filmic apparatus, referencing the film as a production by including performances within the diegesis—and the films stare back at the spectator. My argument proceeds by showing this series of connections between partial and whole objects, progressing steadily in the name of the ambivalent relationship that the cinematic partial objects by Godard and Jia have to the social whole of France and China, and—by a final synecdochic extension—the larger world under neoliberal globalization.

There's an inherent violence in the severing of partial objects from whole objects, an inherent violence, therefore, in synecdoche. Recall the Kleinian baby's sadistic impulses against the mother's breast and toward the inside of her body. At a later stage of development, the subject, anxious about the repercussions of this early sadism when it recognizes suddenly that "its loved objects are in a state of dissolution—*in bits,*"[29] tries to repair what it imagines it has destroyed. What could be more devastating or more banal than this realization: we tear to pieces the things we love.[30]

In the last pages of her work on the maternal function, Marder ponders how uncanny, prosthetic, technological, nonbiological wombs (e.g., "freezers, case studies, photographs, labyrinths, miniature portraits, dreams, crypts, and tiny coffins") simultaneously "preserve *bits* of death and reproduce new forms of life."[31] She meditates on the ambiguity of the bit, first in English: "Biter or bitten, active or passive or outside, the word resists the possibility of deciding. The word 'bit' is also a bit of the word 'bite.' And it is this bit that designates its aftermath and remainder. The bit is a bit of a bite—its leftover bit—the severed piece that remains—after the event."[32] Next, taking her cue from Jacques Derrida, Hélène Cixous, and Jean Genet, she explores the homonymic affinities of the word in these writers' intertextual dialogue in French: between *mors* (bit), *mordre* (to bite), *morsure* (a bite), *morceau* (a morsel, or a bit), *remords* (remorse), and *mort* (death). Marder warns that to follow these words and their traces as forms of synecdoche would be to err, that "following the word *mors* inaugurates a process that has no predetermined order, no established given boundaries, no given limits, and no end."[33] I want to retain from her work the temporal fluidity of the bit, "the severed piece that remains," which allows me to read the bit as a remnant of refusal to the repression of national trauma, revealing how "the past opens up into the present like a fresh wound" (or bite).[34] However, unlike Marder's navigation among the bits of Derrida, Cixous, and Genet, the bits in this chapter will maintain a synecdochic structure.

In the films of Godard and Jia that respond to cultural and historical trauma, synecdoche is the violent, tragic but necessary figuration of bits or remnants. In Godard's *2 ou 3 choses* and Jia's *The World*, the carving (or Kleinian "scooping") out of a space on the margins of the national capital directs an affective ambivalence against the nation. At the same time, these films also signify an attempt to repair and put back together, even if in a new way, a sense of national identity that has been lost. This reparation requires the resuturing of the map of the capital with the fragments of images, sounds, and feelings that are left behind, resulting in a patchwork aesthetic composed of remnants of refusal.

The ambivalence in these films runs deep; a foundational questioning of how films respond to history tears at the narrative continuity and leaves the films in "bits." I dislodge these remnants in order to emphasize the

violence of ambivalence as the inheritance of national trauma and neoliberal globalization. In some instances, as argued in the work of Garrett
Stewart, these sequences will emphasize the materiality of film and make
cinema's reliance on the photogram ("the individuated photographic unit
on the transparent strip that conduces in motion to screen movement")
felt.[35] Once again, this is an issue of synecdoche: how to divide the part
from the whole (like the severing of the breast from the mother), but also
one of parentage (as in the Kleinian mother's figural decapitation by her
child). In this vein, I would borrow from Stewart, too, the emphasis on
cinema's phylogenetic relationship to photography, describing "the fric-
tive tension in film's *ongoing* relation to a parent (if no longer apparent)
medium, which survives within it by way of the descendant medium's new
combinatory makeup."[36] The photogram's "jagged seriality conduces to the
unruffled flow of movement in screen action" and only becomes visible by
way of meta-reference—the appearance of a physical photograph in the
film's mise-en-scène (what Stewart terms a "phototopan")—or by seemingly
severing individual images from the flow of continuous movement, as
in a freeze-frame or by use of a jump cut.[37] As already suggested, I will
draw attention to the inclusion of the physical photograph, which Jean
Ma has termed "a form of prosthetic memory, a souvenir" and Marder
argues "petrifies the body of the living subject who is mummified by its
uncanny powers," in the mise-en-scène of Jia Zhangke's films in order to
emphasize the ghostly presence of absent human bodies.[38] In Godard's
films, meanwhile, the juxtaposition of flattened images (posters, advertisements, isolated text), use of jump cuts, and emphasis on the mechanism
of projection all lay bare the seduction of the spectacle and probe new
methods of demystifying the filmic image.

As in my first chapter, the "French" and "Chinese" expressions of
ambivalence vary. In the case of the "French," exemplified by the cinema
of Jean-Luc Godard, this ambivalence will register in a decision to begin
anew, start over, try again, throw everything but the baby out with the
bathwater. For the "Chinese," illustrated by Jia Zhangke, the fabric of time
tears, ushering in the return of ghosts. In other words, Godard's films
show that the best way to work through ambivalence is to create something new, while Jia's films reveal that ambivalence cannot be resolved but
rather persists and extends temporally backward and forward, extracting
stories and characters from the past to haunt the present. I'd term these
two methods of breaking with the present first *zero as departure*, and
second, *zero as destination*.

Godard: Cranes over La Courneuve, or *Zero as Departure*

"Space" (*espace*) became a catchword in the realm of urban planning in France in the 1960s, and Godard's *2 ou 3 choses que je sais d'elle* discloses how new spaces formed in the Paris region are linked to the country's figural prostitution to the laws of capitalism and the collective forgetting of historical trauma.[39] In this first section on Godard, I analyze his film *2 ou 3 choses* by offering a tour of sequential spaces: first, the French (or more narrowly, Parisian) landscape that Godard takes as his film's subject; second, an early sequence in a brothel, which underlines the economic problems of the globalizing present; and finally, the film's last moments, which connect these problems of the present to the traumatic past and announce Godard's intent to take a new approach in his future filmmaking.

2 OU 3 CHOSES: LA RÉGION PARISIENNE, 1966

Godard took his inspiration for *2 ou 3 choses* from several studies published in 1966 in the magazine *Le Nouvel observateur*, which treated the phenomenon of occasional prostitution in Paris and its surroundings. These studies indicated that young women, sometimes married, found this intermittent employment practical for covering household expenses. In a television debate during the autumn following the filming of *2 ou 3 choses*, Godard clarifies his belief that occasional prostitution goes hand in hand with the demands of life in the capital: "Today in the Paris region, we all live more or less in a state of prostitution."[40] The physical prostitution, Godard suggests, is prompted by a vicious moral disease, that of the rise of consumption in French society during the Trente Glorieuses.

Furthermore, Godard saw his own work as a director during this period as akin to prostitution, and he thus identified the figure of the filmmaker with the women protagonists of these films.[41] Money, he understood, dictated the rules of film just as it did with sex work, reducing human bodies and the fruits of their labor to a common economy, one that Georg Simmel would term that of "pure means."[42] In his essay on prostitution, Simmel expounds on the cold nature of money, as well as its ability to reduce metaphor to metonymy by turning every human activity into fungible labor: "The indifference with which [money] lends itself to any use, the infidelity with which it leaves everyone, its lack of ties to anyone, its complete objectification that excludes any attachment and makes it suitable as pure means—all this suggests a portentous analogy

between it and prostitution."[43] Such "infidelity" and "complete objectification" exacts violence on relations in the present, while sweeping away (with
total "indifference") any mourning of the unprofitable past, which comes
to be seen as unproductive waste. Caught between the traumatic past and
the calculating present, thus, *2 ou 3 choses* explores the new landscape of
postwar Paris, the new economic pressures exerted on its inhabitants, and
the difficulty for a film to intervene and challenge the rules of the game.

Godard's *2 ou 3 choses que je sais d'elle* begins by situating the
spectator in a precise moment, the summer of 1966, and a specific place,
the Parisian suburbs. After the opening titles and a *tricolore* intertitle
clarifying that, initially, "Elle" will refer to a municipal body, "La région
parisienne," the film's first shot is static—the camera nearly level with an
overpass mid-construction, another tier of building up or tearing down
taking place on the ground below with the help of a backhoe, Jean-Luc
Godard starts his whispered voice-over: "On August 19, a decree concerning the organization of state services in the Paris region was officially
published" (figure 2.1).

Godard builds the scene bit by bit, as if reanimating a decapitated
body. Over three more static shots—the underbelly of an overpass with
its concrete ribs stark against the backdrop of a row of advancing vehicles

Figure 2.1. Opening of Godard's *2 ou 3 choses*: "Elle: La Région Parisienne." *Source*:
Godard, Jean-Luc, dir. *2 or 3 Things I Know About Her* (*2 ou 3 choses que je sais
d'elle*). 1967; New York: Criterion Collection, 2009. DVD.

and a cloudy sky, then more highway traversed by lories and an even larger expanse of cloudy sky, and finally a dark concrete block of shops in the courtyard of a new housing project—Godard continues his narration: "Two days later, the government appointed Paul Delouvrier prefect of the Paris region, which, as the official release claimed, now enjoyed specific new infrastructures" (figures 2.2, 2.3, 2.4).

Delouvrier, who served as a general minster to the Paris region from 1961 to 1969, was appointed prefect of urban planning in 1966. He is credited with many of the changes in urban planning beginning

Figure 2.2. Godard describes the new construction taking place in the Parisian suburbs (1 of 3). *Source*: Godard, Jean-Luc, dir. *2 or 3 Things I Know About Her (2 ou 3 choses que je sais d'elle)*. 1967; New York: Criterion Collection, 2009. DVD.

Figure 2.3. Godard describes the new construction taking place in the Parisian suburbs (2 of 3). *Source*: Godard, Jean-Luc, dir. *2 or 3 Things I Know About Her (2 ou 3 choses que je sais d'elle)*. 1967; New York: Criterion Collection, 2009. DVD.

Figure 2.4. Godard describes the new construction taking place in the Parisian suburbs (3 of 3). *Source*: Godard, Jean-Luc, dir. *2 or 3 Things I Know About Her* (*2 ou 3 choses que je sais d'elle*). 1967; New York: Criterion Collection, 2009. DVD.

in the 1960s, including the *villes nouvelles*, new towns, primarily in the province of the Île de France accessible from Paris by one of the Réseau Express Régional (RER) trains. These suburbs resulted from the massive migration to the national capital following the Second World War and fallout of French colonialism.[44] The escalating housing crisis led to the erection of large, quickly constructed apartment buildings in the Parisian suburbs, known as *grands ensembles*. Though these tower blocks provided necessary housing for the influx of blue-collar workers and repatriated French citizens from Algeria, they also segregated these subjects. Living en masse on the edges of the capital, these citizens constituted a semi-marginalized population. Jean-Luc Godard's *2 ou 3 choses* highlights some of the inequities inhabitants of the *grands ensembles* faced in this period of alleged largesse.

2 OU 3 CHOSES: CHALLENGING THE PRESENT

After building the scene, rejoining the skeleton of the film's location, Godard introduces twice, by way of jump cut, the second "Elle" in the film's title, the actress Marina Vlady and the women protagonist she incarnates, Juliette Jeanson (figure 2.5). "Elle"—and perhaps this is the third piece of "knowledge" promised by the title *2 ou 3 choses*—also offers a pun of the English word "hell," and if hell is the incessant noise of construction, trucks forever hauling and dumping, highways expanding and endlessly

Figure 2.5. The introduction of Juliette Janson/Marina Vlady, a second "Elle."
Source: Godard, Jean-Luc, dir. *2 or 3 Things I Know About Her* (*2 ou 3 choses que je sais d'elle*). 1967; New York: Criterion Collection, 2009. DVD.

coiling, the ubiquity of tower cranes standing above it all like indifferent mechanical demons, then *2 ou 3 choses* shows us hell.

An early sequence of the film provides a collection of details stressing the ambivalence in this globalizing period of seeming plenty. Our heroine, Juliette, arrives at the humble Parisian apartment of Monsieur Gérard, whom we gather has turned his home into a joint brothel-daycare as a way of making ends meet in the city. The walls have posters advertising global cities and foreign nations: Bangkok, Israel, Japan, Greece, Spain, India. These posters signal the growing prominence of the spectacle following the Second World War and its flattening of physical places into glossy images. In the context of the brothel, such images simultaneously reveal how the tantalizing foreign destinations function as both lure and motivation to earn more capital (figured as prostitution). They also implicate Godard's filmmaking—replete with lovely images, attractive women, moments of unironic splendor—in this same economy. Later, Godard would term this the "fatale beauté" of cinema: the crime that damns the cinema but from which it will not escape—an ambivalent double-bind—that of covering over the ugly truths of history with distracting, beguiling images.

The room includes another important poster, an image of actress Anna Karina as the prostitute Nana in Godard's *Vivre sa vie* (1962), an earlier story of the passage to prostitution as a means of scraping by in 1960s Paris. This spectral image of the actress, however, also highlights how a succession of women shaped Godard's vision in 1967 after his rupture with Anna Karina, his failed courtship of Marina Vlady, and his budding relationship with Anne Wiazemsky.[45] It is, therefore, not simply "two or three things" but also two or three "hers," a biographical detail that simultaneously expands the allegorical reading of the film to denote a fable of 1960s Parisian womanhood writ large (figure 2.6).

In the apartment, Monsieur Gérard opens a bedroom door, revealing a man stroking a woman's bare thigh on a bed. He reminds the couple that they only have seven minutes left for their pleasure (figure 2.7). When

Figure 2.6. Juliette drops off her daughter Solange. Behind them is an illustration of Nana (Anna Karina) in Godard's *Vivre sa vie* (1962). *Source*: Godard, Jean-Luc, dir. *2 or 3 Things I Know About Her* (*2 ou 3 choses que je sais d'elle*). 1967; New York: Criterion Collection, 2009. DVD.

Figure 2.7. A prostitute and client at Monsieur Gérard's apartment. Airline advertisements for foreign destinations. *Source*: Godard, Jean-Luc, dir. *2 or 3 Things I Know About Her* (*2 ou 3 choses que je sais d'elle*). 1967; New York: Criterion Collection, 2009. DVD.

the doorbell rings and Juliette enters with her young daughter Solange, the adults exchange scant words, but the little girl's cries dominate on the soundtrack. After Juliette exits, Solange wanders the space, wailing, demanding her mother, hurrying to the front door whenever another prostitute enters. After Monsieur Gérard gathers Solange onto his lap and begins reading a storybook to her and the other children, the camera pans to show us Juliette working the sidewalk below. Solange cries throughout the film. The querulous little girl and her precocious older brother Christophe—who recounts a dream in which North and South Vietnam, figured as estranged twin brothers, reunite—work as clues throughout the film that Godard's wider response to the Trente Glorieuses in *2 ou 3 choses* lies in the promise of new beginnings. The question of how to begin anew, however, is still posed with ambivalence, caught between Solange's choice of violence (the wordless cry as pure demand) and Christophe's preference for reparation (the restorative potential of language in story-telling) (figure 2.8).

2 OU 3 CHOSES: THE PAST IN THE PRESENT

The final sequence of shots in *2 ou 3 choses* definitively announces Godard's decision to beginning anew and, thereby, attempt to shed his ambivalence. It begins with an extreme close-up of the tip of a cigarette, which Juliette has lit in the previous scene. Godard's whispered voice-over

Figure 2.8. Juliette with her two children, Christophe and Solange. *Source*: Godard, Jean-Luc, dir. *2 or 3 Things I Know About Her* (*2 ou 3 choses que je sais d'elle*). 1967; New York: Criterion Collection, 2009. DVD.

accompanies the camera's curious, penetrating gaze. The cigarette seems to become extinguished and then to reignite—oscillating between black and red—as it is smoked by the unseen Juliette. Godard narrates: "I listen to commercials on my transistor radio. . . . Thanks to E-S-S-O, I depart without a care on the road of dreams and I forget everything else. I forget Hiroshima . . . I forget Auschwitz . . . I forget Budapest . . . I forget Vietnam . . . I forget about the minimum wage . . . I forget about the housing crisis . . . I forget about the famine in India."[46] Godard illustrates here a possible consequence of the tyranny of the spectacle: the annihilation of history and class consciousness. The phrase "Thanks to E-S-S-O" rings with the artificiality of advertising language as if the citizen encountering neoliberal globalization of the Trente Glorieuses has lent his mind and voice to the service of the spectacle.[47] The fluctuation of black and red on the cigarette's smoldering end, this punctuation by breath, visualizes menacingly the forgetting that Godard promises. Yet it simultaneously calls to mind apocalyptic destruction: burning cities, furnaces filled with corpses, the dark and smoldering mouth of hell (figure 2.9). As his narration speaks of amnesia, his images remind us of what cannot be erased: the return of the repressed. Commodity fetishism, Godard explains, helps us to expunge the memory of modern historical traumas, and to assuage our sense of responsibility or culpability, but his film does the opposite of this. Throughout, he conjures up uncanny connections between objects and subjects, words and meanings, and human beings in the past and

Figure 2.9. As Juliette smokes, Godard's whispered voice-over speaks about forgetting. *Source*: Godard, Jean-Luc, dir. *2 or 3 Things I Know About Her* (*2 ou 3 choses que je sais d'elle*). 1967; New York: Criterion Collection, 2009. DVD.

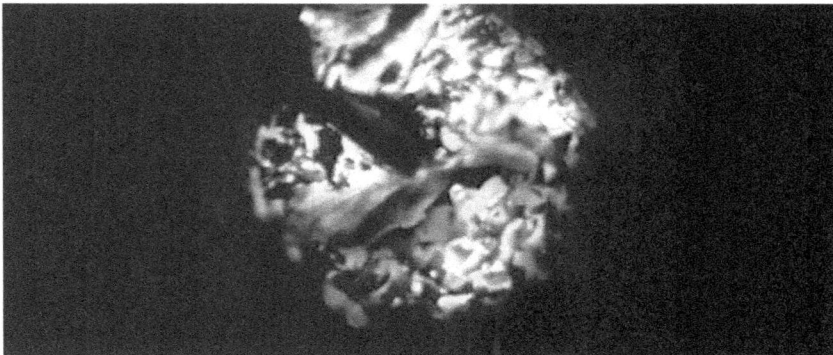

present. He urges the spectator to hold these categories accountable to each other, and to take on the responsibility of history.

Godard reveals a world forged by forgetting in the film's final shot. Beginning in a close-up of a happy couple advertising Hollywood chewing gum, the shot zooms out, exposing a collection of other rectangular consumer products arranged on a lawn. The advertisement of the couple rests amid boxes of Lava soap, Omo laundry detergent, Dash, Ajax, Schick razors, Lustucru pasta, and various brands of cigarettes. The arrangement of these boxes brings to mind the various rectangular structures comprising the housing project, the *grand ensemble*, in which Juliette and her family live. Godard draws a direct comparison between the world inhabited by his filmic characters (and by extension his compatriots) and that of the couple in the Hollywood gum advertisement. Not only does consumerism now structure the lived environment, but the living have also become indistinguishable from their simulacra. In attempting to live the impossible dream of capitalism prescribed by the spectacle, the spectacle threatens to replace social reality (figure 2.10).

Yet the spectacle dominates *2 ou 3 choses* and Godard's earlier Nouvelle Vague films, with their simultaneous condemnation of and passion for beautiful, fleeting pleasures, and their criticism of and fascination with prostitution. At the end of *2 ou 3 choses*, Godard vows to take a new approach. The film concludes with a theory of escape from the falsification

Figure 2.10. The final shot of *2 ou 3 choses*: the world forged by forgetting; the spectacle replaces social reality. *Source*: Godard, Jean-Luc, dir. *2 or 3 Things I Know About Her (2 ou 3 choses que je sais d'elle)*. 1967; New York: Criterion Collection, 2009. DVD.

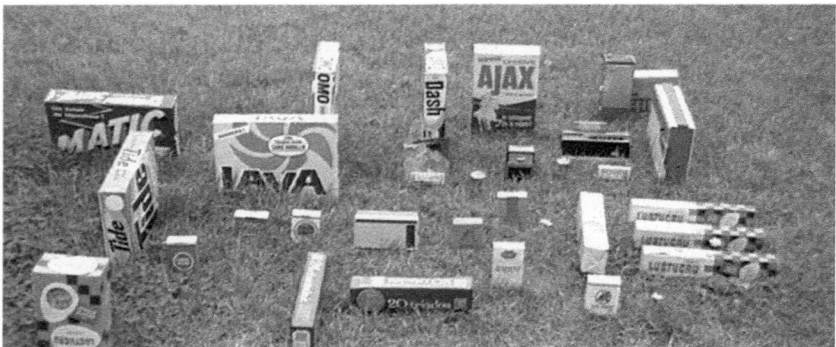

imposed by the spectacle. Godard whispers the film's final lines: "I forgot everything, accept that, since I have been reduced to nothing (à zero), it is from there that I must start again."

Godard alludes to Roberto Rossellini's 1948 film *Germany Year Zero* (appearing in French as *Allemagne année zéro*), while announcing a rather literal departure from his current mode of filmmaking in response to historical devastation.[48] His Nouvelle Vague era ended just a year later, in the summer of 1967. In the summer of 1966, Godard shot two of the last films of his Nouvelle Vague period, *Made in USA* and *2 ou 3 choses que je sais d'elle*. The following year, he ends his 1967 film *Week-end* with a scene of cannibalism—a bourgeois woman eating the cooked carcass of her husband—and then declares in an intertitle "end of cinema" (*fin du cinéma*). *Week-end*, therefore, epitomizes the "weak end" of Godard's Nouvelle Vague period. After announcing the death of cinema, Godard spent the years between 1968 and 1972 making films differently: polemical political pieces that form the corpus of the Dziga Vertov Group. The year 1968, therefore, can be understood not only as a moment of historical rupture for France because of the events and hopes surrounding *Mai '68* but also as marking a rupture and shift in Godard's oeuvre.

Thus, Godard's *2 ou 3 choses* proposes a rhetoric grounded in synecdoche, the logic of "bits" or remnants derived from ambivalence. The film zeros in on the capital region and one day in the life of its inhabitants as a means of revealing larger trends in postwar France. The new mandate for expansion (infrastructural, manufacturing, economic) in the Trente Glorieuses demands that citizens like Juliette Jeanson/Marina Vlady increase their cashflow to keep up. As unconstrained growth requires a constant exchange of buying and selling, Godard suggests that the distance between items, brands, and humans has collapsed into a market of pure means. This competition stresses more over less and future over past, overlooking the destruction it leaves in its wake. Fed up, Godard vows to opt out, to start over, to exit the playing field and only to return with a fresh strategy, eschewing narrative and outside of commercial filmmaking.

Jia: The Undead in New Worlds, or *Zero as Destination*

While Godard's answer to the problems of the present generation in France is to begin anew, Jia Zhangke's 2004 *The World* proposes ghosts in the place of babies, the haunting of the past in the place of the break

toward the future. In this way, I read the Chinese response to the trauma
of Tiananmen and the emphasis on building and expanding in post-1989
China as one of exploding temporal boundaries, whereby the dead mingle
with the living as remnants of refusal. Not only does the future remain
a shadow on a shifting horizon, but the movement toward this future
relies—in Jia's film—on the bodies of dead workers.[49] This figure of the
worker emerges in its contemporary form in tension with Chinese history.
As Corey Kai Nelson Schultz has shown, the characters in Jia Zhangke's
films can be categorized as descendants of five Chinese class types: those
glorified during Maoist China—such as the soldier (兵; *bing*), worker
(工; *gong*), and peasant (农; *nong*)—and those celebrated in China's pre-
Communist past and rehabilitated in the reform period post-1978—such
as the scholar gentry, or contemporary intellectual (士; *shi*), and the mer-
chant, or today's entrepreneur (商; *shang*).[50] All of the central characters
in *The World*, for example, have transformed from Mao-era peasants (农;
nong) into rural-to-urban migrant workers (民工; *mingong*). In this way,
Jia's work emphasizes how ambivalence is built on the unsettled remains
of the past and thus challenges the emergence of the new.

Jia Zhangke's *The World* attempts to carve out hope in the postmodern
dystopia overtaking Beijing, but Jia's vision of China's capital is grounded
in his origins as an underground filmmaker and in stories set in his home
province of Shanxi. At twenty, Jia Zhangke went to Taiyuan, the provincial
seat of Shanxi province, to study painting. During this time, he attended a
screening of Chen Kaige's 1984 film *Yellow Earth* (黃土地; *Huang tudi*) which
inspired the young art student to change course and pursue filmmaking.[51]
Yellow Earth is set on the Loess Plateau in Shaanxi province in the late
1930s, a place and time most famous for marking the end of Mao's Long
March. From 1936 to 1948, Mao and his army occupied Yan'an, spreading
enthusiasm for their Communist vision for China, as well as for their
impending victory over the Japanese and Chiang Kai-shek's Guomingdang
(GMD/KMT) army. This period has traditionally been glorified in Chinese
media and artistic depictions. However, Chen's *Yellow Earth* questions the
practical impact that Mao's ideology had on the lives of peasants and challenges the stock characters and narratives that the Communist Party used
to portray Revolutionary-era China. Jia Zhangke describes the transforma-
tive impact the film had on him in 1990: "To be frank, my understanding
of film then came entirely from the long period of propagandistic official
films. I thought film should always be dramatic, didactic, and formulaic
in dialogue and characterization. . . . But as soon as I saw *Yellow Earth* I

suddenly realized that film could be made in different ways."[52] In 1993, Jia matriculated to Chen Kaige's alma mater, the Beijing Film Academy. As the filmmakers of China's fifth generation, the first post–Cultural Revolution class of filmmakers to graduate from Beijing Film Academy in 1982 (including Chen Kaige) gravitated increasingly toward big-budget fantasy epics and historical costume dramas, the strong ideological and aesthetic rift between their work and Jia's own cinematic direction became increasingly evident. Like other members of China's sixth-generation filmmakers, Jia's cinematic approach "eschews the temptations of melodrama, fantasy, comedy and other commercial forms in favor of a realist aesthetic that highlights the plight of the everyman."[53] His primary aesthetic models are not his fifth-generation predecessors but the post-socialist realism movement in Chinese film of the 1990s and international art cinema.[54]

After graduating from the Beijing Film Academy, Jia Zhangke directed his first feature films, termed his "hometown trilogy": *Xiao Wu* (小武) in 1997, *Platform* (站台; *Zhantai*) in 2000, and *Unknown Pleasures* (任逍遥; *Ren xiao yao*) in 2002. All three films are set in small cities in Jia's home province of Shanxi and explore the lives of ordinary young people cast against the background of China's dramatic transformation from the late 1970s to the beginning of the twenty-first century. Every one of these films failed to pass the censors and obtain the "dragon seal" of the Chinese Film Bureau, and so all three were banned from general distribution in China. While Jia's films enjoyed critical acclaim at international film festivals, it was not until 2004 with *The World* that the filmmaker saw his work in cinemas in his own country. *The World* was co-produced by the official Shanghai Film Group and approved for domestic commercial release. Yet Chinese audiences would be evaluating a film that differed in a significant way from Jia's "hometown trilogy;" *The World* brings a cast from Shanxi to Beijing.

Like Godard's *2 ou 3 choses*, Jia's *The World* is situated on the margins of the Chinese capital. My discussion of *The World* begins by evaluating how the characters' lives in this space illustrate an ambivalence toward the possibilities for working-class, particularly rural-to-urban, migrant Chinese in the new era of neoliberal globalization. Next, I examine how the film posits the relationship of Beijing's suburbs to the rest of the world and to France in particular, allowing for a transnational unearthing of repressed historical traumas. Finally, I show how photographs ("bits" or remnants of film) of absent children and lovers suggest a material separation between striving in the difficult present and arriving in a productive future.

THE WORLD: BEIJING'S FENGTAI DISTRICT, 2004

As I introduced in the opening pages of this chapter, the narrative of *The World* centers on a dancer, Zhao Xiao Tao (played by Jia's future wife and muse, Zhao Tao), who has come from Shanxi to Beijing by securing a job performing at Beijing's World Park, a theme park composed of simulacra of world monuments. In an interview, Jia Zhangke explains that the story of the film was inspired by Zhao Tao's own experience as a dancer at a similar Chinese park, Shenzhen's Window of the World, where Zhao was assigned to work after completing her studies at the Beijing Dance Institute.[55] Jia explains that he was intrigued by Zhao's description of her frustration as a park employee: "On the one hand, the park is dazzling and beautiful, filled with all kinds of sights and sounds and imbued with the feelings of freedom and openness, but for those people who actually work there, it is still like some backward corner cut off from the world."[56] This contrast between the "worldly" image of the park and the isolation of its employees is one of the central sources of ambivalence in the film (figure 2.11). *The World* further troubles this dichotomy and enhances a formal affective ambivalence by blurring the modal edges between narrative and documentary: drawing from the real life of Zhao Tao—to the point of giving her character the same name—making use of amateur actors (such as Jia's cousin Han Sanming, who plays important roles in several of Jia's films) and capturing the dramatic destruction and reconstruction of Beijing starting in 2001 after the city's successful bid for the 2008 Olympic Games

Figure 2.11. The worldly image of the park contrasts to the confinement of the characters. *Source*: Jia, Zhangke, dir. *The World* (世界; *Shijie*). 2004; New York: Zeitgeist Films, 2006. DVD.

and acceptance into the World Trade Organization. The film focuses on the theme park as an ambivalent synecdoche for post-Tiananmen China, a place full of possibilities, but also one where the future is foreclosed. In fact, as Schultz points out, some of the migrant workers in *The World* "end up dying in pursuit of their dreams."[57] While the characters left difficult situations behind in their childhood villages, the migration to the capital has certainly not allowed for unconditional mobility.

The World takes place in Beijing's Fengtai District, a suburb that is home to both an enormous migrant population and to Beijing's World Park. This location, a theme park in an urban suburb, is demystified in the film. Nick Stanley notes that critics "regard the phenomenon of theme parks as a crucial development in economic and cultural imperialism as well as in the enslavement of young people's imaginations."[58] Stanley further explains that many theme parks, including Beijing's World Park, represent a conjunction of technological advances and Americanism.[59] The result is a highly controlled, utopian landscape: "The surveillance and policing of the parks ensures that nothing occurs to upset this dream. There are no poor, few members of minority communities, and despite the visible facilities for the handicapped, few young or old who are fit enough for the grueling pace of the day's endurance test."[60] Thus, the theme park encapsulates the phantasmagoria of possibility and enclosure that defined state Chinese ideology in the years following 1989. The young workers in Jia's film serve as fantasy objects—dressed in costumes aligned with the park's featured locations (kimonos for the Japanese tea house, flight attendant uniforms for the grounded model airplane), performing choreographed dances in approximations of Indian Lehenga Cholis—trapped, immobilized as the park's product: a neoliberal dream vision in which foreign places and people are reduced to commodities. Though *The World* shows that some characters achieve minor career advances or take actions that show a faith in the future, the film expresses cynicism toward these "vertical" movements: the dancer Youyou (Xiang Wan) is promoted as a result of her affair with the park's director, and dancing couple Wei (Jing Jue) and Niu (Jiang Zhongwei) are married toward the end of the film largely to mitigate Niu's paranoid jealousy.

The objectives motivating migration to the capital also stand in tension to traditional Chinese values centered on kinship. After the death of the young migrant worker known as Little Sister, Jia's film dramatizes this relationship to kinship by including a side story of the dead man's parents, who travel from Shanxi to Beijing to honor their son's memory. As other scholars have noted, this chapter of the film, demarcated by the intertitle "Tokyo Story" (東京物語; *Dongjing Wuyu*), adapts some of the themes of country vs. city and family vs. career from Yasujirô Ozu's 1953 eponymous film.[61] In addition to these thematic similarities, Jia subtly interweaves Ozu's soundtrack and uses several rhyming images to make the comparison between the films plain: the horizon of the Tokyo suburbs is striated by smokestacks while Beijing's is streaked with construction sites (figures 2.12, 2.13); both the elderly Japanese and Chinese parents appear

Figure 2.12. Smokestacks in Tokyo's suburbs in Ozu's *Tokyo Story* (1953). *Source*: Yasujirô Ozu, dir. *Tokyo Story*. 1953; New York: Criterion Collection, 2013. Blu-ray Disc.

Figure 2.13. Construction in Beijing's suburbs in Jia's *The World*. *Source*: Jia, Zhangke, dir. *The World* (世界; *Shijie*). 2004; New York: Zeitgeist Films, 2006. DVD.

profoundly out of place, old-fashioned, and immobile when placed beside the migrant urban young people (figures 2.14, 2.15). Ozu's film laments the cultural fallout wrought by the early years of the Japanese economic miracle; Jia's film likewise questions what has become of time-honored beliefs as China enters the age of neoliberal globalization.

In a shot that encapsulates the gap in social mores between socialist and post-socialist China, Little Sister's father, dressed in a Mao suit and

Figure 2.14. Immobile older couple in Ozu's *Tokyo Story*. *Source*: Yasujirô Ozu, dir. *Tokyo Story*. 1953; New York: Criterion Collection, 2013. Blu-ray Disc.

Figure 2.15. Immobile older couple in Jia's *The World*. *Source*: Jia, Zhangke, dir. *The World* (世界; *Shijie*). 2004; New York: Zeitgeist Films, 2006. DVD.

hat, the anachronistic uniform of the latter-day proletariat, wipes tears from his eyes as he pockets his son's back payments (figure 2.16). How does one reconcile, the film seems to ask, China's sudden valorization of personal economic gain over peasant solidarity and cohesive family bonds? And at what price? However, in this way, *The World* also partakes of the following paradoxes of Chinese visualization of familial sentimentality in the age of neoliberal globalization proposed by Rey Chow:

> Is kinship, defined as an inviolable interiority of familial/familiar relations . . . in essence the last vestige of morality (and of humanity) felt in an utterly amoral world? At the same time, is not such commitment to kinship bonds, so deeply rooted in Chinese societies as to be associated with, and reaffirmed as, conscience itself, precisely complicit with some of the worst xenophobic . . . practices in the contemporary world. . . . Ironically, then, the Chinese sentimental attachment to *home* . . . stands in this analysis as an instructive case in point of the modern and contemporary world condition of homelessness.[62]

What Chow suggests—namely, that contemporary images of a Chinese attachment to the imaginary of an "inviolable" "home" rely on the belief

Figure 2.16. Little Sister's father, dressed in an anachronistic Mao suit and hat, cries as he pockets his son's back payments. *Source*: Jia, Zhangke, dir. *The World* (世界; *Shijie*). 2004; New York: Zeitgeist Films, 2006. DVD.

in a prosperity of an "us" (the insider, the family, class, or national unit) regardless of (and sometimes dependent on) the victimization of a "them" (the outsider, the nonrelation, the migrant worker, the foreigner), which illustrates the increasing alienation of the global human condition—crystallizes in the story of Little Sister's death in *The World*. The logic of the neoliberal globalizing age depicted in the film seems to dictate that personal and family success requires exactly the acts—moving to the city, working in dangerous conditions, and sending money back home—that caused Little Sister's demise. While most of the characters accept this paradox, the female protagonist Tao questions it, her ambivalence to her current situation amplified by the tragedy. As Dudley Andrew notes, "Tao, like Norika in Ozu's masterpiece, realizes she belongs with these old people and their traditional ways, more than with the young who have banded together in the crowded city. . . . This scene of mourning and this solidarity with the old couple lead Tao to ask Taisheng about marriage, but too late."[63] Tao's death comes before her ambivalence—or the film's—can be resolved.

THE WORLD: PARIS IN THE BEIJING SUBURBS

The World converses wordlessly through its images with France and, to a lesser degree, with the United States about the occlusion of national traumas and the globalized capitalist spectacles that have come to replace remembrance and reparation. The film's title shot shows the World Park from a distance. The monorail, which carries visitors and workers alike to various parts of the site, is in the background. A simulacrum of the Eiffel Tower sits squarely in the middle. Michelle Bloom comments on the significance of the monument in Jia's film: "The Eiffel Tower's prominent, even central role in this title shot reflects the important position of France. . . . [In fact] France's high profile is conveyed through the visual refrain of the Eiffel Tower, which appears variously in the foreground and background."[64] In the foreground of the title shot, a man wearing a dingy hat and carrying a bag of trash on his back lumbers across the frame. He stops and turns to look directly at the camera, an example of what Schultz terms "the direct *mingong* gaze," a moment during which the migrant worker breaks the fourth wall, which becomes a motif in Jia's oeuvre. Schlutz explains that this direct gaze puts the audience "on the spot in more ways than simply putting us in the moment; rather, it also puts us 'on the spot' in the sense that we are called to judgment and are prompted to respond. . . . In this gaze, we are being 'held' for our (possible crimes) . . . as a member of the audience who has been complacent and uncomplaining about the *mingong*'s wretched situation."[65] The words "A film by Jia Zhangke" appear above the man's head (figure 2.17). The "director," figured by this character, is represented as someone who collects the unwanted, the discarded. The man turns and continues on his way.[66] The film's title, "The World," is now posted in the center of the frame. This allows the spectator to appreciate the park's true location in the suburbs of Beijing and offers a glimpse of another of this suburb's inhabitants, the indigent. It also suggests that the true "world" of Jia's film is the composite of wealth and poverty, futuristic and ancient, international and local that characterizes the double-bind of a neoliberal globalizing world.

An early section of the film, entitled "Paris in Beijing Suburb," opens with the same scale and location of the shot from the title sequence. Tao and Taisheng have been fighting. After a chilly confrontation near the Arc de Triomphe, the couple eventually makes up in the Arcades. The next day, two migrant workers from Taisheng's home village come to visit him at the park before taking up their construction jobs in the city. Taisheng points to an island covered in miniature skyscrapers on one side of a manmade lake. "That's America," Taisheng explains proudly. "The Twin Towers were

Figure 2.17. Title shot from Jia's *The World* includes both the skyline of the World Park and another kind of inhabitant of the area. *Source*: Jia, Zhangke, dir. *The World* (世界; *Shijie*). 2004; New York: Zeitgeist Films, 2006. DVD.

bombed on September 11. We still have them." Then he gestures to the right side of the frame: "And that's France's Eiffel Tower." Finally, he points directly at the camera, as if the film is waving—or pointing its figural finger accusingly—at its international spectatorship: "That's Notre Dame. Heard of it?" His friend walks toward the camera and replies, "I've seen it in the movies." Here, another instance of Schlutz's "*mingong* gaze," we understand that Jia is also giving his international spectatorship an ironic wink (figure 2.18).

In this sequence, Jia Zhangke echoes a question that Godard takes up with his consumer product simulacrum of an apartment complex in the last image of *2 ou 3 choses*: What happens when the copy replaces the original? What happens when an image of something effaces its referent? The World Park is not Paris, but it is *a* Paris in the Beijing Suburbs. The sparkling lights of the Arcades work their magic without needing the aura of the original. The World Park is "superior" to Manhattan because it still has two of Manhattan's most iconic structures. But, when Taisheng points to Notre Dame, looking directly at the camera, breaking the fourth wall, like the trash collector during the title sequence, the spectator realizes that Jia Zhangke is also wondering again about his own role in image making. By shattering its own diegetic plenitude, the film announces its broader ambivalence to pleasing illusions.

Figure 2.18. Taisheng points at the camera: "That's Notre Dame. Heard of it?" *Source*: Jia, Zhangke, dir. *The World* (世界; *Shijie*). 2004; New York: Zeitgeist Films, 2006. DVD.

THE WORLD AND STILL LIFE: NO FUTURE

In *The World*, Jia Zhangke introduces the porousness between our world and the spirit world through photographs of the absent, which function as physical remnants within the diegesis. In an early sequence in *The World*, Tao washes Taisheng's uniform in the employee's dormitory. When Anna enters to wash her own clothes, Tao lends her detergent and offers her hot water. After Anna perceives that Tao is washing men's clothes, she inquires (by drawing contrasting male and female stick figures) if she's married. Tao replies in the negative. Anna indicates her rejoinder by revealing her wedding ring and shares with Tao a photograph in which she and two young boys sit beaming in front of a Christmas tree. Anna points and gives their names, "Igor and Alyosha" (figures 2.19, 2.20). These are the

Figure 2.19. Anna shares a photograph with Tao. *Source*: Jia, Zhangke, dir. *The World* (世界; *Shijie*). 2004; New York: Zeitgeist Films, 2006. DVD.

Figure 2.20. The photograph shows Anna's absent children. *Source*: Jia, Zhangke, dir. *The World* (世界; *Shijie*). 2004; New York: Zeitgeist Films, 2006. DVD.

only children we see in the film, but we are only given their photographic image, emphasizing their physical absence within the world of the film. They exist as flickering, isolated fragments, like ashes. Anna, driven by economic necessity, has left these children in order to earn more money in China. With Anna, Jia Zhangke suggests that the demands of neoliberal globalization drain the vitality of the future, not just for regular Chinese citizens and migrant workers but for the world's unprosperous migrant workers more generally.

In *The World*, the spirit realm merges with the land of the living with the photograph of Anna's children and when Qun shows her lover, Taisheng, a photograph of her husband. Qun hasn't seen her spouse since he left five years earlier. The photograph shows the man in front of the Belleville metro station in Paris, a site belonging to one of the city's Chinatowns.[67] Qun and Taisheng praise the name, "*Belleville*, beautiful city" (figures 2.21, 2.22). The photograph brings to life the specter of Qun's marriage to this absent man in this foreign place. Is Belleville accessible? Is the man still waiting? What will become of Qun should she make it to Paris and be reunited with her husband? In *The World*, the gap between dreams and reality reveals ambivalence. The photograph—a remnant, an image of a character ripped and excised from the plot, like the Kleinian loved objects torn to "bits"—marks this ambivalence.

In Jia's next film, *Still Life* (三峡好人; *Sanxia Haoren*) (2006), photographs also serve as the characters' only connections to absent loved ones. At the beginning, we follow the male protagonist Sanming (Han

Figure 2.21. Qun shows a photograph to Taisheng *Source*: Jia, Zhangke, dir. *The World* (世界; *Shijie*). 2004; New York: Zeitgeist Films, 2006. DVD.

Figure 2.22. The photograph shows Qun's absent husband in front of the Belleville metro station in Paris. *Source*: Jia, Zhangke, dir. *The World* (世界; *Shijie*). 2004; New York: Zeitgeist Films, 2006. DVD.

Sanming) as he travels to Fengjie, a town on the Yangtze River, which is quickly being inundated after the damming of the Three Gorges. Sanming is in search of his daughter, whom he hasn't seen since his wife left him sixteen years earlier. Unable to track down his wife and daughter at the municipal authority office, he asks nearly every inhabitant he comes across if they know his estranged relatives. He finally meets a makeshift brothel Madame whose own child was at school with his daughter. Sanming begs to see a photo, and she produces it: rows of children in uniforms. She points out Sanming's daughter (figures 2.23, 2.24). Like the photographs in *The World*, this image, a bit, a remnant, offers the viewer a moment of the undead. Sanming never succeeds in finding his daughter. In a film about the disappearance of the old—villages covered by the rising river waters—Jia Zhangke shows equal pessimism about his country's care of their young. A young migrant worker called Brother Mark befriended by Sanming is murdered and buried under rubble on a demolition site; Sanming's daughter remains for him a distant memory, a ghost. In *Still Life*, then, ambivalence is attached not so much to the future but to the dead and the haunting past. The characters cannot tear themselves away from their past lives because the future has been foreclosed, turned into an image or spectacle from which they (and their dead, their pasts) are absent.

The World, likewise, concludes with the dead and in the dark. Tao and Taisheng have just been carried out of an apartment asphyxiated

Figure 2.23. A woman shares a photo with Sanming. *Source*: Jia, Zhangke, dir. *Still Life* (三峡好人; *Sanxia haoren*). 2006; Atlanta: Big World Pictures, 2019. DVD.

Figure 2.24. The photo contains rows of school children, Sanming's daughter among them. *Source*: Jia, Zhangke, dir. *Still Life* (三峡好人; *Sanxia haoren*). 2006; Atlanta: Big World Pictures, 2019. DVD.

by a gas leak and laid on the ground, side by side, wrapped in blankets like mummies; the film closes with a long take of the couple. As the camera fades out, the viewer is left in darkness, and suddenly Taisheng speaks. He asks if they have died. Tao responds: "No. This is just the beginning." This final space in *The World*, a haunted space, bridging life and death, is ironically and ambivalently charged with more hope and creative potential than any other in the film. The creative potential will be actualized in Jia's future films, in which characters like Taisheng and Tao return, their ghosts generating new stories from the ashes. Zhao Tao, of course, returns as lead actress in all of Jia's subsequent films. Significantly, Jia's 2018 film, *Ash Is the Purest White* (江湖兒女; *Jianghu ernü*), works both as a sequel to Jia's third feature film *Unknown Pleasures* (2002) and to *Still Life*, returning to Hu Bei province and resuscitating Zhao Tao's character Shen Hong (from *Still Life*) as the ex-convict Zhao Qiao Qiao (a grown-up Qiao Qiao from *Unknown Pleasures*). As in *Still Life*, Qiao Qiao has traveled to the Three Gorges region to settle her score with a man, Guo Bin (played in *Still Life* by Li Zhubing and in *Ash Is the Purest White* by Liao Fan). In *Still Life*, Guo Bin is a philandering businessman, while in *Ash* he is an aging gangster, a former triad boss. Thus Jia, by way of this wry alliance of commerce and crime (the Chinese title, literally "the sons and daughters of rivers and lakes," refers to traditional Chinese fantasy stories, the martial arts community in Wuxia narratives, or the world of organized crime most typically seen in Hong Kong gangster films with its "male and female outlaws"), continues his sly assessment of capitalist machinations in contemporary China.[68] By focusing on the woman protagonist's long incarceration and later having her take an aborted train journey to Xinjiang province, the site of the current concentration camps set up to "reeducate" the region's Muslim Uyghur population, *Ash* can be read as issuing a contemporary critique of Chinese policy and ushering forward a new cast of hidden, detained bodies, and their ghosts. Like Tao in *The World*, Qiao Qiao in *Ash* (and, intertextually, by way of *Unknown Pleasures* and *Still Life*) exemplifies how Jia Zhangke's cinema draws women as ambivalent figures, poised between past, present, and future. Jia explains of the woman protagonist in *Ash*: "I feel like we don't have that many good things from the past that we have preserved for ourselves today. All of the good things seem to somehow be sealed in the past. Perhaps Qiao Qiao is one of the few people who is hanging on to something from the past for us."[69] Thus the women played by Zhao Tao in Jia's cinema, embodying the bridge between the old and new, the sentimental attachment to family and the jockeying for economic position and power, figure the ambivalence of China in the age of neoliberal globalization as remnants of refusal.

David Der-wei Wang's *The Monster That Is History* offers insight into the meaning of ghosts in contemporary China. In the book's final chapter, Wang tries to account for the reappearance of ghosts in Chinese literature at the end of the twentieth century. He notes that these apparitions run counter to the main thrust of modern Chinese literature. Why, then, do the ghosts return? Wang explains that the return of the ghosts reveals a new variety of realism, one tied to the past as well as the present and accepts the uncanny as an integral part of the daily: "Phantasmagoric realism—a realism ironically deriving its effect of verisimilitude from the incantation of apparitions, phantoms, hallucinations, and so on—can be regarded as a special discourse with which late-twentieth-century Chinese writers lay bare 'the illusion of the absolute reality of the unreal.' "[70] The haunted space in *The World*, the dark limbo in which Tao and Taisheng rest, suggests an uncertainty between the boundaries of life and death, the present and the past. In this way, Jia's *The World* points to the convergence of temporalities at work in contemporary China: the simultaneous experience of socialism and capitalism, ancient tradition and modernity, limitations and freedom. *The World* treats this convergence with ambivalence and offers itself up as a remnant of refusal (figure 2.25).

Figure 2.25. The final shot of *The World*: "Are we dead? No. this is just the beginning." *Source*: Jia, Zhangke, dir. *The World* (世界; *Shijie*). 2004; New York: Zeitgeist Films, 2006. DVD.

Woman as Ambivalent Heroine: *Le Trou* and the True

Though directed by men, Godard and Jia's films echo with women's steps and women's voices. The central position of women characters prompts a larger consideration of the different ways in which men and women mediate history and memory, the interventions by those traditionally aligned with public action vs. those relegated to domestic duty.[71] The films of Godard and Jia chronicle women's shifting historical movement from home to workplace in eras of emerging neoliberal globalization.

Godard attaches the conflicting image of womanhood in *2 ou 3 choses* to his ambivalence with the cinematic spectacle. As Laura Mulvey writes of *2 ou 3 choses*, "I was struck by the analogy that Godard seemed to suggest, simultaneously, as it were, *misogynist and anticapitalist*, between femininity and commodities as seduction and enigma, with both premised on an appearance fashioned as desirable, and implying and concealing an elusive, unknowable essence."[72] However, Mulvey goes on to specify: "This dualism also reflects Godard's passionate and conflicted relationship to the cinema—as both a site of fascination and the erotic and something to be exposed as mystification and delusion."[73] If Godard's enterprise always relies on deciphering what cinema can and cannot accomplish (and simultaneously acts as a meditation on the ways in which cinema has succeeded and failed throughout history), it is with stories of women—both as active subjects and as objects of cinematic gaze—that the filmmaker works through these questions. I'd take this a step further: in Godard's films of this era, women reveal the state of the world; women are Godard's agents of change.

The sequence "Chez l'américain" occurring midway through Godard's *2 ou 3 choses* captures the distinctly Godardian ambivalence and the ambivalence of his heroines during the final year of his Nouvelle Vague period. The film's protagonist Juliette and her friend Marianne (Anny Duperey) enter a posh Parisian hotel room. Marianne calls out "Paul?" and later "Johnny?" Juliette stands aside and addresses the camera. She asks what happens when we doubt the correspondence of our thoughts and an external reality. Johnny, the "American," ironically played by the French producer Raoul Lévy, appears sporting a T-shirt decorated with an American flag. He explains that he worked as a war correspondent in Saigon with the *Arkansas Daily*; "They're all crazy down there," he laments (first in accented English, then in French). Marianne lounges on the hotel bed reading a French translation of Ray Bradbury's *A Medicine for Melancholy* (1959). The women then parade before Johnny wearing tote bags advertising American airlines (Pan Am and TWA) over their heads (figure 2.26). Mid-procession, there is a long, static take of a construction site. Afterward, Marianne goes to bed with Johnny while Juliette stands apart, speaking to the camera about what it means to think, her image intercut with those of the violence in Vietnam. This space degenerates into the sound of a camera quickly snapping stills, like that of a machine gun, rat-a-rat-tatting, over more journalistic photographs of Vietnam—victims of napalm, survivors of bombings, dead bodies—while Marianne repeats in voice-over "L'América über alles." This last statement, reminiscent of the first line of the German national anthem ("Deutschland, Deutschland über alles, über alles in der Welt") ties together France's recent past to the present, the German Occupation of France to the Trente Glorieuses. The Germans cut all but the third stanza of the song (beginning with "Unity and Justice and Freedom") after the end of the Second World War and the fall of the Third Reich. In Godard's film, it is the United States that takes up the mantle of villainous invader, not only because of its barbaric foreign war in Vietnam but as a result of its governing influence over a spectrum of spheres including, but not limited to, economic policy, commercial exports, and cultural products.

Though more than one moment from this sequence speaks to the contradictions at play in France in the late-1960s, I want to return to the marching women, heads replaced by American airline companies. And,

Figure 2.26. Juliette and Marianne wear tote bags advertising American airline companies. *Source*: Godard, Jean-Luc, dir. *2 or 3 Things I Know About Her* (*2 ou 3 choses que je sais d'elle*). 1967; New York: Criterion Collection, 2009. DVD.

inserted into the middle, a scene of construction: the destruction of an old building, the erecting of a new one.[74] Presenting this sequence as a collection of Kleinian "bits" or remnants, Godard rejects diegetic plentitude by emphasizing the interstitial (what is between two images) and offering only incommensurability. The parade of Marianne and Juliette as brands is not equivalent to the dramatic urban growth of Paris during the Trente Glorieuses. Both the increasing influence of America and multinational capitalism and swelling urban development are hallmarks of the period and treated critically by Godard. The incommensurable—a lack of correspondence, the not comparable—renders the frontier between these images an ambivalent protest. The image of Juliette and Marianne presents us with a new enemy—America and the tyranny of spectacularized capitalism—encroaching over the body of the nation, here figured as the woman's body, a feminist remnant of refusal.

The ambivalence of women in Godard's cinema, as well as its ambivalence to women and their forms of refusal, has been critiqued by Geneviève Sellier in her sustained study of the "masculine singular" form of address in the auteur cinema of the Nouvelle Vague.[75] According to Sellier, the images of women in the work of filmmakers such as Godard, François Truffaut, Louis Malle, and Claude Chabrol are most frequently "the phantasmatic concretization of a male conscience torn between its desire for autonomy and its fascination for the female Other. Women are mysterious and troubling, objects of both desire and mistrust, if not fear, who must be eliminated in order for the male to survive, if they do not ultimately succeed in destroying the hero, wittingly or not."[76] As relates specifically to Patricia Franchini, the protagonist of Godard's first feature, À bout de souffle (1959/60), Sellier remarks on the choice of casting Jean Seberg, whose "American accent and . . . status as a Hollywood star confer . . . [on her] an aura that Godard deploys with ambivalence."[77] According to Sellier, Patricia's foreignness marks her as an even more complete Other to the film's male protagonist Michel Poiccard (Jean-Paul Belmondo): "This alterity is for the most part ambivalent, that is to say, alternately fascinating and threatening. But the status of the woman in the filmic story is that of an object (of the gaze, of male desire), not of the subject (of her own story)."[78] I agree with Sellier that casting Seberg as Patricia marks her with the ambivalence tied to Godard's love and growing distrust of Hollywood cinema. However, both the women and men protagonists in the film—as in all of Godard's Nouvelle Vague films—are marked by Hollywood. À bout de souffle is commonly read as a tribute to American actor Humphrey Bogart, who died in 1957. André Bazin, in his 1961 essay "Mort d'Humphrey Bogart," describes Bogart as a man with death written on his visage. Bazin quotes Robert Lachenay, who says of Bogart, or "Bogey": "The tension in his jaw irresistibly evokes the grin of a gay cadaver, the last expression of an unhappy man who passes away while smiling. This is indeed the smile of death."[79] Godard seized upon this image of a man grinning after having been condemned to death in order to fashion the protagonist of *À bout de souffle*. Michel mimics Bogart's gestures, particularly his habit of dragging his thumb over his lips. Furthermore, Godard's film is littered with other references to the dead actor: a shot of Michel examining a poster showing Bogart in Mark Robson's 1956 *Plus dure sera la chute* (*The Harder They Fall*), and an ironic homage to Raoul Walsh's 1941 *High Sierra* (also starring Bogart) in the film's closing sequence.

I disagree with Sellier, therefore, that Patricia is any less a "subject" or any more an "object" than Michel, Bogart's juvenile refraction. In fact, the film strategically undermines the possibility that cinematic characters might exist as subjects rather than objects: whether in the sequence of jump cuts over shots of the back of Patricia's head and Michel's off-screen panegyric ("I have a girl with a very pretty neck, very pretty breasts, etc.") or in the scene in Patricia's hotel room in which both characters take turns mugging in front of the mirror—as if their ontology is confirmed only by seeing themselves flattened and framed. In other words, in opposition to Sellier, I read both the men and women protagonists in *À bout de souffle* (and the men and women in Godard's Nouvelle Vague films more generally) as "mysterious and troubling, objects of both desire and mistrust."[80]

I read woman's ambivalence through Patricia's conflicting efforts at forging a place for herself in the world. Sellier labels these Patricia's "contradictory ambitions and desires" and concludes that "the film is happy to deride her professional ambitions in order to reduce her once again to a pretty face, all smiling complicity."[81] Here, again, I disagree: with Patricia, Godard begins problematizing the paradox that women face when they try to claim space in the world. When Patricia reports Michel to the police, who subsequently shoot him dead in the street, her "betrayal" of Michel and the "tragedy" of his death are undercut by the fact that Michel is an aimless petty criminal and that Belmondo is clearly playing an exaggerated character role: a satiric, teenage imitation of the rugged noir heroes incarnated by Humphrey Bogart. On the lamb, Michel grasps at Patricia like a drowning child, and Patricia chooses her own future over his.

À bout de souffle and *2 ou 3 choses* both feature heroines who examine what it means to exist in the world as women; these characters and their questions have only continued and deepened over Godard's career. From 1968 to 1972, Godard attempted a new kind of filmmaking with Jean-Pierre Gorin and their Dziga Vertov Group. After its dissolution, Godard embarked on a new partnership with his companion Anne-Marie Miéville, who wrote the screenplay for their 1975 film, *Numéro deux*. This film is a Godardian post–Nouvelle Vague, post–Dziga Vertov sequel to the question of woman: she who is "number two" to the man's "number one." While it could be argued that in *2 ou 3 choses* Juliette/Marina is still caught between fetish object and active protest, Sandrine (Sandrine Battistella), the housewife protagonist of *Numéro deux*, moves from dissatisfaction to revolt. The film, shot in Grenoble during Godard's and Miéville's residence there, also allows a larger discussion of France: from the capital to the southeastern margins. *Numéro deux* is both a meditation on the processes of filmmaking and on family life in France. The film takes place in Godard's studio, where the filmmaker is surrounded by film and video equipment. Video monitors in the studio show an apartment in a social housing complex in Grenoble occupied by a family of four.

The film foregrounds the processes and materials of cinematic production in order to consider the issue of social reproduction more broadly, the relationship between "the home" and "the factory." As Kaja Silverman points out:

> The film's images are unlike any we have seen before. Most of them were shot in video, then reshot in 35 mm as they played on video monitors. Often two monitors are shown together. Because the 35 mm image is always larger than the video images, those images swim in a pool of blackness. But at the beginning and end of *Number Two*, the full 35 mm image is deployed for the purposes of sketching out another "scene," one which is usually foreclosed from the cinematic text: the site of production. It shows us Godard at work in his studio, surrounded by the tools of his trade, and the material he is in the process of weaving into a film. The 35 mm image also depicts something even more remarkable: a filmmaker interrogating and attempting to transform the relationship between himself and the film he is in the process of making.[82]

Godard's new relationship to his work entails an attempt at stripping himself of authorship. Elise Adami and Alex Fletcher emphasize Godard and Miéville's focus on amateurism and the phases of postproduction in *Numéro deux* as an effort to make noncommercial cinema: "The place of the home and their practice of small-scale film production . . . represents an attempt to explore an alternative mode of production to the one that the metaphor of the factory typically designates."[83] By the end of the film, woman protagonist Sandrine emerges as her own author (speaking simultaneously as actor, character, and film spectator).[84] Sandrine's transformation comes about after she recognizes herself as a part of a collective: *women*, not simply *a woman*. This allows her to understand herself as where she ought to be, taking up space, speaking for herself, and as a member of a group; a new position she triumphantly defines as "number three."[85]

An early sequence from *Numéro deux* gives the viewer a glimpse of the diegetic world of Sandrine's apartment. We see our heroine ironing a man's blue work shirt. Her head is cut off by the frame, her bathrobe open, breasts and pubic hair exposed. Her young daughter Vanessa leans on the ironing board, but then begins to pace, back and forth, behind her mother (figure 2.27).

Figure 2.27. Sandrine irons while her daughter Vanessa asks pressing questions. *Source*: Godard, Jean-Luc and Anne-Marie Miéville, dirs. *Numéro deux*. 1975; Chicago: Olive Films, 2012. DVD.

Her mother asks her to stop. Vanessa then crouches down behind Sandrine and becomes invisible to the audience until she reappears, popping up from between Sandrine's legs, mimicking childbirth. She asks, "Will I have blood between my legs when I'm big?" Her mother says, "Yes. You'll need to be wary of boys." We see on-screen the word "Réglage" ("Adjustment") morphing into "Montage," then the image of a Sandrine's husband Pierre (Pierre Oudrey) anally raping her in the kitchen. The daughter's face slowly emerges in double exposure over her parents. She says, "Sometimes, I find what mom and dad do pretty, and sometimes I think it's poopy." Ambivalence—Sandrine's bodily relation to her husband and Vanessa's mixed feelings epitomized in "Sometimes I find what mom and dad do pretty, and sometimes I think it's poopy"—is the motor behind rebirth. *Numéro deux* proposes that it is only when the world allows women to claim their difference (which little Vanessa identifies in the film as "le trou," the *hole*, or vaginal opening) and collectivity (the "truth" or *whole*), that we break new ground.[86] (See figure 2.28.)

In the films of Jia Zhangke, women also form a collectivity; however, while Godard points with some optimism to the new beginnings built by

Figure 2.28. Vanessa gives voice to her ambivalence over an image of her father anally raping his mother: "Sometimes, I find what mom and dad do pretty, and sometimes I think it's poopy." *Source*: Godard, Jean-Luc and Anne-Marie Miéville, dirs. *Numéro deux*. 1975; Chicago: Olive Films, 2012. DVD.

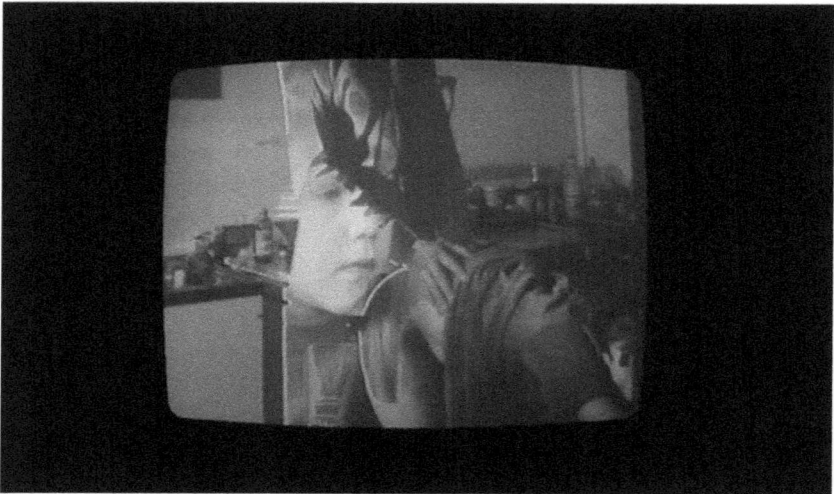

ambivalent heroines, Jia's work has grown increasingly pessimistic about the promise of tomorrow. In Jia's oeuvre, women fuse across films—as in the exhumation of Zhao Tao's character Shen Hong in *Still Life* and Qiao Qiao in *Unknown Pleasures* as Zhao Qiao in *Ash Is the Purest White*—or act as foils of one another within individual films. In *The World*, this could be Tao and Anna, Tao and Wei, Tao and Youyou, or Tao and Qun. Yet this isn't a women's collective empowered by their solidarity. Instead, *The World*, with its multiplicity of women of different nationalities and speaking a range of languages and Chinese dialects, shows the vanishing margins of possibilities for the world's disenfranchised.[87]

Zhao Tao's character in *The World* might also be easily traced back to her earlier role as Lin Ruijuan in Jia's 2000 film *Platform*. Though primarily set in Fenyang in Jia's home province of Shanxi, this film too focuses on the lives of young performers, in this case dancers and musicians who make up the local Peasant Culture Troupe. We first encounter these characters at an earlier historical juncture, in 1979. The Cultural Revolution and Mao's death are three years in the past, and Deng Xiaoping has started to reopen China to the West and to introduce a free-market economy. In Ying Xiao's writing about sound and music in Jia's film, she analyzes the opening sequence in the film, which features the Troupe at work: "Jia's masterful tableau framing and an extreme long shot of a trite musical performance, *A Train Heading for Shaoshan* . . . explicitly sets the beginning of the narrative at a crossroads between the downfall of the Maoist period and the advent of a new epoch of reform. Shaoshan is the birthplace of Chairman Mao and has been unanimously cited as the revolutionary cradle in socialist films and various performances."[88] The first moments of the film are seized in four long takes, capturing the three-step chronology (the before, during, and after) of the troupe's show.[89] The opening of the film uses a stage performance, in other words, to represent the experience of cinematic spectatorship. This meta-filmic dimension is common in Jia's work: made visible by the ludic insertion of theater and—as I've previously argued—the melancholic presence of absent characters in photographs, as well as by television and other instances of entertainment on small screens (monitors, cell phones) within the frame. Later in this chapter I will point out that *The World* also opens with the framing of the three-step chronology of a gaudier spectacle. *Platform*'s first shot shows villagers gathered in the lobby before the performance, exchanging bawdy chitchat about the sex lives of other locals. In the next shot, we are in the theater, as if looking out at the audience from

the back of the stage. A young woman in a blue Mao suit, two neat pig-
tails on either side of her neck, marches onto the stage to announce the
act. Then the extreme long shot described by Xiao captures the rest of
the young performers jerking forward on stools, crudely simulating the
motion of a traveling train. In the next shot, we join most of the cast on
a bus. Mr. Xu, the troupe leader, takes attendance and chastises one of
the male protagonists, Cui Mingliang (Wang Hongwei), when he is late.
Mr. Xu also criticizes Mingliang's work in the performance, mocking
him for his inability to accurately impersonate the sounds of a train.
Mingliang responds that he's never been on a train. This detail signals
the provincial, working-class milieu captured in the film.[90] Mr. Xu turns
away with annoyance, looking directly at the camera. In this final shot,
the camera is in the front of the vehicle, a joking reminder that Jia, the
director, is in the "driver's seat." As the screen goes black, the voices of
the young people on the bus rise in a raucous chorus of train whistles,
which accompany the film's title sequence.

 Platform concludes in darkness with the sound of a kettle whistling,
approximating more closely and menacingly than the title sequence the
sound of an oncoming train. The playful, youthful solidarity we see at the
story's outset has been vanquished over the ten years the film chronicles,
and the film ends on a mixed note. The women protagonists give us two
potential trajectories for the ambivalent Chinese heroine in the early films
of Jia Zhangke. One, Zhong Ping (Yang Tianyi), disappears in the aftermath
of her fallout with her childhood sweetheart, the second male protagonist,
Zhang Yun (Liang Jingdong). The film shows Zhong Ping betrayed twice
by her lover: first, when he pushes her to have an abortion, and later, after
they've been detained for suspected premarital sex, he cowardly admits
to the cops that they are not married. Through these first two characters
we learn about the paradoxes young lovers faced in China's 1980s: on the
one hand, as China opened up, young people wanted to experience more
sexual freedom and to sample the products of other countries (exemplified
in the film by the popular music of Taiwanese singer Teresa Teng or by
home-sewn bellbottom pants); on the other hand, the implementation of
new legislation urging family planning (later colloquially referred to as the
One-Child Policy) and the persistent policing of premarital sex made it
difficult to taste this freedom.[91] Zhong Ping as ambivalent heroine reveals
the double-bind faced by women. And her story points to a pessimism in
the future (figured as children) in post-1989 Chinese cinema.

The second woman protagonist, Ruijuan, whom I've already introduced as a double to Zhao Tao's character in *The World*, has a different
ambivalent outcome. The young dancer does not initially accept the
advances of her childhood crush, Mingliang. Instead, heeding her strict
father, she rebuffs the boy. In fact, when her father falls ill, filial Ruijuan
leaves the troupe and takes a job as a tax collector to earn enough money
to support her family. At the end of the film, however, her father has died
and Mingliang has returned to Fenyang. By the film's conclusion, the two
have been married and have a young son. In *Platform*'s final long take,
Ruijuan comes into the apartment holding the baby and cooing. The
television plays loudly in the background as Mingliang slouches, dozing
in a chair (figure 2.29).

As the kettle on the stove boils, the sound morphs into the blaring,
nondiegetic sound of a train horn. The sound grows louder and louder.
As the screen goes black, the foreboding whistle of the train nearly
blocks out the baby's happy squeals. Much of Jia's work, as I've argued
throughout this chapter and as Kin-Yan Szeto has pointed out, focuses
on disintegrating social relations among members of the working class:
"With films set amidst an accelerating market economy, Jia explores the
increased challenges and displacements—regarding love, communal and

Figure 2.29. Ruijuan soothes the baby while Mingliang dozes at the end of Jia's
Platform (2000). *Source*: Jia, Zhangke, dir. *Platform* (站台; *Zhantai*). 2000; New
York: New Yorker Films, 2005. DVD.

marital relations and interdependence—that now confront the nation's marginalized groups."[92] Unlike in *The World*, in *Platform*, Ruijuan is granted the love object and the home she wants, but the ominous ending makes it impossible to judge her story truly happy.

The World, meanwhile, tracks women protagonist Zhao Xiao Tao's increasing ambivalence and eventual disillusion with her career and romantic prospects. The film starts—as it concludes—with a darkened screen and off-screen voices, a parallelism that both bookends the filmic space with ghostly echoes and suggests the opening and closing of stage curtains

In *The World*, the opening sequence draws attention to the gap between polished performance and messy reality. Tao's voice calls through the darkness, "Does anyone have a Band-Aid?" Then we see her in a green costume, an Indian Lehenga Choli, walking toward the camera down the hall of an underground, backstage space. The camera tracks backward, giving us Tao's movement through the bowels of this building and introducing us to the other characters who populate it: guards, dancers, all young. Tao continues to call out, soliciting the Band-Aid. An off-screen woman's voice retorts, "Stop shouting, you'll bring ghosts." Here, again, the film gestures toward its haunted conclusion. Tao's reply, "Ghosts? I'll kill them," also paints her as a pluckier character than the depleted one with whom we are left at the finish. Another dancer finally offers the needed Band-Aid, and Tao begins to affix it to her ankle when her friend Wei barges in, frantic because her costume has a broken zipper (figure 2.30). Though it's clear that the performance is about to start, Tao helps Wei before attending to her ankle.

Figure 2.30. Tao fixes Wei's zipper before the performance begins in *The World*. *Source*: Jia, Zhangke, dir. *The World* (世界; *Shijie*). 2004; New York: Zeitgeist Films, 2006. DVD.

The music for the performance starts as nondiegetic, and then with a cut, the film shows a location in the park that we won't recognize until later, a simulacrum of Manhattan partially illuminated by searchlights. The next shot gives us the audience in the auditorium, and finally a reverse shot reveals the start of the show. Women walk the stage like a catwalk, showing off the various regional fashions that have inspired their costumes—Indian, Korean, and so on. Tao dances forward and moves to the center of the frame. Then an abrupt cut returns us to a tracking shot through the building's backstage as the cheering crowd is heard overhead. The frenzied hustle, the last-minute adjustments, the humble subterranean space of the backstage are in stark contrast to the professional smiles, the coordinated movements, and the dramatic lighting of the performance, emphasizing the gulf between the world occupied by park workers and the world seen by park visitors. Cui Shuqin too has analyzed Jia's attention to the gap between various social classes in contemporary China: "The gulf between rich and poor, center and periphery, elite and ordinary widens as rapidly as globalization itself spreads. The significance of Jia Zhangke's films lies in the deep concern for those marginalized by the forces of globalization: economic outsiders, youth subcultures, and 'floating' migrants, for example, are left behind by the increasingly affluent main-stream."[93] Over the course of the film, this gulf becomes more apparent, and the once spirited Tao becomes more pliable and finally despondent, her ambivalence giving way to exhaustion.

Par exemple, la fatigue: From Ambivalence to Exhaustion

In this chapter, I have chronicled the filmic narratives of women charac-ters from France and China and argued that these ambivalent heroines, as well as the male director's ambivalence toward images more broadly and images of women specifically, serve as our guides to the world of repressed trauma and exploding globalization. In two separate sequences in Godard's *2 ou 3 choses*, Juliette marvels at a new sensation: "Suddenly, I had the impression that I was the world and that the world was me." Juliette explores her revelation in more detail in the second sequence, explaining: "A landscape is exactly like a face (*Le paysage, c'est pareil qu'un visage*). . . . My facial expression must represent something . . . something that could be detached from the general sketch [of my face]. . . . It's as if it were possible to say: this face has a particular expression . . . and then . . . and then. . . . Actually, it's this one. . . . For example, fatigue (*Par exemple, la fatigue).*" The synecdochic promise of the first pages of this chapter—taking the woman for the nation and these films as visions of the newly neoliberal globalizing world—comes full circle, is exhausted, and shows us an ambivalent world racing against the clock to stasis, fatigue.[94]

Jia Zhangke's *The World* makes this movement from cinematic image to exhaustive global portrait even more explicit; as a neon sign in the World Park promises, "Give us a day and we'll give you a world." Here, the World Park's sign performs an act of synecdoche, giving the park as (and instead of) the world, or at least "a" world, the one available for the price of admission. In bringing together these films by Godard and Jia, this chapter makes legible the encrypted conversation between France, China, and the larger world. These films speak through synecdoche, displaying the nation as torn into ambivalent bits, or remnants, and the cinematic spectacle as wrenched from itself: stilled, ripped from the illusion of narrative, coldly staring the viewer directly in the eyes with its attitude of refusal.

Jia Zhangke's *The World* shows Tiananmen only once, and pairs it with another vision of Paris. I will show how the affective ambivalence to the repressed historical trauma of the June Fourth Massacre once again flickers to the surface with the juxtaposition of these sites. After an argument with Taisheng at a dirty, unromantic hotel, Tao travels back to the World Park by bus. A monitor inside the bus plays a montage of world monuments. The Eiffel Tower appears, and the camera pans to the left and reveals Tao looking out the window. After several seconds, we realize that the bus is passing Tiananmen Square as the shot's background reveals the iconic portrait of Mao on the Tiananmen Gate to the Forbidden City. Tao's face is impassive (figure 2.31).

Figure 2.31. Tao traverses Tiananmen Square by bus. *Source*: Jia, Zhangke, dir. *The World* (世界; *Shijie*). 2004; New York: Zeitgeist Films, 2006. DVD.

She looks at her phone. Here, the film shifts to animation, a technique Jia uses at several moments in the film in order to offer the spectator access to a character's subjective experience of an interaction with technology. We see an animated shot of Tao's cell phone with a message from Taisheng: "How far can you go?" Or, perhaps more literally: "Let's see how far you can run."[95] His message, which the film reiterates again and again, does not need a response: both Tao and Taisheng know that she can't go far. She's exhausted. The constricted daily and local spaces in *The World* show the near impossibility of freedom from routine. In the bus sequence, Tao is visually situated between the unreachable world beyond the spectacle (Paris, the Eiffel Tower) and the unacknowledged world of the traumatic past (Tiananmen Square and the 1989 Massacre). What is this middle space? It is the ambivalent bind of toiling in the logic of neoliberal globalization while recognizing that this logic produces only unremitting desire, unattainable pleasure, and exhaustion. In my next chapter, we will further explore how the melancholy and ambivalence in France during the Trente Glorieuses and in China following 1989 culminates in anti-portraiture, an exhaustion of character and narrative form.

Chapter 3

Exhaustion

I, too, fought against something menacing to restore a kind of
harmony. . . . It was an entire universe in miniature, there before
us. . . . And we tried to master something very strong, indestructible,
unbearable.

—Nathalie Sarraute, *Le Planétarium*

It seems that time is exhausted.

—Chen Ran, *A Private Life*

Beginning in the late nineteenth century, the medical diagnostics of
exhaustion have fluctuated from George M. Beard's unwieldy, catchall
neurasthenia to Freud's melancholia, from the first Swiss and American
pharmacological "solutions" for depression to contemporary global complaints of stress and burnout.[1] Extending the condition even more broadly,
Elena Gorfinkel adds, "Being in a state of constant exhaustion and wearing
out, of 'energy departing,' is what many theorists of our economic and
affective present describe as the basic condition of the postindustrial,
information driven, neoliberal global economy."[2] The exhausted, which
Gilles Deleuze famously called "a whole lot more than tired," takes the
affective form of depletion, lassitude, apathy, disillusionment, or with-
drawal.[3] Freud's essay "Mourning and Melancholia" (1917), has served
as a manual unlocking the symptomological logic of this book and it is
again useful here in describing how I frame exhaustion. Freud explains
that melancholia results when something has been lost, but instead of

125

a cleansing period of grief, hostility and sadistic torment are directed obsessively back onto the self. The ambivalence to the lost loved object proves stronger than the ego's self-love. Since the ego now harbors the lost object within itself, the subject's hatred for the object is directed inward, and this self-abuse can have extreme consequences: "It is this sadism alone that solves the riddle of the tendency to suicide which makes melancholia so interesting—and so dangerous."[4] We have arrived, then, at the wicked end of this chronicle of melancholia: spewing self-reproach, savagely hacking away at the subject until nothing remains. As affective forms of protest, or remnants of refusal, to the repression of mourning in France following the German Occupation and in China following the June Fourth Massacre at Tiananmen Square, this book has shown that feminist authors and women protagonists counter with stubborn melancholy, violent ambivalence, and now savage exhaustion. In this chapter, I will argue that novels by Nathalie Sarraute and Chen Ran employ an affective form of exhaustion in response to the ideological "energetics" of capitalist expansion in France and China.

Sarraute's *Le Planétarium* (1959) discloses the lives of a young bourgeois couple in postwar Paris, Alain and Gisèle Guimier. The novel has two main plotlines. One is devoted to Alain—an aspiring writer—and his attempts to be accepted by the literary circle lorded over by Germaine Lemaire, a thinly-veiled fictionalization of Simone de Beauvoir. The second features the couple's efforts to oust Alain's childless Aunt Berthe from her large apartment so that they may take up residence. The relative banality of these humdrum subjects and their concerns are rendered dramatic by Sarraute's writing, which does away with conventional characterization and narrative by navigating daringly between different perspectives and threads of thought, offering, as in this chapter's epigraph, "an entire universe in miniature."

Chen Ran's *A Private Life* (1996) tells the story of Ni Niuniu, a young woman who comes of age in Beijing in the late 1980s. The novel chronicles her unhappy childhood, friendships, love affairs, and eventual breakdown, after which she renounces the world and elects to remain cloistered and idle in her apartment, having concluded that even "time is exhausted." Aesthetically, the exhaustion in the work of Sarraute and Chen results in the dissolution of tradition narrative and character as an antidote to the meaningless mundanity of classical novelistic form when compared to the phantasmagoria of recent national trauma and burgeoning neoliberal globalization.[5]

Anti-Portraiture: Strange True Becomings in Defiance of Homogeneous Empty Time

The January 7, 1986, radio broadcast of "La Nuit sur un plateau" featured Agnès Varda in conversation about her recent film *Sans toit ni loi* (1985) with Nathalie Sarraute, the author to whom the film was dedicated. During the broadcast, Varda praises the elusiveness of Sarraute's writing, "trying to capture what isn't capturable, the spaces between things, delving into feelings before they are put into words and actions."[6] Before arriving at the final title for her film, Varda explains that she and the crew called it "To grasp" (*saisir*), "because I told myself that the film itself was elusive, in the process of being grasped."[7] She likens the experience of making the film to a kind of wandering, an experience shared by the film's itinerate protagonist, Mona (Sandrine Bonnaire). In an attempt "to grasp," like Sarraute's prose, the "spaces between things," Varda focuses on the images and sounds that express what others see and think about the protagonist. Mona, on the other hand, never gives a thorough account of herself. Why does she wander? What drives her? After the film opens with Mona's dead body in a ditch, *Sans toit ni loi* pieces together her story through the past-tense recollections of those who've encountered her along the road. The goal, Varda claims, is "through a play of prisms and mirrors to understand by reading between the lines (*en creux*) Mona who refuses her own character."[8] By withholding a motive for Mona's life and death, resisting the reassurance of narrative closure, Varda's film simultaneously reveals the impossibility of grasping another person's subjectivity and the exhaustion of classical narrative modes in the cinema.[9] The fact *Sans toit ni loi* takes its as subject and borrows its aesthetics from a woman's refusal makes the film's exhaustion a feminist position. As Susan Hayward explains, "Her [Mona's] rejection of social and sexual productivity, which her choice implies, erases the hegemonic image of women—she leaves no trace, as Varda's voice-over comments: 'this death leaves no traces.' "[10] In what follows, I argue that novels by Nathalie Sarraute and Chen Ran, like Varda's film, operate through two related forms of feminist affective exhaustion. First, the exhaustion of the classical narrative's ability to fully grasp and make their characters knowable. Second, the exhaustion of narrative form itself, especially of movements toward closure. I will introduce each form below.

By retracing our steps over the pages of this book—remembering the systematic repression of traumatic mourning and rising neoliberal

globalization from West to East (and back again) since the end of the
Second World War—we've ended up among exhausted characters. In
chapter 2, I demonstrated that the ambivalence toward the nation in
films by Jean-Luc Godard and Jia Zhangke registers a refusal to accept
the present and leave the past behind. When ambivalence is given form,
it presents as subjects in conflict with themselves. I trace this ambivalence
to the nation through the violent severing of objects in the films, and the
concatenation of synecdochic relations between the subsequent partial
and whole objects: primarily, capital to nation, woman citizen to national
populace, and single image (photogram) to moving picture. Faced with
ambivalence, Godard decides the only recourse is to begin again, "from
zero"; he determines to try differently and to employ new methods. Jia
shows no such faith in new beginnings. Instead, he allows time to split
open: the past enters the present, the old resurrects and replaces the new
with the stillborn.

This chapter takes the path of destruction wrought by ambivalence a
step further. While the films in chapter 2 still offered characters, however
ambivalent, the novels in this chapter show a greater suspicion to figural
representation. Sarraute dissolves firm distinctions between characters
and Chen slackens the line dividing her heroine's dreams from reality. In
this chapter, then, I move from ambivalence to exhaustion, and from the
literary trope of synecdoche to the intermedial genre of anti-portraiture.

To clarify what I mean by anti-portraiture, let's return momentarily
to Agnès Varda's description of Sans toit ni loi's aim: "To understand by
reading between the lines (en creux) Mona who refuses her own character." Taken figuratively, this adverbial phrase, en creux, denotes something
implicit, prompting my above translation ("reading between the lines").
As a description of art and architecture, en creux literally refers to a
work in counter-relief or something hollowed out. This may remind the
reader of the "blanks" (des blancs)—holes in signification—in Marguerite
Duras's prose treated in the first chapter of this book. Indeed, as Hayward
clarifies of Varda's feminist filmmaking in Sans toit ni loi: "Her particular
approach of textural intertextualization (a mise-en-abyme of different textures: painting, sculpture, photography, etc., cinépeinture as she calls it) is
equally counter-cinematic in that it works 'in opposition to the naturalized
dominant male discourse to produce textual contradictions which would
de-naturalize the workings of patriarchal ideology' (Cook 1985, 198). These
textual contradictions create gaps in representation 'into which woman's
representation can insert itself' (ibid.). Varda makes frequent reference

to the painterly quality of her films and to her desire to leave gaps, *des creux*."[11] Thus, Varda's *Sans toit ni loi* serves an exemplar of anti-portraiture: it forms Mona's character by focusing on what surrounds her. By chipping away at what others have seen, Mona herself takes shape.

I argue that the anti-portraits explored in this chapter reveal the workings of affective exhaustion in post-traumatic periods of historical erasure. In Nathalie Sarraute's *Le Planétarium*, characters disintegrate and bring to the forefront collective rather than individual psychology and emotion, thereby offering an unflinching anti-portrait of France during the Trente Glorieuses. Chen Ran's *A Private Life* (私人生活; *Siren Shenghuo*), though told through the first-person perspective of a young woman protagonist Ni Niuniu (倪拗拗), offers an anti-portrait of China in the era of neoliberal globalization.[12] Paradoxically, Chen Ran's story of Niuniu's sexual coming-of-age both aligns with the new consumer appetite in 1990s post-socialist China for salacious women's literature that objectifies femininity and complicates or opposes these market trends as Niuniu shatters under the weight of history until she becomes simply "a broken fragment in a fragmented age."[13] Just as the solidity of Cartesian characters no longer exists in Sarraute and Chen's work, the norms and boundaries dividing genders also come into question. Thus, I argue that anti-portraiture, in the case of Sarraute and Chen, first results in an exhaustion of characters as knowable individual, gendered subjects.

The history of anti-portraiture in the twentieth century often begins with Pablo Picasso, Joan Miró, Marcel Duchamp, and other figures of the European avant-garde who undertook new modes of representing subjects in order to combat the greater naturalistic authority of photography and cinema.[14] The ability of new technologies to capture iconicity has provoked philosophical and artistic critiques over the course of the twentieth century and shows no signs of abetting today: from challenges to mass publicity in the 1960s to questions about digital contact tracing of COVID-19 in 2021. While I have already treated the interrogation of the spectacle in the wake of historical trauma and amid capitalist expansion during my discussion of the films of Godard and Jia in chapter 2, this chapter focuses more specifically on critiques of the construction of the literary subject and narrative. However, just as anti-portraiture relies on combating and reframing the rules of artistic practice, pushing the boundaries of genre and media, this chapter will extend the intermedial approach I have employed throughout this book, allowing the literary and filmic to speak together.

Sarraute's and Chen's refusal of literary mimesis takes on an added political charge when we consider it as a rejection of emerging neoliberal modes of subjectification in postwar France and post-Tiananmen China. These authors' literary characters cannot be deciphered and coded, or easily identified, swallowed, and digested. Their aniconic portraits resonate with the critique of faciality—the imposition of a readable subjectification, which can be effectively ciphered by "certain assemblages of power"—proposed by Gilles Deleuze and Félix Guattari.[15] The anti-portrait questions dominant contemporaneous forms of representation; and, in attempting to show otherwise, endeavors to create new modes of understanding. Deleuze and Guattari write:

> If human beings have a destiny, it is rather to escape the face, to dismantle the face and facializations, to become imperceptible, to becomes clandestine, not by returning to animality, nor even by returning to the head, but by quite spiritual and special becomings-animal, by strange true becomings that . . . make *faciality traits* themselves finally elude the organization of the face—freckles dashing toward the horizon, hair carried off by the wind, eyes you traverse instead of seeing yourself in or gazing into in those glum face-to-face encounters between signifying subjectivities.[16]

In its deliberate dodging of classical literary form and exhaustion with "glum face-to-face encounters between signifying subjectivities," anti-portraiture under the pen of Sarraute and Chen escapes and dismantles the face. Both authors work earnestly—with humor, irony, at the risk of despair—to do the impossible, to achieve these "strange true becomings."

Sarraute and Chen, however, do not simply decompose the subject; they launch a full-scale assault on dramatic plot structure, particularly the classical narrative demand for closure. Both Sarraute's *Le Planétarium* and Chen's *A Private Life* unhinge linear temporality and challenge the order and fact of events. Thus, I propose that in their texts exhaustion also works as a form of protest in defiance of the orderly, temporal progression of a common national narrative and the flow of capital.[17]

Benedict Anderson's famous theorization of the birth of nationalism at the end of the eighteenth century relies on the members of each "imagined community" sharing in a sense of simultaneity, what Walter Benjamin termed homogeneous empty time. According to Anderson, this mutual understanding of national time, measured by dates on the calendar and the position of hands on the clock, arose as a result of the proliferation of two popular forms: the novel and the newspaper.[18] Novels present concrete worlds peopled with acquaintances and strangers of which any combination may breathe the same air, in the same city, on the same day, and yet be capable of vastly different experiences. Like the idea of the nation, novels offer "sociological entities of such firm and stable reality that their members . . . can even be described as passing each other on the street, without ever becoming acquainted, and still be connected."[19] Newspapers, likewise, relay events based on the coincidence of their calendrical occurrence (the date below the masthead), and unite their readers in a secular daily ritual tied to the rhythm of the market: "At the same time, the newspaper reader, observing exact replicas of his own paper being consumed by his subway, barbershop, or residential neighbours, is continually reassured that the imagined world is visibly rooted in everyday life."[20] Today, the notion of homogenous empty time—perhaps best embodied by social media platforms—remains central to our shared participation in the idea of the nation and the global market: a belief in a dubious shared modernity, or contemporaneous contemporaneity. Even if, as Harry Haroontunian explains, "A historical present filled with mixed temporalities has always been a condition of capitalist modernization, even as its copresent uncanniness was suppressed by both the authority of the future perfect and the expectations of progress that vowed to raise all societies to the same level."[21]

When the identity of a nation is threatened by national trauma, national leaders may attempt to revive nationalism by suturing citizens to each other and to a fictitious common narrative of the traumatic past. In the years following the German Occupation of France and the Tiananmen Square Massacre in China, each government sought to control the memory of the events by focusing on national economic development. This involved an active repression as well as subtler forms of manipulated forgetting and conscious installation of sinister reminders that served as warnings to those who might be tempted to invoke their own memories for political ends. In endeavoring to (re)write history and destabilize memory, each government warped its discourses with results resembling a heap of logical contradictions. This resulted in what Julia Kristeva later terms in *Les Nouvelles maladies de l'âme* "the modern crisis of values," leading to "an unease brought about by the use of language that finally feels 'artificial,' 'empty,' or 'robotic.' "[22] Exhaustion in Nathalie Sarraute and Chen Ran takes its form in anti-portraits, which strike out against fictious homogenous empty time. Their narratives make use of the power of anti-portraiture to eschew progressive forward movement, preferring to loiter in the spaces between thought and action. Such slack temporality allows for events to happen twice from different points of view, or for events to simply be imagined. Sarraute and Chen encourage the reader to linger in memories, to question the present along with the past, and to unearth the repressed.

Nathalie Sarraute and Chen Ran share similarities that I have emphasized in my analysis of the authors and filmmakers in chapters 1 and 2. Like Marguerite Duras and Wang Anyi, as well as Jean-Luc Godard and Jia Zhangke, Sarraute and Chen blend their personal experiences and episodes (or personages) from their private lives into their fictional oeuvre. Like these others, Sarraute and Chen create largely outside and against the mainstream; their work breaks new aesthetic ground and stands in opposition to dominant national discourse, offering what I have been terming feminist remnants of refusal to the changing shape of the nation and the repression of national trauma. Finally, this work—like that covered in chapters 1 and 2—commingles the literary and the filmic. Sarraute's psychological treatment of the Parisian bourgeoisie following the Second World War in *Le Planétarium* acts like a roving camera, capturing every vibration in the interior landscape of the city's inhabitants, rendering the novel a breed of *ciné-roman*. The evocative, dream images that fill Chen's *A Private Life*, meanwhile, approach filmic oneirism. Both authors' work productively rhymes with concerns taken up by filmmakers; some final thoughts in conversation with Agnès Varda's films will bring this chapter to a close.

However, Sarraute and Chen make possible new avenues of discussion. This book has heretofore argued against the viability of direct witness accounts to capture the affective conditions of post-traumatic history; however, Sarraute and Chen complicate matters. I argue that the experiences of Sarraute, as a Jew in hiding during the German Occupation of France, and Chen, as an inhabitant of Beijing during the period that culminated in the Tiananmen Massacre, uniquely impacted these authors and their writing. Though their work does not overtly treat the traumatic periods, direct references crop up in their oeuvres. My discussion of the novels of Sarraute and Chen, therefore, and their exhaustion of narrative, character, and gender, will be firmly grounded in each author's historical moment and personal, lived experience.

Living Substance: Sarraute's Tropisms

Nathalie Sarraute's *Le Planétarium* takes place among a collection of bourgeois Parisians following the end of the Second World War. As I've already introduced, the plot involves two main conflicts: First, the young couple at the novel's center, Alain and Gisèle Guimier, covet the large apartment belonging to Alain's childless, widowed Aunt Berthe. Second, Alain, a hapless doctoral student, yearns to be accepted into the literary circle presided over by Germaine Lemaire, a character based on Simone de Beauvoir whose mannerisms and literary style Sarraute critiques in the novel.[23] At the end of *Le Planétarium*, the Guimiers have successfully expelled Aunt Berthe from her apartment and claimed it as their own, and Alain has gained entry into Lemaire's inner sanctum. However, the way Sarraute portrays these characters—with no real protagonists or antagonists, each with their own insecurities gnawing at the shallow bank of confidence on which they stand—gives readers access to a communal psychological realm.

In the 1964 preface to her collection of essays on the novel, *L'Ère du soupçon*, Sarraute describes this shared psychological realm as made up of rapidly shifting, unconscious movements, which are "the origin of our gestures, our speech, the feelings that we express and that we believe we feel," and, therefore, "the secret source of our existence."[24] These movements, which Sarraute terms tropisms, emerge through the novels' depictions of social encounters—"our conversations, the character that we seem to have, who we are in the eyes of others"—but "these superficial dramatic actions which form the plot are only the conventional framework that we apply to life."[25] The tropisms, not the characters nor the events making up the story, are Sarraute's true subject, "the living substance of all my novels."[26]

Focusing on the delicate, fluctuating psychological vibrations beneath the surface of quotidian human life makes Sarraute a notoriously demanding author. Moving seamlessly between interior monologues (what she terms "sous-conversations") and dialogue, Sarraute smudges the line dividing characters and the landscapes they inhabit.[27] In some ways, this recalls Jean-Luc Godard's *Numéro deux*, in which the children question whether the landscape is their mother or their mother a landscape, or his *2 ou 3 choses que je sais d'elle*, in which Juliette Jeanson/Marina Vlady twice marvels at the revelation "that I was the world and the world was me." In Sarraute's work, each movement, object, and interaction are filtered through the perspective of one or more positions, which creates an exterior world reliant on interior worlds. Physical "reality" changes depending on the flickering focalizer; the objective hangs on the subjective. Scenes are relayed from different points of view, but—like those evenings when we lay sleepless, ruminating over some unpleasant interaction, thinking, "If only I'd said that!"—Sarraute also writes scenes with several hypothetical outcomes.

In his 1947 preface to Sarraute's second novel, *Portrait d'un inconnu*, Jean-Paul Sartre praises her difficulty and her insistence on breaking down the distinction between the objective and subjective, "by showing the incessant back and forth between the specific and the general . . . she clarifies a technique which allows one to attain . . . human reality in its very essence."[28] Sartre's preface also classifies Sarraute as a writer of "anti-novels," signaling her work's formal disruption, and hinting at its tendency to provoke adherents and antagonists, and the obsession with classification that would surround it ever after.[29] In 1957, Émile Henriot's scathing *Le Monde* review of Robbe-Grillet's *La Jalousie* classified a group of fellow writers published by Les Éditions de Minuit—which included Nathalie Sarraute—as authors of the *nouveau roman* or "new novel."[30] This would be one year after Sarraute's *L'Ère du soupçon* appeared as a collection of essays published by Gallimard. The aesthetic distance that Sarraute's essays establish between her work and that of the existentialists (principally Sartre and Beauvoir) parallels the publication story of these essays.[31] While Sartre applauded *Portrait d'un inconnu* and approved of her essay "De Dostoïevski à Kafka," his passion for the literature of commitment soon eclipsed his earlier appetite for a diversity of literary styles. Sarraute believed her essay "L'Ère du soupçon"—whose title was taken from a sentence from Stendhal's *Souvenirs d'égotisme* (1892), "The genius of poetry is dead, but the genius of *suspicion* has entered the world"—only appeared in *Les Temps modernes* because Maurice Merleau-Ponty served as editor of the journal while Sartre was away in Dakar.[32] She attributed *Les Temps modernes*'s 1954 rejection of "Conversations et sous-conversations" to the influence of Simone de Beauvoir, whom she suspected perceived (not incorrectly) in the essay a critique of Beauvoir's recently published novel *Les Mandarins*.[33]

It is undeniable that Sarraute and other writers loosely (sometimes reluctantly) aligned with the nouveau roman deliberately parted company with Sartre's literature of praxis and Beauvoir's realistic depiction of social realities. François Dosse's enumeration of the set of formal and thematic considerations underlining the nouveau roman makes plain its contrast to the literature of commitment: "The elimination of the subject, with the exclusion of the classical novelistic characters a preference for a space where observed objects were cast in different configurations; a defiance of dialectical time in favor of suspended temporality, a slack presence that dissolved as it revealed itself."[34] While Sarraute did not deconstruct character, space, and time to the same extent as, say, Alain Robbe-Grillet (who offers a "purely synchronic approach whose inner logic was to be discovered") or Samuel Beckett (who goes so far as to destroy progressive logic, leaving the pages of his novels covered in a dust of murmuring words), her work foregrounds the same exhaustion with classical novelistic form.[35] Dosse further unites the authors of the nouveau roman as a group that "turn[ed] to the social sciences, drawing its inspiration from their decentering of the subject, their protest against Eurocentrism, and a configuration that substituted the figure of the Other for the quest for the Same."[36] The critique of these Cartesian, centered forms of knowing resonated with other anti-Enlightenment philosophical and literary inquiries, which flourished following the Second World War.

Roland Barthes, for example, responded with enthusiasm to the work of Robbe-Grillet and the nouveau roman, considering it parallel to the form of criticism he hoped to advance in his own work.[37] During the same years that Sarraute published the first essays of L'Ère du soupçon, Barthes embarked on his treatise on the state of writing in 1950s France. By opening his book, Le Degré zéro de l'écriture (1953), with a chapter entitled "Qu'est-ce que l'écriture?" Barthes jousts with Sartre and his manifesto on the literature of commitment, Qu'est-ce que la littérature (1947). Both Sartre and Barthes wonder if French writers could escape their bourgeois condition and serve leftist politics. While Sartre proposes that literature must find a way to speak plainly to the masses, Barthes ponders the possibility of "a writer without Literature."[38] With the structuralist impulse that characterizes much his work, Barthes defines three central concepts of language, style, and writing: "Language and style are blind forces; writing is an act of historical solidarity. Language and style are objects; writing is a function: it is the relationship between creation and society, the literary language transformed by its social destination, form realizing its human intention and thereby connected to the grand crises of History."[39] While language (the field of all possible discourse) and style (the individual form by which each person communicates) are historically and biographically foreclosed (or, "blind forces"), Barthes argues that writing must always take a moral position. According to Barthes, following the 1848 Revolution, the French bourgeoisie found themselves in a new historical position. Hereafter, neither bourgeois ideology nor literature—a product of the bourgeoisie—could claim universality. Barthes extends this history of French letters from 1848 to the present:

> It is from this moment that modes of writing began to multiply. Each one, henceforth, whether it be practiced, populist, neutral or colloquial, takes as its initial task that the writer acknowledges or rejects his bourgeois condition. Each one is an attempt to respond to this Orphean problem of modern Form: writers without literature. For one hundred years, Flaubert, Mallarmé, the Goncourt brothers, the Surrealists, Queneau, Sartre, Blanchot, or Camus have drawn—and are still drawing—means of integration, rupture, or naturalization of literary language; but what is at stake is not some adventure of form, successful work of rhetoric, or bold use of vocabulary. Each time the writer assembles a network of words, it is the very existence of Literature that is called into question; what modernity has given us to read in the plurality of modes of writing, is the dead end of its own History.[40]

Writing cannot escape its bourgeois history unless it puts aside its literary aims. As soon as a writer has achieved something unique and untainted, the familiar "Orphean problem of modern Form" arises: the work immediately appears fabricated, just another phony literary gimmick. Barthes's skepticism about the possibility of creating anything new clashes with Sartre's emphatic conscription of literature in the service of politics. This suspicion with authenticity preoccupies Barthes until the end, and always contains a melancholic aspect; consider *Camera Lucida* (1980) and his formulation of the photograph's *punctum* as a means of eulogizing his late mother. Sarraute's suspicion with authenticity grows out of a similar exhaustion with prevailing literary forms and their impotence to compete with the disasters of history. She asks, "What invented tale could rival that of the confined woman of Poitiers, or those of the concentration camps, or the Battle of Stalingrad?"[41] Sarraute's attempt to offer a "living substance" and tap into the "secret source of our existence" in her writing arises out of her own experience reckoning with the messiness of history.

Sarraute *La Sauvage*: Historical Stains and *Le Planétarium*

After France fell to the Nazis during May and June of 1940, Nathalie Sarraute found herself in an increasingly precarious situation. Jewish ancestry played so little role in the family's self-definition that her own children initially had no knowledge of their background. Biographer Ann Jefferson recounts an anecdote relayed to her by Sarraute's eldest daughter Claude about the discovery of her Jewishness during a conversation with her grandfather Ilya at the age of ten: "Complaining one day to her grandfather that school dinners were horrible, she explained that this was because the catering manager was a Jew. When Ilya asked her what she thought a Jew was, Claude was happy to sketch the anti-Semitic stereotype of an unwashed miser, complete with hooked nose and protruding ears, at which Ilya revealed to her that both he and she were Jewish. The revelation came as a shock, and it cost her friendships at the École Alsacienne, where she remembers the children being free with anti-Semitic insults."[42]

Under Occupation, anti-Semitic legislation increased apace. In September of 1940, the so-called Liste Otto outlawed a collection of books regarded as "unsavory," in many cases because of Jewish authorship. Sarraute's first book *Tropismes* (1939) escaped ban; however, as she had complied with the German ordinance requiring Jews in the occupied zone to register, further publications were now out of the question. By late March of 1941, Sarraute, who worked as an attorney during these years, was removed from the French bar owing to her "foreign birth."[43] As the instatement of additional Vichy anti-Jewish laws (Statut des Juifs) threatened Nathalie's lawyer husband Raymond, due to his mother's Jewish background the couple divorced in January 1941 to weaken his association to Jewishness and safeguard his employment. This measure didn't fully shield Raymond, however. He was arrested and interned twice over the course of the Occupation: first, for presumed Jewishness, and later, for his connections to left-wing figures. This second arrest so upset Raymond's father Joseph that he committed suicide. Nathalie and her children attempted to attend the funeral without Raymond "only to be turned away by Joseph's family for reasons she interpreted—no doubt correctly—as anti-Semitic: Joseph's mistake was to have married a Jew and to have raised a son who repeated the error."[44]

When the first deportations of Jews began in March 1942, Nathalie and Raymond—divorced only in the eyes of the law—decided it prudent for Nathalie to leave Paris. She spent the summer of 1942 in a gardener's

cottage in the village of Janvry. Both Raymond and Nathalie were active
in the Resistance; they first joined Sartre's Socialism and Freedom group
in 1941. While in Janvry, Nathalie housed two members of the Resistance
cell Gloria SMH, Samuel Beckett and his partner Suzanne Deschevaux-
Dumesnil. (Beckett and Sarraute—though later grouped together in large
part due to Mario Dondero's so-called nouveau roman photograph, taken
of authors published by Les Éditions de Minuit outside of the press in
1959—disliked each other fervently.) When Nathalie moved to the village
of Parmain from late 1942 until the spring of 1944, she was again called
upon by the Resistance as a translator (she spoke English as well as Russian and French) for a group of Canadian parachutists.

In both Janvry and Parmain, Nathalie kept her Jewish identity a
secret. In Parmain, she lived under the fake name (complete with fabricated
identity card) of Nicole Sauvage, which allowed her to preserve her real
initials. Ironically, the surname *Sauvage* (meaning wild, feral, untamed,
barbarian)—though adopted as a means of concealing her identity—befits
Nathalie's biographic and literary trajectory. After her parents separated
when she was two and later remarried, Nathalie felt like an outsider in
her family. As a Russian, she was an outsider in France. Under the Occupation, her Jewishness elevated her outsider status to that of a criminal
in hiding. History bequeathed Nathalie with the name Sauvage, and she
imprinted her texts with a fierce, feral brutality.[45]

In her essay "De Dostoïevski à Kafka," Nathalie takes ownership of
her otherness in France by aligning herself with those she termed the two
fathers of the modern novel: Dostoyevsky, the "Russian," and Kafka, the
"Jew." After her description of a passage from Dostoyevsky's *The Brothers
Karamazov*, she praises his mastery of the psychological: "All of these
strange contortions . . . all of these chaotic leaps and grimaces are the
precise outward translation, produced without indulgence or the desire
to please . . . these subtle, barely perceptible, evasive, contradictory, tran-
sitory movements, weak rumblings, hints of timid appeals and retreats,
pale, sliding shadows, whose incessant play constitutes the invisible thread
connecting all human relations and the very substance of our lives."[46] Sarraute's description of these "movements" under the skin that serve as "the
very substance of our lives" sounds very much like her characterization
of her own tropisms, the "secrete source of our existence." While Dostoyevsky mastered the psychological novel, Kafka's prose, which Sarraute
aligns with the so-called *roman de situation*, describes with icy finesse the
ritualized social conventions and mores that make human life practicable

(and unbearable).[47] Though both writers present the reader of any time or place with familiar feelings and worlds, the miracle of Dostoevsky and Kafka lies in their ability to see how real historical situations could unravel. In other words, by understanding human nature in the universal as well as the particular, Dostoevsky and Kafka saw the complexities of the present and predicted the future. Sarraute ends her essay on this note:

> With the divinatory powers belonging to certain geniuses, the same that made Dostoyevsky foresee the fraternal impulse of the Russian people and their unusual destiny, Kafka, who was Jewish, and lived in the shadow of the German nation, fore-told the fate that awaited his people, and understood certain fundamental features of the German character that were of Hitler's Germany and would lead the Nazis to conceive and carry out a unique experiment: this consisted of yellow satin stars distributed upon receipt of two coupons cut from the textile ration-card; of crematory ovens on which hung adver-tisement posters giving the name and address of the sanitary firm that had built the model; and of gas chambers in which two thousand naked bodies (as in *The Trial*, their clothes had previously been 'carefully put aside and folded') writhed under the gaze of well-strapped, booted, and decorated gentlemen, sent on a mission of inspection, who watched them through a window to which they approached, one after another, respecting precedence and exchanging polite glances. . . . We can neither remain where Kafka left off nor attempt to go further. Those who live in the human world can only retrace his steps.[48]

Any reader can recognize the similarity between Kafka's inhuman bureau-crats and these "gentlemen" inspecting the gas chambers, "respecting prece-dence and exchanging polite glances." Sarraute marvels at the bravery that lent Kafka his perspicacity and allowed his fiction to skate on the razor's edge of human horror. Beyond this edge, all meaning dissolves; and yet, one cannot step back from the precipice and away from the calamitous vision once it's been revealed. Given the catastrophes of history, Sarraute contends that the writer's only recourse is an impossible "retracing" of Kafka's footsteps. The writer must communicate the dark truths that can only be accessed by resting on the edge, dipping the cup of inspiration into the exhaustive traumatic void.

I argue that Sarraute *la Sauvage* takes up this task in *Le Planètarium*: her barbarous pen, dipped in the blood of the Parisian bourgeoisie, ferociously lambastes French society following the Second World War amid the Trente Glorieuses, sparing no one, herself included. Hannah Freed-Thall has also pointed to the figuration of history in Sarraute's novel, arguing:

> *Le Planétarium* provokes an interpretive crisis by trailing dirty fingers all over a familiar Balzacian inheritance plot. Historically specific images of war, occupation, and collaboration surface bizarrely throughout the novel, unattached to any metatextual interpretive frame, blatantly inappropriate to the conventional social dramas they appear to metaphorize. *Le Planétarium* does not suppress history, but dramatizes its own messy assimilation of recent historical events, presenting complicity (in its etymological sense of a folding together) as both a thematics and a readerly effect.[49]

My argument differs from Freed-Thall's in that I see Sarraute's novel as rebelling against the "assimilation of recent historical events." Sarraute's unrelenting attack, an exhaustive inventory of human foibles which reveals all characters to be equally fallible, acts as a remnant of refusal to the repression qua assimilation of national trauma. The traumatic past cannot be neatly preserved, and sorted into authorized pageants of memorialization, museumified and pacified. Neither can it be comfortably digested through habit (displaying a wreath, lighting a candle, hanging a flag, etc.). In Sarraute's novel, the traumatic past appears unbidden. It is the incessant itch under the skin, the dull gnawing of conscience. Though she couldn't foretell the future like Kafka, Sarraute reveals how the outlines of the past underlie the present, allowing history to crop up again in all its ugliness.

Le Planétarium begins in the apartment of Aunt Berthe. Without profession, husband, or children, Aunt Berthe obsesses over the redecoration of her home in the chic Passy neighborhood of Paris. As the novel opens, she returns to the apartment, reflecting on its new velvet curtains "in a deep green, simple and understated . . . and at the same time, a warm luminous shade," and the beige wall, which "looks just like skin. . . . It's as soft as chamois."[50] She congratulates herself on taking such pains in selecting the materials, the colors, choosing always "exactly what was required."[51] She thinks with excitement about her newest acquisition—an oval oak door, which will separate the pantry from the dining room—inspired by a model glimpsed during an otherwise dull summer visit to a cathedral. It was this door, in fact, that set her new interior design scheme into motion. As she climbs the stairs to her apartment, she marvels at her achievement: "This summer, ideas came one after another, and everything turned out better than she could have hoped. The result will be delightful, and the door will be the best part."[52]

However, when Aunt Berthe rushes into her apartment and lays eyes on the door, her confidence instantly dissolves. The door itself appears "ugly, common, and trashy."[53] But this is not all: the workmen have attached a nickel-plated door handle and an aluminum fingerplate, making the whole effect vulgar, and transforming what she had hoped would be her crowning achievement into "a real bathroom door."[54] Whereas Berthe had previously applauded her own good taste and the efforts of the workmen, she now doubts both. She suspects the workmen of conspiring against her; "There's a cold and hostile will, some insidious malice"[55] When she confronts the workers, they promise her that the door looks just as it should: "Come on now, it's only a question of habit. You'll get used to it; you'll see. . . . It's very nice, pretty in fact."[56] Feeling gaslit, Berthe imagines that she is now being punished for her collaboration with this enemy, conquerors, "who ravage and disfigure the country, vandalize works of art, tear down dear old buildings and erect blocks of cement in their place."[57] Here, with its curious reference to collaboration and the subsequent war—which Berthe imagines leaves her "the sole survivor of a destroyed world, alone among foreigners, enemies"—the events of the recent war and Occupation first appear in Sarraute's text.[58] Once the workmen leave, Berthe recovers from her paranoia only to tumble into a new obsessive frenzy. Seeing marks left on the baseboards and along the walls by the workmen's hands, she sets about trying to carefully scrub away the dirt. She gently wipes the offending areas until she feels confident that "the stain (*la tache*) has disappeared."[59]

The stain, however, only spreads. As Freed-Thall suggests, "As the text slides from decorating crisis, to an allegory of the Occupation, to a crisis of modernity itself, we lose all sense of proportion. . . . We cannot escape the sense that we, too, are implicated in Berthe's obsessive attempt to efface the stains left by those, who, in following orders, have destroyed the world."[60] The escalation of the crisis begins innocently enough in the second chapter as Aunt Berthe's maniacal behavior makes a reentrance as dinner party fodder. At the insistence of his mother-in-law, Alain reluctantly launches into the story of his aunt's misadventures in interior decorating, continuing the saga of the oval oak door. Alain explains—much to the amusement of the dinner guests—that his aunt recently telephoned him at eleven in the evening to insist that he come to her aid. When Alain arrives at his aunt's apartment, he sees the door, which he describes as "a frightful new door like one sees everywhere, the pretentious interior decorator's variety."[61] The fingerplate and handle have been removed, leaving tiny holes, which Aunt Berthe now furiously rubs with polish. Even though they will most likely go completely unnoticed—Alain admits that he himself wouldn't have perceived them if his aunt hadn't pointed them out—Berthe refuses to shrug off the blemishes. As long as she knows the holes exist, the whole effect is ruined for her; precisely what she cannot abide is "this tiny fault, this miniscule problem, this small wart on the face of perfection."[62] A similar mania emerged, Alain explains, with a broken bedpost two years back, which—though the missing shard was adequately matched and replaced—tormented his aunt until she finally swapped out the entire bedpost. However, Alain concludes by expressing sympathy for his aunt, who has lost her husband and whose own death awaits her soon: "All of her accumulated anxiety attaches to that shard, to these holes in the wood, everything is concentrated on a single spot—it's a lightning rod, really . . . I, myself, confess that after a minute, I scrubbed . . . I, too, fought against something menacing to restore a kind of harmony. . . . It was an entire universe in miniature, there before us. . . . And we tried to master something very strong, indestructible, unbearable."[63]

Alain's words show how the desire to purify the sullied, to wipe clean the slate, comes up against the reality of imperfection and the stains of history. Through Alain's narration Sarraute lampoons the anguished struggle of aunt and nephew against the blemished oak door, while simultaneously likening it to battles fought on a grander scale. On the one hand, Alain sees their difficulty as akin to that of mastering forces of ill fortune or evil (the "very strong, indestructible, unbearable"); and, here, the reader may sympathize, for who can deny that small obstacles sometimes take on an unreasonable weight in the mind of the sufferer? On the other hand, there is an undeniable absurdity in the door, this pockmarked imitation of a starry sky, taking on the appearance of "an entire universe in miniature." Thanks to their myopia, Alain and Berthe may battle the insignificant and forestall those larger battles extending beyond the door and the apartment: just like all (of us) who hide their heads in the sand when historical disaster knocks. The reference to "an entire universe in miniature," of course, recalls the novel's title. Is a planetarium simply a shoddy simulation of the real universe, or does it offer a sense of scale and

reveal the distance between the parts and the whole? Here, as is typical
of Sarraute's writing, biting irony exists alongside empathy: models, like
extended metaphors, distill truths, and truths—for Sarraute—are always
and only subjective, dependent on one's fallible point of view.

This leaves the characters and the reader on shaky ground; such
is the brutal egalitarianism of Sarraute that the stain threatens to touch
everyone. The novel formalizes exhaustion in its unhierarchized accumulation of data, as it spins out toward historical refraction. This obsessive
build-up both mimics and ironizes the exhaustive cataloging by the Nazis
as well as the preoccupation with and the exhaustion of the commodity in
France during the Trente Glorieuses. Alain's story casts from the amusing
and trivial (silly, eccentric Aunt Berthe) to the tragic (the poor old woman
cannot face her own misery and so displaces it onto superficial problems)
to the ontological and phenomenological (questioning the nature of the
universe and humanity's position within it). Deciding that the story has
gone off the rails, that its shifts in tone render it unsuitable as dinner
party gossip, Alain's mother-in-law tries to wind things up. She laughs and
wags her finger at Alain: "But, be honest, it's an obsession of yours, too,
it enthralls you. . . . Your aunt fascinates you You understand her only
too well. You take after her, in fact."[64] If Alain and Berthe share the same
traits, if their obsessions and anxieties can be relegated to the domain of
family eccentricity, of inheritance, then the others can relax.

The subject of the stain as inheritance stretches beyond the con-
fines of the narrative in Le Planétarium, connecting the novel with other
texts associated with the nouveau roman. One thinks immediately of the
continual evocation of the "blackened stain (une tache noirâtre) marking
the location of a crushed millipede" in Robbe-Grillet's La Jalousie (1957),
which serves as a metaphor for the jealousy that taints the perception of a
suspicious husband.[65] However, it also evokes the stained face, "the bloody
grimace," of the unnamed man who murders his lover in the opening
pages of Duras's Moderato cantabile (1958), an event that captivates the
novel's protagonist, Anne Desbaresdes, and provokes her foray into her
own murky desires.[66] Thus, I am suggesting that the stain is a wider figure
for exhaustion during this period.

These Les Éditions de Minuit novelists break with the formal
restrictions of the classical novel to address a common thematic concern:
how to describe the intricate workings of human psychology, memory,
and desire in a literature that incarnates the disintegration of bourgeois
consciousness following the Second World War. In other words, in a

literature of exhaustion where subjects frequently lack names or bleed into each other, where plot and temporality crumble under unending repetition and a suspicion that blurs the division between objective and subjective viewpoints, these novelists consider what's left on the carcass of the novel, and how the death of the Cartesian subject allows for a new perspective on the stain that muddies the invisible line separating the self from the other. The presence of the stain in the nouveau roman, then, emerges as collective, historical inheritance or as something contagious, a historical illness.

In *Le Planétarium*, too, immediately after Alain and Berthe have been isolated from the others by their unseemly obsessive traits, Sarraute turns the tables once again and implicates everyone. Alain enthusiastically agrees with his mother-in-law that he resembles his aunt: "We are two peas in a pod (*comme deux gouttes d'eau*). . . . Otherwise, she wouldn't interest me so much."[67] However, he goes on to level an accusation at the others: "It wouldn't interest you, either, if you, and all of us here, didn't have a little something, somewhere, well hidden in a closely sealed recess."[68] This insinuation brings the dinner party to an abrupt end: "They all stood, this time, for good. Scandalous! This boy is impossible."[69] The novel proposes that the characters possess a shared culpability, a common stain, something both transmissible and transgenerational. That Alain's suggestion of this shared "little something" prompts such outrage and denial among the guests only makes its truth plainer. In *Le Planétarium*, this "little something" appears through its symptoms: a fascination with what I've been terming the stain, which could be otherwise stated as a preoccupation with that which sullies our human interaction with others and the world. Taking this a step further, I am suggesting that the root of this exhaustive and exhausting fascination, the illness prompting this symptom, is the traumatic impact of history.

In the early pages of the novel, Alain appears almost heroic in his contempt for the bourgeois mores that restrict how much truth-telling is acceptable in polite company. He admits his faults and asks his mother-in-law and the other dinner guests to consider their own. Alain's role as social rebel, however, quickly gives way to reveal less laudable character traits: insecurity, greed, and desperation to appear cultured and gain acceptance in literary social circles. He becomes, in other words, no better or worse than any other voice in the novel. By a practiced self-deception, Alain convinces himself that he deserves his Aunt Berthe's large apartment. With the encouragement of his wife, he visits Berthe to first suggest, then to demand, that she turn over her home. He recalls a school friend who once told him that his aunt was hard and contemptuous. When his aunt looks at him reproachfully, he uses this memory as arsenal against his mounting feelings of guilt: "He was liberated. Saved. Embraces. Tears of joy. People surround him: Your aunt is hard. She is contemptuous. It's a fact. It's how she is. It's her nature. Now he need only call out and they run to his side. She is encircled, captured a large crowd assembling around her and scrutinizing her, pointing at her, look: she is hard, con-temptuous."[70] Imagining himself flanked by these agents of reason who condemn the "hard" and "contemptuous," who believe one has a right to live and flourish and fight those who stand in their way, Alain continues to push his aunt. As she remains unmoved, she reminds Alain of other "lawbreakers" he vaguely recollects from his youth:

> Escaped prisoners, members of the Resistance, Jews hidden under fake names were basking in the sun, chatting in village squares, seated on the edge of fountains, drinking together in bistros, as if nothing had happened, cunning, troubling prey, slyly forcing the others, the pure who had done nothing, the strong who had nothing to fear from anyone, into a disgust-ing complicity, luring them into their debasement, scoffing at the law, overturning order, until one fine morning, a person got up—after all someone had to take it upon themself and do it—left his house and ran along the walls, kowtowing, to denounce them.[71]

In this passage, seemingly unprompted, the traumatic past comes directly into view. Sarraute—whose own experiences we recognize in the first few lines ("Jews hidden under fake names," etc.)—aligns Alain with German collaborators and proffers a collaborator's logic that might rationalize and "excuse" denunciation. Many took advantage of the Occupation to seize Jewish property. Sarraute's own father, Ilya Tcherniak, in fact, left his fac-tory in the Parisian suburb of Vanves in the hands of an Aryan business acquaintance, a certain Demarteau (whose name Sarraute borrowed for her 1953 novel *Martereau*), during the Occupation, and had to take legal action after the War to repossess what Demarteau, whom he previously regarded as his friend and savior, had claimed as his own.[72] The shadows of the Occupation still cover Sarraute's Paris in *Le Planétarium*, and Alain adopts the logic of collaboration, callously denouncing his aunt for "scoffing at the law," which demands that the old and weak bow to the young and shameless. The novel's most chilling echo of the traumatic past occurs later, when the Guimiers successfully take over the apartment and Aunt Berthe's final whereabouts are left, like many of those deported during the Occupation, unaccounted for, disappeared without a trace.

Sites of Action: Gendering Equality

Sarraute's novel makes every character guilty, but also dislodges the guilt from the individual, rendering it a shared, free-flowing virus, a common stain. Even the family name of the central couple, Alain and Gisèle *Guimier*, suggests the collapsible quality of these characters. *Guimier* is a near homonym of the French *guillemet*, commonly used in the phrase *entre guillemets*, meaning "quote unquote" or "so-called." As in English, this phrase often attaches a whiff of sarcasm or irony. (Take, for example, a sentence like "He was a so-called expert.") This play on words between *Guimier* and *guillemet* helps to further transform Alain and Gisèle into floating signifiers, part of a larger strategy of anti-portraiture. They are *called* Alain and Gisèle, but they might as well be named otherwise. They might be someone else. They could be any one of us.

Le Planétarium also makes every character equally capable of small moments of redemption. Even the vilest subject is allowed a flash of heroism. For example, at the beginning of the novel, the role of hero is temporarily granted to Alain. At *Le Planétarium*'s conclusion, however, Sarraute gives the final word to Germaine Lemaire, the parody of Simone de Beauvoir whom she has unmercifully skewered throughout the novel. In the last pages, Alain mocks a fellow writer for his apparent hypocrisy. He tells Germaine an unflattering anecdote about a recent run-in with this writer who at first pretended to be disinterested in complimentary press about his work before quickly revealing that he cared very much after all. Alain hopes that Germaine will laugh and jeer the other writer for his vanity. However, her response surprises Alain (and the reader): "She doesn't move. She plunges a hard gaze deep into his eyes: 'Oh, that, really. . . . You're severe. I think we are all, really, a bit like that.' "[73] This quote ends the novel and condenses one of its central messages: according to Sarraute, deep down, all human beings resemble each other.

This extreme egalitarianism, what I am terming an exhaustion of character, extends to gender. In *Le Planétarium*, Sarraute attributes genders to her characters, but these genders constitute only a superficial surface. Over the course of her life, Sarraute would extend the gender-neutral philosophy of her fiction and even apply it to her own outward presentation. Ann Jefferson comments that by the end of the 1980s, Sarraute "now always wore trousers, unisex cardigans, a silk cravat, flat shoes, and men's shirts. . . . Her hair was still cropped and she continued to abjure makeup."[74] Sarraute's growing gender neutrality in life as well as in literature sheds some light on her close friendship with lesbian feminist Monique Wittig (who famously declared "Lesbians are not women").[75] "From the mid-1970s," Jefferson explains, "in line with this refusal of femininity, Nathalie had called Wittig by the ungendered name Théo, which Wittig had taken to using in preference to Monique."[76] Annabel L. Kim too has argued that Sarraute and Wittig took the position of "anti-difference French feminism" in their lives and literary work.[77] Sarraute and Wittig both witnessed and reviled how emphasizing gender difference had impeded women's economic and social freedom.

Wittig also drew inspiration from Sarraute. Kim explains how both authors resist categories of gender identity in their work and, instead, "hollow out difference and rework our subjectivity."[78] In her 1984 essay "Le Lieu de l'action," Wittig praises the equality Sarraute grants her characters. Wittig terms these characters "interlocutors," as they are "called forth by dialogue . . . and disappear like meteorites or like people we pass in the streets."[79] According to Wittig, Sarraute's literature of "interlocution" reaches beyond dialogue to include all action occurring between people before, during, and after speech. In other words, not just the words spoken but the fluctuating inner substance (Sarraute's tropisms) that produce such words, as well as the outward pauses, gestures, and moments of silence. Thus, the "site of action" referred to in the title of Wittig's essay does not designate a sociotemporal universe in Sarraute's fiction (especially in her later work, in which realistic space is rendered completely indistinguishable); rather, action occurs in "any unspecified place where one speaks, perhaps even in those mental spaces with imaginary interlocutors."[80] Wittig's description, though largely drawn from her reading of Sarraute's 1980 *L'Usage de la parole*, corresponds with my analysis of Sarraute's *Le Planétarium*, in which the significant "action" occurs between obsessive, anxious thoughts and aggressive or defense dialogue.

Wittig's praise of Sarraute's narration of multiplicity—"like some kind of ancient Greek choir, not tragic but sarcastic, commenting on the fortuities of the discourse, of the dynamic gathering of all the elements in a unique movement that accrues them all away"—rather than a privileged, textual "I," aligns with her larger strategy as a materialist feminist.[81] Wittig connects the leveling of difference in Sarraute's writing to the utopian vision of Rousseau's social contract, under which all people would exist freely and equally. She imagines a "first language," before signification has silenced the words between the words and has cemented difference. In this language "there are neither men nor women, neither races nor oppression."[82] However, the social contract has a terrible flaw, "a worm in the fruit," which banishes us forever from this neutral and neutered paradise.[83] Wittig explains that the language of the social contract necessitates an "I," which carries along with it a grasping for power over speech. The repercussions of this desire to control speech reverberate into the social world as a feverish grappling by every subject to claim position.

Wittig's essay ends with a lament but again applauds Sarraute's fiction: "The paradise of the social contract exists only in literature, where the tropisms, by their violence, are able to counter any reduction of the 'I' to a common denominator, to tear open the closely woven material of the commonplaces, and to continually prevent their organization into a system of compulsory meaning."[84] Sarraute's anti-portraits yield exhaustion like a pair of claws, ripping apart "the closely woven material of the commonplace." In *Le Planétarium*, the refusal of assimilation and of "compulsory meaning" bars characters and situations from settling comfortably into themselves and into recognizable spaces. A persistent stain circulates in the site of action as the affective form of exhaustion.

Transcending Gender: Chen Ran's Fluidity as Defiance

In 1990s China, following the June Fourth Massacre at Tiananmen Square, dominant social discourse championed independent, apolitical, gendered subjects. In the place of such solid, desiring individuals, Chen Ran's fiction offers exhausted characters whose wandering yearnings never settle on one gender nor on a single plane of existence. In what remains of this chapter, I will argue that Chen's anti-portraits of bisexual heroines who drift between dream and waking life constitute remnants of refusal to the structured forgetting of history in Chinese society.

Maoist codes demanded that personal desires be subordinate to the ongoing revolutionary project of the nation. The death of Mao and the beginning of economic liberalization in the 1980s and 90s contributed to the advent of new conceptions and conventions of sexuality and gender identity. Lisa Rofel's ethnographic study of China in the 1990s argues that these "desiring practices" allowed Chinese citizens to distance themselves from the real and imagined strictures of Maoist socialism and redefine themselves as properly cosmopolitan subjects.[85] According to Rofel, Chinese aspiring to be such cosmopolitan subjects articulated their project as adopting a consumer identity invested in making China worldly ("domesticating cosmopolitanism") as well as transcending Chineseness; the resulting individual would, thus, (at least figuratively) straddle the local and global world. In her analysis of what she terms "cosmopolitanism with Chinese characteristics," Rofel describes the bind young Chinese women face in fashioning themselves into such subjects: "in post-Mao China, it is imperative to make radical distinctions between femininity and masculinity and yet the cosmopolitan self one should embody is both implicitly nongendered and easier for men to achieve."[86] In the 1980s and 90s, essentialized gender identities came back into vogue and reappeared on the consumer market in order to dismantle what was believed to be the flattening of gender difference (masculinizing women and emasculating men) under Mao. However, only for the Chinese man was the position of the universal subject available. The marketization of gender difference, newly adorned with the discourse of individual freedom and personal choice, reinscribed much of the system of compulsory meaning lamented in the West by Monique Wittig.

A number of Chinese women writers in the 1990s—Wang Anyi and Lin Bai, among others—tackled this system of compulsory meaning, but perhaps none so paradoxically as Chen Ran, whose work seems to conform to post-Mao market trends as well as challenge them. While Nathalie Sarraute's gender neutrality narrows the separation between her characters, rendering them all equal players across her novels' site of action, Chen Ran directly attacks gender binaries in her lectures, essays, and fiction. Many of her bisexual women characters engage in romantic relationships with men and women. They delight in both femininity and androgyny. Same-sex desire and lesbian activity complement discussions of gender inequity and female solidarity. Tze-Lan D. Sang argues that while Chen's writing can be viewed simply as one example of the "reemergence of the taxonomy of homosexuality into discussions in the PRC [and, therefore, as] . . . part and parcel of the 'sexing' of Chinese society and culture after Maoism," Chen's works, in fact, "challenge the facile hypothesis that there has been a liberation of gender and sexuality in China after Maoism."[87]

Sang explains that Chen Ran's 1994 university lecture, "Gender-Transcendent Consciousness and My Creative Writing," highlights two distinct and somewhat conflicting ideas: "One is the notion of *transcending gender*, which refers specifically to the ability to choose a partner of one's own biological sex instead of being limited by the social imperative to procreate and, hence, to choose a partner of the opposite sex. The other is the notion of a radical indifference to anatomical sex and social gender that downplays sex/gender altogether."[88] While one aspect of Chen's "gender transcendent consciousness" focuses on choice of sexual partner and the other on gender identity, both emerge out of a frustration with heterosexual relations and the gender hierarchy imposed by patriarchal society. Sang suggests that "Chen's ideal is probably closest to a genderless utopia."[89] Chen's characters share this contradictory position: bucking against essentialized notions of gender yet valorizing lesbian relationships and female friendships over mixed gender relations. Such fluidity rejects strict definitions, proposing exhaustion as a languid form of defiance.

The roving desire in Chen Ran's work serves as an example of what Wendy Larson terms the author's "awkward postmodernism." Larson explains, "This atomized, disembodied desire references the postmodern discourse of desire, yet simultaneously speaks to the distance between China and the postmodern West. Chen Ran's characters know of the revolutionary past and wistfully acknowledge its presence, but in their lives, its power becomes a residual trace."[90] The women characters in Chen Ran's fiction act out of desire, but this desire does not solidify into a feminist ideology of triumphant otherness. Unlike the western models of the laughing medusa or the chimeric cyborg, Chen's women characters remain marginal without claiming otherness as a maxim of strident, public activism. With the decline of the Maoist revolutionary project, the violent rebuke of popular political engagement at Tiananmen in 1989, and the rise of neoliberal globalization in the early 1990s, utopian longings in Chen Ran's fiction have been replaced by affective exhaustion.

In Chen Ran's 1995 short story "Breaking Open" (破開; *Pokai*), the reader enters the mind of the narrator Dai'er, crossing spatiotemporal, conscious and unconscious frontiers. Dai'er and her friend Yunnan, two thirty-something women, travel from the south to the north of China. The story follows the precepts of road fiction: beginning in an airport lounge and concluding in a busy city square in a northern metropolis, Dai'er not only journeys across the country but also reaches new understanding and maturity. On the one hand, "Breaking Open" is a coming-of-age tale. On the other hand, Daï'er—a semi-autobiographical character who reappears in several of Chen's stories—remains mid-metamorphosis and destined to linger on the periphery, always slightly out of step and adrift.[91]

Over the course of the story, the relationship between Daï'er and Yunnan develops in tandem with the women's reflections on gender and intimacy. Yunnan explains that she dislikes the descriptor "female" for Daï'er; "Instead, commenting on what she saw as my natural and unrestrained calm, she said that she liked my air of 'little-brother-like kid sister' or 'kid-sister-like little brother.'"[92] Daï'er remarks that one of the most beautiful forms of address she has heard "came from an old lover of mine, a painter, who once called me in public 'Brother Dai,'" which in Chinese is a near homonym for the name Daï'er.[93] To others, therefore, Daï'er appears to fall outside traditional gender binaries. Her own desires also no longer conform to heterosexual restrictions:

> To exist in this antagonistic world brimming with antagonism, a woman must choose a man in order to join the "majority" to be "normal." It is a choice that comes from not having any other choice. However, that is not how I feel. I am willing to disregard a person's gender identity in favor of their personal qualities. I do not care anymore about the difference between male and female, and I do not care about being part of a "minority" either; I do not even see it as "abnormal." I feel that an affinity between two people does not only appear between a man and a woman but that it is indeed also a kind of latent vital energy that has long been neglected among us women.[94]

Exhausted by the rules of the "majority," Daï'er shrugs off these shackles and charts her own uncertain path. Increasingly compelled by the "latent vital energy" drawing her to Yunnan, Daï'er describes the other woman's effect on her using the language of lovers: "The innate beauty of her words sets me aflutter with emotion."[95] Daï'er and Yunnan have grown closer as a result of their partnership in establishing a woman's association. The association seeks to break down the male norms that permeate social and cultural spheres and transcend "any consciousness of sexual difference."[96] After rejecting the name "The Second Sex," they decide to call the association "Breaking Open." By the story's end, Daï'er and Yunnan break with the strictures of platonic friendship, confess their feelings for each other, and resolve to cohabitate.

Thus, Chen Ran's story takes the action of "breaking open" as a central aesthetic and thematic concern. Daïer's meandering narration offers bits and pieces of her life story—difficult moments from her childhood, assorted observations about literary and historical figures, the account of her blossoming love for Yunnan—and reveals that her journey has involved a series of breaks from convention. She likens her life to a marginal daily newspaper that she prefers to *The People's Daily*, the official mouthpiece of the Chinese Communist Party: "These [marginal daily] papers are a little like my life. I slowly walk alone in a quiet little side street, always beyond the hurly-burly of crowds."[97] Daïer breaks away from the mainstream and breaks open the barrier keeping her on the side of the "normal." Her rejection of the status quo, however, does not take place in the public domain. Daïer reacts to the fervent clamoring after fame and fortune that surrounds her—what she describes as being "a wooden puppet on this huge stage"—with exhaustion.[98] She tarries in her own mind, "driven into distant corners of hopelessness and plagued by extremities of feeling."[99] This personal pilgrimage works as a remnant of refusal to the steady march forward in progressivist neoliberal time.

In the last pages of the story, Chen Ran breaks open Daïer's unconscious. As Daïer drifts into sleep on the plane, we follow her into a dream. The dream begins violently with Daïer's death as the plane malfunctions and falls from the sky: "The whole plane melts down among the clouds as it tumbles up and down amidst the collapsing rose-colored sun. Time is caving in, on the verge of disappearing altogether . . . I am leaving my physical body. I crash into a pitch-black tunnel, which leads to a powerful source of light."[100] In this timeless, bodiless space of nonbeing, Daïer receives the message that will propel her to action in her waking life. She encounters an old woman who urges her to take Yunnan home with her and together to tend to Daïer's mother: "You must work together, close as sisters, like mouth and teeth, like hair and brush . . . like barrel and bullet, because only women can really understand women."[101] Upon awakening, she recounts the dream to Yunnan who reveals that the woman resembles her own mother who passed away thirteen years ago. Emboldened by this blessing by spectral matriarchy, the two women resolve to always face the world together from this point forward. After disembarking the plane and standing in the city square, where the women's inner rhythm contrasts to "a male rhythm that has become a public standard," Daïer is startled to find a souvenir—a pile of baby teeth—that the old woman from her dream has left in her pocket.

This abrupt introjection of the bodily ab ect at the end of "Breaking Open" suggests that affective exhaustion in Chen Ran's fiction—with
its sleepy subjects lost in society, drifting in and out of thoughts and
dreams—works its own savage disturbance. Though her work is primarily
relegated to stories of women's private lives, Chen Ran shows that women's
bodies, minds, and intimacies can oppose the dominant discourse of the
public sphere. In other words, that what comes from within may trouble
what is without.

Women's Discourse of Privacy:
Active Spaces of Feminist Refusal and Chen's *Private Life*

Chen Ran's confessions of women's secrets exemplify the discourse of privacy
appearing in Chinese women's writing in the 1990s—part of a broader
transition in Chinese cultural expression from the 1980s to the 1990s.
Chinese literature of the 1980s functioned largely within the trope of the
father-son patriarchal order. In this dyad, the "sons" (elite experimental male
writers and fifth-generation male filmmakers), spawned allegorical work in
which young men protagonists struggle against the emasculating nation,
figured as the father's generation and its parochial cultural expectations.
In such narratives, women are marginalized, relegated to the position of
object of male desire or, as a Dai Jinhua puts it, featured only as "blockage
or obstacle that spurs the young male protagonist/'son' to go outside the
bounds of history."[102] Elite male authors overwhelmingly believed that the
nation was progressing steadily in the direction of a modernity in which
the totalitarian government (the "father's" PRC) would cede its place to
one more favorable to the plight of the individual and personal freedom
(the "son's" PRC). However, the 1989 Tiananmen Massacre (which Dai
refers to euphemistically as "the last historical catastrophe in 1980s China")
aided in crushing these hopes.[103]

The trauma of the June Fourth Massacre was compounded by the
modernization and globalization processes beginning in the early 1990s,
which Dai wryly claims "clearly pointed to a future saved by materialism
that pompously flaunted an avaricious pragmatism."[104] As a result, "The
cultural landscape of the mainland in the early 1990s suffered from the
torments of aphasia."[105] No longer able to speak about themselves, elite
male authors and filmmakers displaced their anxieties about the nation
onto women protagonists who were doomed to suffer abuse. However,

some women writers emerging in the 1990s, carved out a cultural space for women outside of these national allegories authored by men.

These writers, Chen Ran among them, drew from their private lives and from personal stories of sexual awakening. In the case of Chen Ran's work, as we have seen, these narratives of early sexual experience often include the homoerotic. Although, these women writers allowed their work to be " 'packaged' by male publishers and critics in such a way as to wet the voyeuristic whistle of the commercial market, Dai argues that their writing, nevertheless, acts as a form of resistance:

> Not only did women have an unprecedentedly clear and powerful voice of resistance, but it was also fully conscious of the existential gendered state of women, which included profound introspection on women; moreover, it yet again sought to surpass and overthrow gender order at a new cultural level. Sisterhood was no longer homoeroticism in a narrow sense or merely a female utopian evasion of reality, but became a clear expression of a cultural space for women and an ideal society for women.[106]

The story "Breaking Open" draws on introspection and sisterhood in order to carve out such an alternative realm for women, an active space of feminist refusal. Chen's 1996 autobiographical novel, *A Private Life*, likewise, pits the public against the private and reveals the latter as a site of affective exhaustion: a place of repose where rest is protest.

Chen Ran directly references Chinese women's discourse of privacy (隱私; *yinsi*) in the title of *A Private Life* (私人生活; *Siren Shenghuo*). Lingzhen Wang clarifies the shrewdness of this tactic: "Chen's choice to put the word *si* in the title of her novel signaled a conscious appropriation of the existing discourse on women, privacy, and consumption; it also made a public statement about a gendered, personal reinscription of terms and concepts produced in Chinese tradition and in the 1990s consumer market."[107] While *A Private Life* invites the reader to consume salacious passages from a young woman's diary, it simultaneously makes the society of consumption a target of critique.[108] This promised entrée into a woman's "private life" operates as lure, but the novel's narrator deconstructs herself, serving up her "private self" as a heaping portion of fragments. Niuniu, the novel's central protagonist and narrator, explains, "For so many years, time seemed to be speeding by. But now it's tired and wants to slow down. It has stopped in my apartment. It has also stopped in my face. It seems that time is exhausted."[109] This untimely woman, out of synch and in seclusion, spends her days in the bathtub or on her bed, which "is my castle amid a confused and disorderly world. It is my man and my woman."[110] Chen Ran's *A Private Life* serves as an anti-portrait of Niuniu: culled through her musings from her island of exhaustion, just another "broken fragment in a fragmented age."[111]

Written primarily in the first-person, Chen's *A Private Life* takes the form of an autobiography of a disintegrating subject. Bookended by the present when Niuniu is in her late twenties and living in isolation in her Beijing apartment, the novel's second chapter flashes back over ten years when the narrator was "eleven or possibly younger."[112] Born in Beijing in 1968 amid the Cultural Revolution, Niuniu's childhood features few friends or adult figures. A loner by nature, the child prefers the company of her own thoughts. As in the story "Breaking Open," antagonism between the sexes structures her social world. Niuniu explains, "I couldn't count on my father. That was very clear to me. He was an arrogant and pushy civil servant who never got very far."[113] Easily angered by the smallest slight, Niuniu's father sends away her nanny and banishes the family dog Sophia Loren. In an act of involuntary frustration and symbolic castration, little Niuniu cuts off the legs of her father's freshly pressed trousers. She reflects on how women's social conditioning allows them to be dominated by men: "Father's cruelty, his despotic ways, and absolute power were freely given to him by mother, nanny, and me. We handed him the power to oppress us through our gentleness and submission. The more tolerant and obedient we were, the more violent and dictatorial he became."[114] Niuniu and her father never develop a close relationship, and her parents quarrel incessantly. Finally, as Niuniu finishes secondary school and takes the entrance examinations for college, her parents divorce, and her father disappears from her life.

A Private Life gives the reader a chronical of China in transition through the eyes of this singular young woman. With the reinstatement of university entrance exams in the late 1970s, Niuniu perceives that the old spirit of collectivity among students has been replaced by one of fierce competition between individuals. Never one to idealize the past, she comments instead on how the misplaced priorities of the present emerge as a result of historical missteps: "When I think back on it today, the collectivism of our youth, which ignored the individual, was in fact the hotbed that nurtured our present inhumanly arrogant individualism.

Any phenomenon that is carried to an extreme will gradually lead to the emergence of its opposite."[115] As Beijing continues to transform over the course of the 1980s, Niuniu and her mother receive official notice that their house will be demolished to make way for construction; they, along with the other inhabitants of their neighborhood, move to apartments in a new high-rise.

The novel places Niuniu's personal evolution and later devolution in parallel with the shifts taking place in the public sphere. After going through puberty at the age of fourteen, Niuniu charts her own body's maturation with fascination. Chen Ran, therefore, "centers a bildungsroman on a diverse array of erotic relationships instead of the traditional grand themes (in the Chinese context at least) of the Communist Revolution and nation building."[116] No sooner does Niuniu move into her own apartment in the new high-rise than she receives a visit from her first sexual prospect, her old secondary school teacher Mr. Ti. Like Niuniu's father, Mr. Ti occupied a hostile position in Niuniu's childhood. He made her schooling miserable, and at first, she's appalled by his sexual advances. However, curious about the new feelings his touch awakens, she loses her virginity to him later in the summer in a garish, grotto-themed restaurant. In each scene of seduction between Niuniu and Mr. T, the narrator's voice shifts to the third person as if she doesn't recognize herself in the role of participant. During one such passage, she explains: "Her mind and her body had distanced themselves from each other."[117] As in "Breaking Open," therefore, the protagonist's attitude toward the possibility of heterosexual coupling remains wary. Niuniu engages in a more harmonious relationship with Mrs. Ho, a young widow whom she has known since her childhood. Ho lives just two floors below Niuniu in the new high-rise, and the two women often dine together, drink sweet wine, and discuss Chinese and foreign literature. Niuniu comments frequently on the older women's smell, her body, and her gentle hands. One night, she dreams of the two of them meeting at a party: "Our feet moved forward, back, in the crowded space, but we didn't bump into anyone, and so we danced our androgynous dance."[118] The blossoming of Niuniu's polyamorous, fluid desire, however, does not continue unhindered.

In 1989, Niuniu's third year of university, a series of tragedies permanently alter the course of her life: her mother falls ill with heart strain, an ailment that precipitously leads to her demise, and Mrs. Ho perishes in a fire that breaks out in their apartment building. Niuniu refers to 1989 as "that year of death" in which personal and national tragedies wind together: "The evil mists that enveloped that year were more than enough to distort many realities. But nature seemed to think they were not enough, and on that winter evening the choking black smoke obliterated my life. Like the prelude to a tragedy, this opened the curtain onto a more and more savage plot that within several moments had engulfed the entire country."[119] By synchronizing Niuniu's personal heartbreak with the events surrounding the 1989 June Fourth Massacre at Tiananmen Square, *A Private Life* confronts the private with the public; the "choking black smoke" from the high-rise fire simply a harbinger of the "more savage plot" to come. Niuniu's swift degeneration following 1989 reveals the novel's subtle allusion to "a tragedy . . . [which] engulfed the entire country" as one aspect of a larger project composed of remnants of refusal.

Such remnants result from the impact of "a stray bullet," which Chen Ran takes as the title for the chapter following the apartment fire. This "stray bullet," born out of what the novel euphemistically refers to as "the turmoil in my hometown that summer," collides with Niuniu's left calf as she travels across the city to visit her mother in the hospital.[120] Before she's hit, a flood of ominous images of death from Ingmar Bergman's films' *Wild Strawberries* (1957) and *The Seventh Seal* (1957) flash through her mind. Paradoxically, however, Niuniu confesses that she will not see these films until years in the future. *A Private Life*, thus, provides a rejoinder, a second coming, to the predictions in absent moving pictures I pointed to at the conclusion of Wang Anyi's *The Song of Everlasting Sorrow* in chapter 1. In Wang's novel, the protagonist's murder resembles something she's already witnessed: the fictional death of an actress at a Shanghai movie shoot she visited as a teenager. This murder, which she apprehends only as "insipidly familiar," presents itself in the future perfect, in advance of its full eventuality. In chapter 1, I argued that such time out of joint renders the protagonist's death in Wang's novel a melancholic reminder of (and a remnant of refusal to) the violence of June Fourth, whose images were broadcast on televisions nearly everywhere except the PRC. Likewise, in *A Private Life*, although Niuniu physically collides with the events of the Massacre, she cannot experience it directly. The traumatic effect of the violence replaces the immediacy of the fright with foreign film images to be (re)visited upon her in the future. In a final temporal flip, these images occur before the bullet itself strikes. Niuniu describes the impact: "The smoke floated up like curling wisps of incense above an alter toward a silent, unanswering heaven. It was just at that moment that the stray bullet, with complete disinterest, came out of nowhere to pierce my left calf

on one side and exit from the other."[121] This historical agent, which tears
with complete "disinterest" through the lives of private citizens, pierces
more than Niuniu's calf. In the final chapters of Chen Ran's novel, Niuniu
loses her grip on reality; "The wound was like a dark red cave, the mouth
of a living spring."[122] In response to the living, traumatic wound, Niuniu
crawls into the "dark red cave," retreating forever from the public, and
further clarifying that the predilection for private spaces in Chen Ran's
novel complements the position of protest.

Chen's *A Private Life*: The Inner Room

In the final chapters of *A Private Life*, the work of exhaustion completes
the novel's anti-portrait of its protagonist. Niuniu casts off public life
and withdraws figuratively back to the womb. Learning of her mother's
death in 1990, she rejects the news. Instead, she elects to live outside of
normative spaciotemporal relations: "And from that time I have harbored
a quiet secret in my heart: my mother, in actuality, had not left me."[123]
Niuniu understands this period not as one of death, but as a sort of new
beginning, which she terms the "birth of Miss Zero."[124] Rereading Kafka's
Metamorphosis with fresh investment, she feels words like insects swarm-
ing inside her: "It was from that moment that my life of ceaseless writing
began."[125] Here, the reader recognizes that Niuniu's story, the novel that
they hold in their hands, emerges from the narrator's wound, takes form
in response to her mental breakdown.

Chen's *A Private Life* shows how psychological illness stems from
both personal and national turmoil. On the one hand, the novel confirms
the findings in Zhang Li's ethnographic study of psychotherapy, *Anxious
China*, which indicates that the massive changes in post-socialist China
have led to a rise in anxiety among Chinese. Zhang takes this a step further, arguing: "Among various forms of mood disorders, anxiety (*jiaolu*
焦虑), broadly construed in both medical and social terms, has become
an indicator for the *pulse* of contemporary Chinese society."[126] And she
points to what might seem a paradox: "In China, many people are feeling anxious and stressed out rather than optimistic despite the rapid rise
and expansion of the economy."[127] The word "pulse," which likens society
to a living organism, frequently appears in Niuniu's musings about her
psychological relationship to the world around her: "I had also come to
realize that if a person lives within a fragmented world, unless she can

find harmony and completeness within herself, she will walk the same road to perdition as the world around her. Every outward nervous symptom is the product of a fierce conflict between a person's inner needs and the realities of the world around them."[128] Niuniu realizes that the "fierce conflict" between her peace of mind and the "fragmented world" has given rise to her "every outward nervous symptom."

On the other hand, I am suggesting that the impact of neoliberal globalization, as indicated by Zhang, as well as the suppression of national trauma at Tiananmen in 1989 and personal losses, conspire to trigger Niuniu's degeneration in *A Private Life*.[129] Furthermore, Niuniu does not necessarily understand her "illness" as one that needs treatment or healing. In this way the novel both partakes of and distances itself from the so-called psy fever (心理熱; *xinli re*), which began in China in the 1990s. Zhang Li explains, "This popular wave signals a widely shared desire and aspiration among middle-class Chinese searching for therapeutic fixes and self-help techniques in order to attain the good life."[130] *A Private Life* does not arm Niuniu with "therapeutic fixes" or "self-help techniques." On the contrary, the novel shows Niuniu's exhaustion as an affront to such "healthy" desires.

In order to further substantiate that the exhaustion in Chen's writing is representative of a broader trend in post-Tiananmen Chinese aesthetics, I'd like to turn briefly to another example taken up by Mila Zuo in her essay on traumatic boredom in Lou Ye's film *Summer Palace* (2006). Zuo writes, "The post-Tiananmen malaise is a condition of *impossibility*—beyond tiredness, realization, and acceptance. Beyond the threshold of tired lies exhaustion. . . . In post-Tiananmen, beyond the realm of the democratic possible, the state of suspended waiting hosts feelings of bored exhaustion."[131] *Summer Palace* begins shortly after Yu Hong (Hao Lei), a young woman from a city on the Chinese–North Korean border, arrives at a prestigious college in Beijing. Transpiring over slightly more than a decade, the film follows Yu Hong and several of her friends from their heady college days in Beijing during the Tiananmen Movement to their disillusioned young adulthood. The affective boredom that Zuo pinpoints in Lou's film goes hand in hand with "*Summer Palace*'s repetitive, fatiguing fixation on sex."[132] The film conflates a love triangle between Yu Hong and two other students in Beijing with the feelings of betrayal, anger, and disappointment prompted by the fallout of the Tiananmen Massacre. In both Lou Ye's and Chen Ran's coming-of-age stories, therefore, burgeoning sexuality and sex form the backbone. Yet the gratuitous sex in these

Bildungsromans/films does not render them exciting; rather, it becomes part and parcel of the boredom and exhaustion that slowly dissolve the characters' resolve. To this end, Zuo argues:

> Relevant to those who participated in the defeated pro-democracy movement, *Summer Palace* asks how resistance takes shape through the body. Unrooted individuals comprise a disjunctive universe in which corporeal agency constitutes the foundation from which democratic idealism proceeds. However, as the promise of democracy dissipates, so do the characters' sense of purpose and bodily control. . . . Sex, rather than constituting the censored obscene act, stands in for something far more offensive. That the onscene sexual spectacle becomes boring and repetitive reveals that the ob/scene—that which cannot be seen—has drained life of its vitality.[133]

Unable to act or protest the government's response to an event that has been officially denied, Niuniu's isolation now serves as her means of revolt. Alone in her apartment in the final chapter, listening to the radio, her mind seizes on the lyrics of a popular song that claim that the solitary (孤獨; *gudu*) are shameless (無恥; *wuchi*).[134] Niuniu scoffs: "Feudalism and conservativism are finished. The age of openness has arrived. Once it was revolution that shook up society, now it's love. If you aren't part of the trend, you're shameless."[135] Niuniu turns her back on trends and embraces her "shameless" solitude.

Rejecting the "love" on offer in the outside world, Niuniu settles into a spaciotemporal universe of rounded edges and perpetual returns populated by her memories. She explains, "I have a love that runs totally counter to the times—in my bathroom. To be precise, my bathtub."[136] The water, like amniotic fluid, nourishes her: "I leaned against the tub quietly like a thirsting plant nursing its way back to succulent life."[137] Niuniu shape-shifts: both baby and adult woman, both human and plant. Only her mind connects her to the outer world. Lying in the tub, she teases: "I did something to myself. Something you only have to imagine and its done."[138] After masturbating, envisaging her hands to be those of the women and men she has loved and lost, she sinks into dream.

These last pages, located in a private interior space in Niuniu's Beijing apartment, recall an earlier chapter in Chen's novel, "The Inner Room."[139] In this chapter, Niuniu recounts how she first encountered sex: peeping into the "inner room" where her friend Yi Qiu withdrew, giggling with her boyfriend. Niuniu feels compelled to spy, unable to resist the attraction of the inner room. She ties this story to blood. First, she explains how she earlier witnessed her friend's period: finding blood-soaked paper in a trash bag near the toilet, Niuniu felt her heart pound wildly. When she turns fourteen, the same year she peers into the "inner room," Niuniu's own period begins: "Even today, I still believe that Yi Qiu was the catalyst that initiated my passage into womanhood, because when I got out of bed the morning after I had witnessed this, I discovered a small patch of blood, like a living crimson plum blossom, among the printed green flowers on my sheets."[140] This chapter reveals how the "inner room" unites women's experiences, forming them into an alternative history of cycles as opposed to lines, known only by girls and women, private and passionate.

Looking back from the novel's conclusion to this earlier moment, it's no surprise when Niuniu admits that she invented the story of witnessing Yi Qiu's sex with her boyfriend. She explains, "The creative imagination is the *mother* of all memories. . . . The reason that my focus persistently returns to the bits and pieces of the past is that they are not dead pages from history; they are living links that connect me to my ever-folding present."[141] Chen Ran's *A Private Life* celebrates the exhausted retreat to the "inner room," isolated from the clamor of the public sphere, because it is in this space that woman's remnants of refusal materialize.

Womb Work: *Cinécriture*

The affective exhaustion in the writing of Nathalie Sarraute and Chen Ren results in anti-portraits that serve as feminist remnants of refusal to the suppression of national trauma in ages of expanding neoliberal globalization. In the early pages of this chapter, I gleaned my approach to anti-portraiture from Agnès Varda's description of *Sans toit ni loi* (1985), a film she dedicated to Sarraute. However, Varda's practice of anti-portraiture may be traced back to works from the beginning of her career. In her 1958 short film, *L'Opéra-Mouffe*, Varda treats the contradictory feelings provoked by her pregnancy by capturing the faces of strangers at the open market on Paris's Rue Mouffetard. As the title sequence plays across the image of Varda in the nude, her back to the camera, the film announces its strategy of anti-portraiture (figure 3.1). The filmmaker—rendered anonymous without her face—silently watches the theater of humanity on display in the street. She subtitles the film "A Pregnant Woman's Filmed Diary" and structures it into chapters—on emotions ("Anxiety"), figures ("The Dearly Departed"),

Figure 3.1. The opening of Varda's *L'Opéra-Mouffe* (1958) shows the title across the back of the director's nude, pregnant body. *Source*: Varda, Agnès, dir. *L'Opéra-Mouffe*. 1958; New York: Criterion Varda, 2008. DVD.

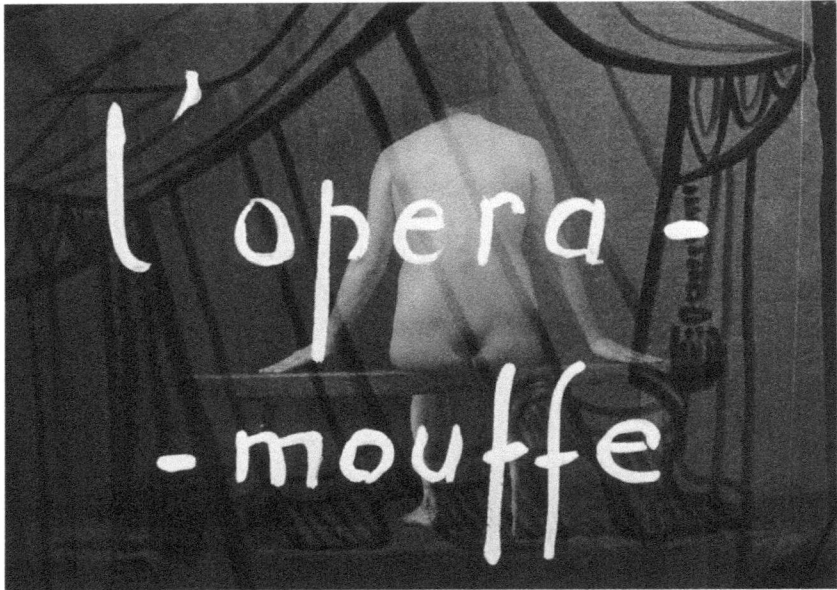

states of being ("Drunkenness"), and so on—capturing her pregnancy by illustrating the jumble of feelings and figures it inspires. Varda called *L'Opéra-Mouffe* "a film about instinct, in the sense that an instinct develops according to a logic of its own."[142] She explains of the film:

> Those faces passing in the street speak so eloquently. And I was the pregnant woman who was looking at them. A look that I call subjective documentary. The subjectivity of a pregnant woman. A look that says, "They were all newborns before becoming old people, bums, blind men. How did people look at them when they were babies? How can one get pregnant when one feels situated between the hope of having a baby—this little bit of tender flesh that we kiss—and the reality of those former babies?" I was incredibly moved since I was doing the filming in the Rue Mouffetard, which relayed back to me all these images of my own feelings.[143]

Varda's "subjective documentary" gives authorship to an expectant mother's feelings. Sandy Flitterman-Lewis explains that the film's insistence on the woman filmmaker's subjective point of view marks it as a significant work of feminist cinema:

> The subjective consciousness, this gaze of the enunciating subject, is thus the unifying factor that weaves the subtle texture of images of daily life through the subjective structures of memory and anticipation. Varda has spoken of *L'Opéra-Mouffe* as a film that works at the limit of modesty and immodesty; it is in this sense that this profoundly personal vision becomes inseparable from the social context that produces it. And it is here that the film's most productive feminist meaning can be ascertained. Varda's comments combine an interest in filmic composition with the problematics of the gaze, and in so doing suggest that cinema is, above all, an articulation of vision which is at once both personal and deeply social.[144]

This womb work, this woman's affect as birthed from personal and social vision, selects the images—the hope and the dread—that reflect its creative contradictions.

Varda's *cinécriture* is motored by women's affect. She explains that her goal of *cinécriture* pushed her to fight since her first film, *La Pointe Courte* (1955), "for something that comes from emotion, from visual emotion, sound emotion, feeling, and finding the shape for that, and a shape which has to do with cinema and nothing else."[145] The anti-portraiture in her cinema is intimately tied to her *cinécriture*. As Hayward writes of the unconventional narrative and character formation in *Sans toit ni loi*: "The digressive structure of Varda's flashback construction and the analogically digressive composition of her tracking shots. These are aspects of her feminist *cinécriture* which are political because—as with feminist writing which refuses to inscribe contours—in their digressiveness they go counter to dominant male film-making practices and are, therefore, counter-cinematic."[146] Varda's *cinécriture* refers to all the work that goes into a film; the boundaries between the initial idea and the script, the cinematography and the editing, blur and come to form this intermedial mode. Varda elaborates, "*Cinécriture* isn't the scenario, it's the ensemble of exploratory walks, the choices, the inspiration, the words that one writes, the shooting, the editing, the film is the product of all these different moments."[147] The film, then, always emerges from the body of labor, or the woman's laboring body, womb work.

Varda's womb work, like that of Chen Ran and Nathalie Sarraute, does not shy away from savagery. *Sans toit ni loi* begins as it ends with its homeless heroine Mona exhausted, dead in a ditch. This womb-like image serves as the viewer's introduction and conclusion to Mona's journey of refusal (figure 3.2). Varda expounds on this structure: "The way the story is told is not to be pitiful, not for understanding, that is not what it's about. It's about what it is to be so much in the 'no' situation—she says no all the time—and I don't know why she ended up on the road and saying no. But I like to see how her 'no' opposed to the society gets reactions in such different ways according to who is meeting her."[148] Varda's respect for Mona's "no," and Mona's refusal to fall in line with society, motivates the distance the film takes from its subject, "trying to capture more or less, less rather than more."[149] The film's tracking shots seize the landscape and allow Mona to enter and exit the frame as she pleases, without caging her defiance. Flitterman-Lewis describes Varda's depiction of Mona as the "riddle of femininity politicized."[150] She writes, "Mona herself, this 'impossible portrait'—this wanderer, this homeless person, this . . . woman. In

Figure 3.2. The womb-like image of Mona dead in a ditch in Varda's *Sans toit ni loi* (1985). *Source*: Agnès Varda, dir. *Vagabond (Sans toit ni loi)*. 1985; New York: Criterion Varda, 2008. DVD.

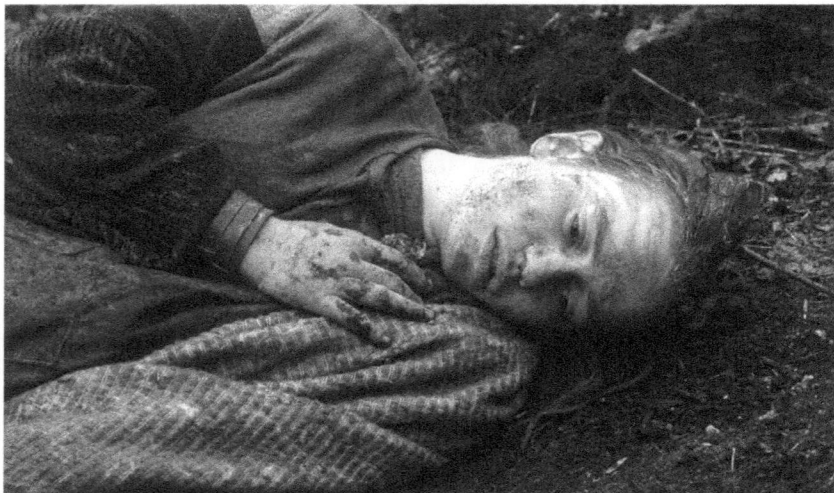

this film, Varda as filmmaker asks the questions—the social and psychic questions of femininity. And in posing a central character who remains an enigma, she offers us, and her characters, the possibility of engaging in the process of meaning construction. The woman is posed as enigmatic precisely to allow us to explore the production of that enigma."[151] Feminist anti-portraiture—by Varda, Sarraute, and Chen—does away with conventional methods of storytelling and character formation and uses this position of exhaustion as the place from which women's affective stories as remnants of refusal might reclaim history.

Conclusion

This book has examined how feminist affects in literary and filmic works from France and China can be read as remnants of refusal to the occlusion of traumatic memory during periods of expanding neoliberal globalization. In chapter 1, I show how works by Marguerite Duras and Wang Anyi function as melancholic feminine allegories. In chapter 2, I discuss how films by Jean-Luc Godard and Jia Zhangke propose ambivalent rejoinders, riddled with violence. Finally, in chapter 3, I argue that works by Nathalie Sarraute and Chen Ran render exhausted anti-portraits. While each chapter is devoted to a different affect and set of authors, the progression over the pages of the book, from melancholy to exhaustion, from the introduction to this conclusion, aims to present a series of rhyming protests constructed in literary and filmic form.

In the pages that follow, I will discuss two events that suggest a break, or at least a pause, an *interlude,* from the periods under examination and the melancholy, ambivalence, and exhaustion in my preceding chapters: the May 1968 revolts in France, and the 2008 Beijing Olympics. Finally, I will end this book with a *postmortem: death of the modern nation* in which I reiterate how reading transnationally might propose other ways of considering trauma not on a national but on a global scale. While I'm not suggesting that this book's central affects no longer function as modes of refusal, I do want to stress that these historical moments reframe the relationship within, between, and beyond nations and allow for the emergence of new responses.

Interlude

Kristin Ross explains that May 1968 "was the largest mass movement in French history, the biggest strike in the history of the French workers' movement, and the only 'general' insurrection the overdeveloped world has known since World War II. . . . France, for some five to six weeks, was brought to a complete paralysis."[1] The events of "May" truly began on March 22, when student protestors occupied an administrative building at the University of Paris at Nanterre. Following the success of this initial action, students and workers gathered to revolt throughout the country. On May 14, while President de Gaulle was on a state visit to Romania, "The *Nantais* factory *Sud-Aviation* was the first to call for a general strike and occupation."[2] However, this was just the beginning: "Other, bigger and more significant factories, including the bastion of the working class—the Renault factory at Boulogne-Billancourt—soon followed suit. By 19 May, up to two million people were on strike and de Gaulle, having cut short his state visit, was clearly perturbed with the state of affairs declaring, 'reform, yes; havoc, no.'"[3] According to May '68 student leader Daniel Cohn-Bendit, the docility fostered by the growing abundance during the Trente Glorieuses gave rise to a distinct generation gap: "In France the situation was such that, on the one hand, we find what I call economic modernization, and, on the other hand, a conception of life and morality that was of another age. Putting this another way, the collision at the end of the 1960s was one between the generation that had not lived through the war and the generation which had built a system coming from the war, thereby conserving the memory [of the war] by radically undermining democracy and liberty."[4] The events of May ended on May 30, when de Gaulle dissolved the National Assembly and announced that he would not abdicate the presidency. The revolts, though achieving some successes for workers at individual factories, failed to incite an outright revolution. Looking back, Kristin Ross identifies May as a crisis in functionalism: "The movement took the form of political experiments in *de*classificiation, in disrupting the natural 'givenness' of places; it consisted of displacements that took students outside of the university, meetings that brought farmers and workers together, or students to the countryside. . . . The political opening to otherness allowed activists to create a rupture with that order, to displace, if only briefly, the places assigned by the police, to make seen what was not seen, make heard what could not be heard."[5] Although a decisive disappointment to its proponents, May '68 marks a rupture in the relative tranquility of the Trente Glorieuses and has retained a firm place in the French imaginary; its repercussions have rippled across France ever since.[6]

Jean-Luc Godard's *La Chinoise* was released the summer before the tumultuous spring of '68. Godard biographer Antoine de Baecque asserts that the commonly held belief that the 1967 *La Chinoise* announces the

May '68 revolution is a misunderstanding, because "the film announces less the hope for change and the student revolt . . . than the disillusionment that follows every frenzied engagement."[7] I would argue that *La Chinoise* is symptomatic of both the coming revolts and their aftermath. Godard himself was experimenting with leftist politics during the late 1960s and would call himself a Maoist by '68. He was also on the brink of forming the socialist-idealist Dziga Vertov cinema group, which marked a radical break with his Nouvelle Vague films, revealing his new commitment to explicitly political cinema. Though released in the same year as *2 ou 3 choses que je sais d'elle*, *La Chinoise* breaks with some of the former film's ambivalence and stands as a sturdier symbol of Godard's personal revolt, as well as that of the students and workers of May '68.

On one wall of an otherwise humdrum bourgeois apartment in Paris's posh seventh arrondissement, the following phrase appears in black: "One must confront vague ideas with clear images" (figure C.1).

With this shot, *La Chinoise* reveals the bourgeois apartment remade into Maoist cell. A later tableau frames the young would-be revolutionaries:

Figure C.1. The Maoist cell-cum-bourgeois apartment in Godard's *La Chinoise* (1967). *Source*: Godard, Jean-Luc, dir. *La Chinoise*. 1967; New York: Kino Lorber, 2017. DVD.

on the left, Godard's second wife, Anne Wiazemsky, incarnating the philosophy student Véronique; in the center, Jean-Pierre Léaud—whose career began at the tender age of fourteen in Truffaut's *Les Quatre cent coups* (1959) and whom Godard employed in many projects thereafter—plays Guillaume, a young actor inspired by Brecht's epic theater; on the right, Juliet Berto, who had a brief appearance in Godard's *2 ou 3 choses que je sais d'elle*, is Yvonne, a country girl who arrived in Paris only several years earlier and now works as a maid, supplementing her income with occasional prostitution (figure C.2). We have, therefore, an ensemble already deeply implicated in the Godardian universe, playing character types (a philosopher, a political artist, a sex worker) common to the filmmaker's work. The significance of recognizing the actors and their roles as belonging to the *famille Godard* lies in the fact that this work, Godard's fourteenth feature-length film, must be understood as another episode in the chronicle of history, personal and universal, that Godard undertakes in his films. As we see repeated numerous times in intertitles throughout *La Chinoise*, it is "a film in the process of being

Figure C.2. Véronique, Guillaume, and Yvonne, the three aspiring revolutionary comrades in Godard's *La Chinoise*. *Source*: Godard, Jean-Luc, dir. *La Chinoise*. 1967; New York: Kino Lorber, 2017. DVD.

made." The film is as much about revolutionary filmmaking, artmaking, as about anything else. It is another step on Godard's long march as an image-maker: here, a step in a new direction.

The title of Godard's film, *La Chinoise*, or *The Chinese Woman*, seems to refer especially to the character of Véronique who seeks to change the world through Maoism (and, finally, terrorism). The colors in the film—white walls, red curtains and a mountain of *Little Red Books*, blue Chinese workers' uniforms on the young women, and a blue shirt on Guillaume—stand out as those most frequently selected from Godard's color wheel during this period of his work (the mid-to-late 1960s). However, the predominance of red in *La Chinoise* of course, carries another significance, in that this film treats a band of young "reds," French youth newly devoted to Maoism and other brands of socialism. The other prominent color in the film is yellow, which Jacques Rancière has suggested completes the palate of primary colors in Godard's film, "which counter the degradation of nuance and the confusion of 'reality.' "[8] In other words, these primary colors provide "clear images." Yet the tableau of the characters that I have described appears too clear, exaggerated. Why so many copies of the *Little Red Book* when they all contain the same aphorisms? Why go so far as to don the garb of Chinese workers? Politics in *La Chinoise* becomes primarily a matter of maximalist mise-en-scène. At the end of the summer, the Maoist cell disbands. Véronique returns to university, and Guillaume sets out on his own, vowing to change the world through theater. Godard's characters, these self-proclaimed soldier-citizens of a revolution that would not gain real momentum in France until 1968, are treated with gentle irony and as "works in progress."

In the twenty-first century, in which transnational Sinophone artistic production has grown both progressively prolific and garnered increasing attention, writer and filmmaker Guo Xiaolu offers a more contemporary response to Godard's *La Chinoise*.[9] Of her 2009 film, *She, a Chinese* (中國姑娘; *Zhongguo guniang*), the filmmaker proclaims in an interview for the Belgian newspaper *Le Soir*, "It's in some ways the Chinese version of *La Chinoise*. A version going in the opposite direction, since my Chinese woman journeys from East to West. It is a slightly cynical reference to Godard, as his Chinese woman no longer exists."[10] While Godard's title may refer specifically to Véronique, it also illustrates his decidedly European romanticization of Maoism in the late 1960s when the Great Proletarian Cultural Revolution called for every member of society to participate in the overhaul of traditional thinking. By 2009, in China's post-reform era, when Guo's *She, a Chinese* appeared in cinemas, Chinese society had moved decidedly away from Maoist revolution. So, indeed, Godard's "Chinese woman" never truly existed in China, and certainly no longer exists.

The year before the release of Guo's film, Beijing hosted a global occasion, the 2008 Olympic Games. That year not only marked an important "coming out" party for China on the world stage but also signaled an anniversary in the history of the PRC. Kate Merkel-Hess explains:

> The year 2008 marked the end of the second major era of the PRC. Scholars of China frequently speak of the period from 1949 to 1978 as "Maoist China," but when Deng Xiaoping kicked off massive economic reforms in the early months of 1979, he turned the collectivizing goal of Mao's China on its head. The period from 1979 to 2008 was one of unprecedented growth for China but also one marked by increasing inequality and insecurity. Privatization, as much as concerns for free speech issues and increased political participation, set the stage for the student demonstrations of 1989, an event that still frames Western interactions with China. And today, a younger generation scoffs at the idealism of the 1989 leaders, seeing economic growth and influence as the only way for each of them—and for China—to get ahead.[11]

It is too early to hypothesize which model—reform China or Mao's China—will enjoy the more enduring legacy, but the overall success of the 2008 Beijing Olympics secured China's place as a dominant world power. In the same year as China faced criticism for contaminated baby food and toys, and after the devastating natural disaster of the earthquake in Sichuan province in May, the Beijing Olympics came to the rescue: providing a seemingly nonthreatening exhibition of a nation ready and able to be accepted among the ranks of the "First World."[12]

Dai Jinhua too marks 2008—citing the global financial crisis, the revelation of China's new middle class who donated money and goods following the Sichuan earthquake, and the Beijing Olympics—as a turning point in China. No longer belonging to the post–Cold War cold war, China "finally joined world time and world history."[13] She explains:

> After this transition in 2007–8, a new social hegemonic discourse was established in China. Most prominent within this

discourse are developmentalism, consumerism, the market, and
fetishism-filled capitalism. . . . For this author, the so-called
rise of China is the most important sign that the world has
entered an era after the post–Cold War. One no longer need
beat around the bush and evade the open secret of China's
total entrance into capitalism and its role as the most active
and lively player in a global capitalism in crisis.[14]

The opening and closing ceremonies of the Olympics—directed by the
design team headed by the world famous fifth-generation filmmaker
Zhang Yimou—provided a stage for China to showcase its "total entrance
into a capitalism, wowing (and troubling) spectators with its thousands
of performers moving in unison to create an awesome mass spectacle."
Geremie R. Barmé explains that Zhang Yimou "presented the world with
a series of golden vistas of invention and amicable exchange. Pursuing
the central theme of the Communist Party, that of harmony (*hexie*; 和
諧), however, the directors of the show created a 'flattened' narrative
that eliminated China's 20th-century history of radical iconoclasm and
struggle, as well as democratic aspiration."[15] Focusing on China's ancient
inventions, Confucian heritage, and contemporary multiculturalism,
the opening ceremonies excised the entire twentieth century from their
sweeping chronicle. Even Mao Zedong garnered only elliptical reference.[16]
Barmé continues, "The Party wanted the ceremonies to be 'outstanding,
innovative, [employ] local colour, [reflect] the spirit of the age and [take]
an international perspective' (*jingcai, xinying, minzu tese, shidai tezheng,
shijie yanguang*; 精彩, 新硬, 民族特色, 時代特徵, 世界眼光). The creative
team had to 'use an international language to tell China's story' . . . but
it was a story that perforce dovetailed with the Party's propaganda."[17] In
other words, "The spirit . . . was best expressed by the slogan that was
on display in the creative headquarters: 'Benefit the motherland above all'
(*zuguode liyi gaoyu yiqie*; 祖國的利益高於一切)."[18] Yet even if the intense
nationalist overtones of the opening ceremonies disturbed some with their
proximity to fascism, the overall valuation of the Olympic Games was
positive. After all, "Better to party en masse than to flex massive military
muscles; better to deck out the PLA soldiers in fluorescent catsuits and
make them undulate in the Bird's Nest than to have them drive tanks into
Tiananmen Square and mow down demonstrators. It is not often that
China is faulted for trying too hard to please. No one, really, minds being
mesmerized by (soft) power."[19] The last time the world turned its gaze to

Beijing was during the tragedy at Tiananmen in 1989; the Olympics strove to replace that dark image with a lighter one, even if critical observers perceived the displacement of Beijingers during the preparation for the event and the mass spectacle of the opening ceremony as new worrying displays of totalitarianism (figure C.3).

As Chinese totalitarianism shows no sign of ebbing, some Chinese artists have left China, hoping to gain freer expression elsewhere. One such example, the aforementioned Guo Xiaolu, grew up in southern China and attended the Beijing Film Academy, before relocating to London in 2002. In an article published in 2008 in London's *The Independent*, Guo tries to understand and explain her roots by using an object, her Chinese identity card: " 'Identity,' most of the time, is something that exists but isn't chosen. And one has to accept it or else lose one's social position. I, too, have a noble piece of plastic—it says: Chinese, Hui Minority, Peasant Household."[20] Although she still possesses a Chinese identity card, Guo is not a permanent citizen of one nation: she divides her time between Europe and China and works in a variety of languages. Hybrid identity, the navigation of the national and the global "self," unsurprisingly, stands

Figure C.3. Mass spectacle as totalitarian display during the opening ceremony of the Beijing Olympic Games in 2008. *Source*: US Army; https://www.army.mil/article/11606/olympic_opening_ceremony_celebrates_one_world_one_dream.

out as a central theme in both her written and filmic work. She concludes the article in *The Independent* by using another object, one perhaps more useful to someone with her peripatetic lifestyle—a map—to describe her unresolvable relationship to the landscapes and languages of her life: "So here I am in decayed Europe, looking at the map of China. A map of China with English letters. That is confusing—when you read your own country's map in a foreign language, you are not sure anymore where those places are supposed to be. I don't really find the China with its cities and towns, all I see are those borders. . . . And on that map I'm still trying to find out why I am a Hui and why a peasant and why I am a Chinese."[21] For Guo, and for a growing number of Chinese in the twenty-first century, the individual no longer needs to belong to one nation; and yet, this nation and its language remain inescapable markers of self.

In addition to her film, *She, a Chinese,* Guo Xiaolu's 2007 novel *A Concise Chinese-English Dictionary for Lovers,* her first work written in English, takes up the issue of contesting identities, telling the story of a young Chinese woman, Zhuang Xiaoqiao, known to her new Anglophone acquaintances simply as "Z," who comes to London to study English and ends up falling in love. The novel, written as a series of diary entries divided by month, charts Z's range of experiences as a foreigner and as a woman in love over the course of a year. The first entry for the month of February, Z's first month in London, begins with a word that frames Z's new circumstances: "**alien** *adj* foreign; repugnant (to); from another world *n* foreigner; being from another world."[22] The novel also performs Z's growing knowledge of English. Another early entry reads, "Windy and chilli [*sic*]. I feeling I can die for all kinds of situation in every second. No safety in this country, I think unsafe feeling come from I knowing nothing about this country. I scared I in big danger."[23] By the end of the year, Z's English has improved dramatically. She writes fluidly. "I think of those days when I traveled in Europe on my own. I met many people and finally I wasn't so afraid of being alone. Maybe I should let my life open, like a flower; maybe I should fly, like a lonely bird."[24] Z's sentimental education is no less dramatic. Beginning the story as an inexperienced, meandering girl who doesn't know what she wants or who she is in the world, Z grows up over the course of her year in England.

Since Guo uses the English language as an aesthetic and structural device in Z's coming of age narrative, it would have been impossible to write the same story in Chinese. Yet, a question remains: by switching to English, has Guo "sold out" in order to cash in on the higher market value of English literature? In his essay, "The Language of Betrayal,"

Ha Jin gives a more general response to this question, using his own choice to write in English—as well as that of Joseph Conrad and Vladimir Nabokov—to structure his argument. Ha Jin asserts: "The ultimate betrayal is to choose to write in another language. . . . Historically, it has always been the individual who is accused of betraying his country. Why shouldn't we turn the tables by accusing a country of betraying the individual? Most countries have been such habitual traitors to their citizens anyway. The worst crime the country commits against the writer is to make him unable to write with honesty and artistic integrity."[25] Jin refers (hardly obliquely) in this passage to the censorship laws imposed on writers in Mainland China. According to Jin, China can no longer claim "betrayal" after having expressly repressed the voices of its people. As a result of such repression, Jin migrated to the United States, and now writes in English. He believes a writer working in a new language "must do everything to find his place in his adopted language, including cracking jokes that are not translatable for his native people. In such a case, he may have to sacrifice his mother tongue, while borrowing its strength and resources, in order to accomplish a style in his adopted tongue. In short, he must be loyal only to his art."[26]

Guo has claimed that her decision to write in English was made as a result of real-life circumstances; as a young Chinese woman living in London, she endeavored to gain proficiency in the language of the place. However, Guo's *A Concise Chinese-English Dictionary for Lovers* differs from Ha Jin's works in that Guo's novel is written between Chinese and English. The tale begins in broken English; even as Z progresses in linguistic ability, she refers to Chinese sayings, and occasionally includes a diary entry written in Chinese. At the end of the section devoted to August, Z begins her entry: "我说我爱你, 你说你要自由"[27] The Chinese remains untranslated on the page, allowing only readers of Chinese access to Z's bilingual story. However, for readers ignorant of Chinese, this gesture highlights the difficulty that Z must encounter when writing in English: the difficulty of existing between languages. The Chinese characters appear in their blunt alterity on the page. The English-language reader must continue to the next page to find the editor's translation, situated in the center of the page: "I say I love you, but you say you want to have freedom."[28] While Guo writes most of her novel in English, the text never gains complete freedom from Chinese. These Chinese remnants serve as an aesthetic reminder of the fate of any person who chooses (or is forced) to live elsewhere. Guo's novel shows the struggle of a Chinese immigrant; but displaced people everywhere have similar stories of living between languages and cultures.

Her tale is a Chinese one, but also a worldly one: nations grow less and less uniform, cultures blend, and languages evolve.

Guo's 2009 film *She, a Chinese* also tells the story of a young Chinese woman's journey West to London (a variation on the plot of *A Concise Chinese-English Dictionary for Lovers*) and breaks with the melancholy I've located in the films and literature under discussion in the chapters of this book. The film follows the trajectory of Li Mei (Huang Lu), a daughter of the Cultural Revolution generation and a young woman with passions shared by other post-1989 young adults. She doesn't care about politics. She listens to pop music on her headphones and yearns to have enough money to travel and live as she pleases. Born in a village, the victim of poverty and sexual violence, she flees to the booming city of Chongqing and later to London. In Chongqing, Mei works as a prostitute. She stays in the city only a few months, falling for one of her clients, a hitman named Spiky (Wei Yibo). After Spiky is killed on the job, Mei finds a large quantity of cash hidden under his mattress and uses it to take a trip with a tour group to Europe. In London, she flees the tour and works various odd jobs under the table, before marrying an Englishman who is old enough to be her grandfather. She flees this new marriage of convenience as well, taking up with another immigrant, Rashid (Chris Ryman), by whom she becomes pregnant. Mei dumps Rashid when it becomes clear that he will never marry a non-Muslim, and the last shots of the film display the heavily pregnant Mei walking along the side of the highway. This retelling may give the impression that this story is a tragedy, but I would argue that such is not exactly the case. Mei stubbornly insists on a life suited to her own desires. She is young, vain (there are many sequences in the film in which Mei examines herself in mirrors), self-centered (she shows no remorse in leaving her parents without a word), and entirely uninterested in engaging politically. These descriptors should not be taken as value-laden judgments: Mei is a young woman trying to shape her destiny on her own terms against difficult odds. In an early sequence in the film, she gazes out of the car window. Mei's gaze is always turned toward what is to come. In this sense she is a profoundly optimistic character. Her revolt, stemming from a dogged determination to flee her limited surroundings, comes at a higher cost than that of Godard's subjects in *La Chinoise*, but is also more courageous. *She, A Chinese* tells the story of a certain kind of ordinary twenty-first-century Chinese women trying to be a person on her own terms, in a world in which Godard's soldier-citizens in *La Chinoise* have been replaced by imperfect, wandering individualists. Guo's engagement in women's struggles for equality and freedom reveals that the battle is slow, painful, personal, and unresolved (figure C.4).

Figure C.4. Mei's gaze is always turned toward the future in Guo Xiaolu's *She, A Chinese* (2009). *Source*: Guo, Xiaolu, dir. *She, A Chinese* (中國姑娘; *Zhongguo guniang*). 2009; London: StudioCanal, 2010. DVD.

While Godard's *La Chinoise* and Guo's novel and film reveal that something new is afoot in France post-1968 and China post-2008, a nation's traumas never truly disappear but are forever reflected on the horizon; journeys away from home return travelers to the enigma of their lost historical origin. In the final section, I will further probe how engaging with the changing face of transnationalism in the age of neoliberal globalization might revitalize our understanding of the dynamic relationships between states and people, collectives and individuals, and history and memory.

Postmortem: Death of the Modern Nation

Cao Fei's 2014 city symphony, *La Town*—shot in the artist's Beijing studio—combines models and wax figurines from a variety of nationalities and time periods, creating a miniature globalized city after its destruction. The camera floats through space like a curious ghost whose vertical and lateral movements and frequent use of racking focus suggest an investigation of the details on each level and plane. A disaster has taken place, and the camera traverses the devastated landscape as if searching for clues. In place of answers, *La Town* offers a collision of historical, geographic, and mythical signifiers. An early sequence of shots circles a derailed high-speed train, still smoking from the impact of a crash, something protruding from its nose. A tighter shot reveals the protruding object to be the legs and body of a reindeer; having narrowly escaped death, Santa in his sleigh sits frozen before the bloodied scene (figure C.5).

Cao Fei's train introduces one level of her city symphony's dialogue with cinematic and global history. Since the train sped into the frame of the Lumière Brothers' 1895 actuality film, the cinema has been simultaneously attentive to the velocity of the new and a testament to the past. One may still arrive at La Ciotat by train (electric or diesel), but not by steam locomotive. Both the particular vehicle and the travelers captured by the Lumières are outmoded, dead. City symphony films of the 1920s feature the train as a symbol of modernity and facilitator of movement. Walter Ruttman's *Berlin: Symphony of a Metropolis* (1927) brings the spectator to the city by rail, Dziga Vertov's *Man with a Movie Camera* (1929) shows the risks the camera operator takes in order to film a dangerous, oncoming train. The perilous train is, of course, invoked in 1920s historiography of another kind explored in the introduction to this book, namely Freud's *Beyond the Pleasure Principle*, in which he identifies the shock of a mechanical accident such as a railway collision and the psychic damage endured during World War I as two sources of traumatic neurosis. The repetition compulsion accompanying traumatic neurosis, the uncanny return in dreams to the situation causing the initial fright, leads Freud

Figure C.5. One of Santa's reindeers has collided with a high-speed train in Cao Fei's *La Town* (2014). *Source*: Cao, Fei, dir. *La Town*. 2014; Digital file courtesy of the artist.

away from the singular reign of the pleasure principle to hypothesize the destructive death drive.

La Town's relationship to the death drive is revealed in the film's epigraph: "Everyone has heard the myth of *La Town*. The story first appeared in Europe, but after traveling through a space-time wormhole, reappeared in Asia and Southeast Asia. It was last seen near the ocean bordering the Eurasian tectonic plate, vanishing in its midst as if a mirage." This story—moving asynchronously across the globe, shifting, reemerging, submerging—is that of the death drive: the cycles of brutality unleashed on the world by neoliberal globalization. The mythic quality of *La Town*'s story also bespeaks the illusive, shadowy properties of the death drive: as if the reason for human self-destruction lay beyond reach, as if humanity couldn't imagine its own accountability. By its very title, *La Town*, an any place whatsoever without regional or national specificity at the crossroads of different languages, suggests that the film's tale won't be a singular one. *La Town*, with its grocery store advertising sausages in German, its movie theater playing an American film (Victor Fleming's 1939 *Gone with the Wind*), and its remnants of a Chinese technology industrial park is both everywhere and nowhere. Or, as the skeleton of a McDonald's insinuates, *La Town* is the kind of anywhere produced by the flattening force of globalization. *La Town* is all towns today or tomorrow (figure C.6).

Figure C.6. Like nearly anywhere in today's globalized world, La Town had a McDonald's. *Source*: Cao, Fei, dir. *La Town*. 2014; Digital file courtesy of the artist.

However, the epigraph—authored by an avatar of the artist, "Cao Fei (Archeologists of Future, 2046)"—writes of *La Town* in the past tense. Its story has been both "heard" and "seen." The tale of *La Town*'s fate cannot be separated from its spectacle. In fact, *La Town* may be no more than spectacle: a familiar spectacle, giving a sense of déjà vu. "Everyone" recognizes it; though, each person may recognize something different. In considering *La Town*'s myth, Roland Barthes would caution that "there is no fixity in mythical concepts: they can come into being, alter, disintegrate, disappear completely. And it is precisely because they are historical that history can very easily suppress them."[29] In *La Town*'s last frames, papery human figures fall through the sky. For viewers of the right age and national origin, this spectacle of the world collapsing cannot help but conjure up other images of falling men from America's not-so-distant history. Perhaps other viewers would be reminded of something different or of nothing at all.

If there's an element of whimsical hope in *La Town*, it exists in the images of its citizens carrying on, surviving in the aftermath of disaster. The portraits of survival in certain shots making up *La Town* can even be understood as belonging to a mode of human love. The voice-over narration of Cao Fei's *La Town*, adapted from Marguerite Duras's screenplay for Alain Resnais's 1959 film *Hiroshima, mon amour*, also suggests love as a means of surviving trauma. *Hiroshima, mon amour*, after all, begins with a series of dissolves, each shot featuring lovers' entangled arms in the film's three primary temporal and spatial locations (Nevers 1945, Hiroshima 1945, and Hiroshima in the mid-1950s) such that the lovers, the locations, and their traumatic histories speak together. The *Hiroshima* intertext also presents another level of dialogue between *La Town* and cinematic and global history. The opening lines of *Hiroshima*, with their syntactical spareness, a melancholic call and response—"You saw nothing in Hiroshima. Nothing." "I saw everything"—are mimicked in the opening lines of La Town: "You saw nothing in La Town." "I saw everything." However, if *Hiroshima*'s first sequences try to imagine a post-nuclear afterlife for the modern city, *La Town* gives the viewer the postmortem of the postmodern globalized city. By the time of La Town, the modern city has already passed away.

Resnais's and Cao's films—with their visions of modern and postmodern urban spaces—question institutions devoted to memorialization. The female speakers insist on the multiple trips they have taken to those museums commemorating the cities' traumas: "Four times at the museum," says Emmanuelle Riva twice in *Hiroshima*'s voice-over; "four times at the late-night museum in La Town," says Céline Allemand twice in *La Town*'s voice-over. With the second utterance of the line, *La Town* shows a dark open space with a large projection of South Korean pop star Psy's 2012 "Gangnam Style" music video in the background. The shadows of museumgoers stand before it, their bodies contorted as if in mid-dance. By placing the memorialization of *La Town*'s mysterious tragedy in the dark rooms of the "late-night museum" and making it as much nostalgic disco as history lesson, Cao Fei, like Resnais before her, levels a sharp critique at the way in which cities and nations communicate the sanctioned version of traumatic events. In these museums, visitors see "everything" but are left with an understanding of "nothing." In the case of the unlit "late-night museum" in *La Town*, seeing is not even guaranteed. The visitors walk around, and the museums offer explanations ("for lack of anything else") as well as exhibits of what remains: in the case of Hiroshima, the fallen hair of radiation victims, in the case of La Town, a life-size model of the high-speed train crash complete with Santa, sleigh, and slaughtered reindeer.

I have already sketched some of the treatments of the train in film history; here, Cao Fei places her vehicular apparatus within a museum, an apparatus of memory. She comments on both physical (within the museum building) and virtual (projected on the screen) archives of memory. The trio of apparatus—train, museum, cinema—in *La Town* and its relationship to traumatic history, as well as Cao Fei's titular nod to Alain Resnais in her 2013 video *Haze and Fog*, necessitates a retreat to Resnais's *Night and Fog* (*Nuit et brouillard*), the 1955 documentary-cum-city symphony of Nazi death camps: with their own hospital, red-light and residential districts, and, yes, even a prison (within a prison). We have withdrawn here at night on Cao Fei's museumified train and on Resnais's death train; in the daytime, in the absence of a real train, we float above the tracks and think of the dead (figure C.7).

How do we remember without being trauma tourists? How do we manage the ways in which historical violence echoes and morphs into the contemporary and future world? This book has responded to these questions by examining the form that feminist affect takes as remnants of refusal to the repression of national trauma. I have augured that the melancholy, ambivalence, and exhaustion in works by Marguerite Duras, Wang Anyi, Jean-Luc Godard, Jia Zhangke, Nathalie Sarraute, and Chen Ran allow us to recognize the gaps between past and present, the violence wrought by both national trauma and the rise of neoliberal globalization.

Figure C.7. Floating over the train tracks with the dead in Alain Resnais's *Nuit et brouillard* (1956). *Source*: Resnais, Alain, dir. *Night and Fog* (*Nuit et brouillard*). 1955; New York: Criterion Collection, 2016. Blue-ray Disc.

As we move toward a further globalized future, a world in which all the world's major cities risk becoming like that depicted in Cao Fei's *La Town*, we must continue to question the flattening force of capitalist expansion and listen for the murmur of ghost trains, which continually return and refuse to be forgotten.

Notes

Introduction

1. Tang's film came out soon after Hong Kong filmmaker Stanley Kwan's *Lan Yu* (藍宇), which also tangentially treats the events of June Fourth.

2. Margaret Hillenbrand convincingly argues that public secrecy continues to contribute to the silences around controversial episodes in Chinese history. See Margaret Hillenbrand, *Negative Exposures: Knowing What Not to Know in Contemporary China* (Durham, NC: Duke University Press, 2020).

3. Sigmund Freud, "Mourning and Melancholia" in *The Standard Edition of the Complete Psychological Works of Sigmund Freud*, vol. 14, *1914–1916: On the History of the Psycho Analytic Movement, Papers on Metapsychology, and Other Works* (London: Hogarth Press, 1964), 253.

4. Shoshana Felman and Dori Laub, for example, consider the historical trauma of the Second World War: "The watershed of our times and . . . not as an event encapsulated in the past, but as a history which is essentially *not over*, a history whose repercussions are not simply omnipresent (whether consciously or not) in all our cultural activities, but whose traumatic consequences are still actively *evolving* (Eastern Europe and the Gulf War are two obvious examples) in today's political, historical, cultural and artistic scene." See Shoshana Felman and Dori Laub, *Testimony: Crises of Witnessing in Literature, Psychoanalysis, and History* (New York: Routledge, 1991), xiv.

5. David Harvey, *A Brief History of Neoliberalism* (Oxford: Oxford University Press, 2007), 2, 9.

6. Wallerstein writes, "Over time the loci of economic activities keep changing. This is due to many factors—ecological exhaustion, the impact of new technology, climate changes, and the socioeconomic consequences of these 'natural' phenomena. Hence some areas 'progress' and others 'regress.' But the fact that particular states change their position in the world-economy, from semiperiphery to core say, or vice versa, does not in itself change the nature of the system. These shifts will be registered for individual states as 'development' or

'regression.' The key factor to note is that within a capitalist world-system, all states cannot 'develop' simultaneously *by definition*, since the system functions by virtue of having unequal core and peripheral regions." See Immanuel Wallerstein, *The Capitalist World-Economy* (Cambridge: Cambridge University Press, 1979), 60–61.

7. Giorgio Agamben, *Remnants of Auschwitz: The Witness and the Archive*, trans. Daniel Heller-Roazen, rev. ed. (New York: Zone Books, 2002), 133–34. Emphasis in the original.

8. Agamben, 120.

9. Agamben, 39.

10. My emphasis on affective forms in literature and film also distances my approach from what Yomi Braester terms bearing witness *against* history, which he defines as "*bearing witness against testimony itself*" (emphasis in the original). Braester argues that "a preponderance of authors have stated or implied that writing can neither reconstitute historical evidence nor demonstrate the significance of events within a larger historical order of things. Moreover, in claiming that writing is divorced from 'history' (understood as the sign of reality, progress, and national destiny), the authors challenge their own capacity to bear witness." See Yomi Braester, *Witness Against History: Literature, Film, and Public Discourse in Twentieth-Century China* (Stanford: Stanford University Press, 2003), ix–x.

11. Jacques Derrida, *Specters of Marx: The State of the Debt, the Work of Mourning and the New International*, Routledge Classics (New York: Routledge, 2006).

12. Michel Foucault stresses that France only truly adopted neoliberal policies in 1972 through the work of Finance Minister Giscard d'Estaing. David Harvey, meanwhile, marks the beginning of China's path to neoliberalism with Deng Xiaoping's implementation of economic reforms in 1978. See Michel Foucault, *The Birth of Biopolitics: Lectures at the Collège de France, 1978–1979* (New York: Picador, 2010), 200; Harvey, *A Brief History of Neoliberalism*, 9.

13. Although Chinese leaders like Hu Jintao and most recently Xi Jinping have marshaled the promise of a New Era (*xinshiqi*) in their political rhetoric, the term "New Era" is commonly applied to the post-Mao era of sociopolitical reforms and avant-garde cultural practices in 1980s China. Xudong Zhang offers the following origin for the term "post–New Era" in reference to Chinese 1990s: "In terms of the minute chronology of terminologies, the circulation of 'post-modernism' is inseparable from the other, more historical marker, namely 'post–New Era' (*hou xinshiqi*). Coined by the literary critic Zhang Yiwu, a controversial, productive, and at times crude and superficial theoretician of Chinese postmodernism, 'post–New Era' is a defiant term that marks the ideological, intellectual and, in terms of taste, habit, and behavior, cultural break from the New Era and its high modernist-humanist discursive mainstream and hegemony." See Xudong Zhang, *Postsocialism and Cultural Politics: China in the Last Decade of the Twentieth Century*, Illustrated ed. (Durham, NC: Duke University Press, 2008), 171.

14. Emily Apter, *Against World Literature: On the Politics of Untranslatability* (London: Verso, 2013), 21.

15. Zhang Zhen, ed., *The Urban Generation: Chinese Cinema and Society at the Turn of the Twenty-First Century* (Durham, NC: Duke University Press, 2007).

16. In her book on Sino-French cinemas, Michelle E. Bloom comments on how the trope of imitation in Tang's film functions as social critique, since most of the characters do not have the possibility to travel abroad. She writes of the classroom language pedagogy sequence, "The reproduction of France in *Conjugation* centers on the teaching and learning of French in China, which makes sense since language pedagogy, like first-language acquisition, entails imitation." And, of the classroom sequence featuring slides of Paris, she comments, "Instead of bringing Paris to life, the images render the city inert. . . . Although two women are in the café, no tourists are seen visiting the Arc de Triomphe and no shoppers frequent the store, which is populated only by headless mannequins in its window. Paris, and by extension France, is reduced to a national monument and two other stereotypically French public spaces: the café, a quintessentially French establishment, and the store, which conjures up the reputation for fashion." See Michelle E. Bloom, *Contemporary Sino-French Cinemas: Absent Fathers, Banned Books, and Red Balloons* (Honolulu: University of Hawaii Press, 2016), 166, 170.

17. Dai Jinhua, "Invisible Writing: The Politics of Mass Culture in the 1990s," *Cinema and Desire: Feminist Marxism and Cultural Politics in the Work of Dai Jinhua*, eds. Jing Wang and Tani E. Barlow (London: Verso, 2002), 215.

18. Bloom, *Contemporary Sino-French Cinemas*, 4.

19. Bloom, 161.

20. Bloom, 24.

21. Yingde Zhang, "La Francophonie Chinoise d'aujourd'hui et l'héritage Du Général Tcheng Ki-Tong," in *Traits Chinois/Lignes Francophones*, eds. Rosalind Silvester and Guillaume Thouroude (Quebec: University of Montreal Press, 2012), 28. Unless otherwise noted, all translations from the French and Chinese in this book are my own.

22. Zhang, 40. Zhang makes this claim because it wouldn't be until the rise of the New Culture Movement (1917–1923) that Chinese writers would relinquish Classical Chinese for the vernacular language. The vernacular quickly became a signifier of modern Chinese literary form.

23. Zhang, 38.

24. Just to take one example, a recent essay by Yuqing Yang treats the French director Jean-Jacques Annaud's 2015 adaptation of Jiang Rong's 2004 novel *Wolf Totem* (狼圖騰; *Lang Tuteng*). See Yuqing Yang, "Cross-Cultural Transactions in the Film Adaptation of Wolf Totem," *Journal of Chinese Cinemas* 14, no. 3 (November 2020): 242–58, https://doi.org/10.1080/17508061.2020.1839245.

25. Shuangyi Li, *Proust, China and Intertextual Engagement: Translation and Transcultural Dialogue* (Singapore: Palgrave Macmillan, 2017), 9.

26. Li, 139.

27. Li gives the following explanation of his choice of the label Franco-Chinese (as opposed to Sino-French): "My choice is a pragmatic rather than political one: 'Franco-' is a shorthand for 'France' as well as 'francophone,' 'Chinese' evokes the writer-artists' ethnicity, cultural origin, and personal ties to mainland China. 'Sino-French' would work less well, the evocation of the sinophone through 'Sino-' is beyond the scope of this study, and this designation may well include native French writers and artists who are interested in China and the sinophone world." See Shuangyi Li, *Travel, Translation and Transmedia Aesthetics: Franco-Chinese Literature and Visual Arts in a Global Age* (Singapore: Palgrave Macmillan, 2022), 17.

28. Li, 8.

29. Worthy of mention is Subha Xavier's *The Migrant Text: Making and Marketing a Global French Literature*, which further expands modes of comparison beyond the Sino-French in her study of French literature by immigrants from China, Haiti, Iraq, Poland, Algeria, and Cameroon published in France and Canada. See Subha Xavier, *The Migrant Text: Making and Marketing a Global French Literature* (Montreal: McGill-Queen's University Press, 2016).

30. Philippe Burrin, *La France à l'heure Allemande: 1940–1944* (Paris: Seuil, 1997), 15.

31. Henry Rousso, *Le Syndrome de Vichy de 1944 à nos jours*, 2nd ed. (Paris: Seuil, 1990), 30.

32. De Gaulle did not serve as president of France from 1944 to 1969. He acted as the provisional president between 1944 and 1946, and then returned as president of the Fifth Republic from 1958 to 1969. From 1946 to 1958, the Fourth Republic saw the presidencies of Vincent Auriol and René Coty.

33. Susan Rubin Suleiman, *Crises of Memory and the Second World War* (Cambridge, MA: Harvard University Press, 2006), 17.

34. Kristin Ross, *Fast Cars, Clean Bodies: Decolonialization and the Reordering of French Culture*, 1st paperback ed. (Cambridge, MA: MIT Press, 1996), 74.

35. Ross, 78.

36. "What is the nature of today's liberal, or, as one says, neo-liberal program? You know that it is identified in two main forms, with different cornerstones and historical contexts. The German form is linked to the Weimar Republic, the crisis of 1929, the development of Nazism, the critique of Nazism, and, finally, post-war reconstruction. The other, American form, is a neo-liberalism defined by reference to the New Deal, the criticism of Roosevelt's policies, and which, especially after the war, is developed and organized against federal interventionism, and then against the aid and other programs of the mainly Democrat administrations of Truman, Kennedy, Johnson, etcetera." See Foucault, *The Birth of Biopolitics*, 78–79.

37. Foucault, 82.

38. Foucault, 85.

39. Foucault, 86.

40. Harvey, *A Brief History of Neoliberalism*, 11, 9.

41. Hillenbrand, *Negative Exposures*, 16–17.

42. Hillenbrand, 9.

43. Hillenbrand, 9.

44. "The prodemocracy demonstrations of 1989 were by far the most extensive outburst of collective dissent in the post-Mao era. According to the government's own figures, demonstrations occurred in each of China's twenty-nine provinces and in eighty-four of its cities. Over two million students from over six hundred institutions of higher learning nationwide participated. In Beijing alone, students from over either different colleges and universities converged on the capital to participate in demonstrations there." See Jonathan Clements and T. David Mason, "Tiananmen Square Thirteen Years after: The Prospects for Civil Unrest in China," *Asian Affairs* 29, no. 3 (Fall 2002): 164.

45. Alan P. L. Liu, "Symbols of Repression at Tiananmen Square, April–June 1989," *Political Psychology* 13, no. 1 (March 1992): 48.

46. Liu, 50.

47. Liu, 57.

48. Liu, 57.

49. A May 4, 1989, student declaration listed the following demands of the government: "Accelerate political and economic reform, guarantee constitutional freedoms, fight corruption, adopt a press law, and allow the establishment of privately-run newspapers." See Andrew J. Natnan, "The Tiananmen Papers," *Foreign Affairs* 80, no. 1 (February 2001): 3.

50. Erin Y. Huang, *Urban Horror: Neoliberal Post-Socialism and the Limits of Visibility* (Durham, NC: Duke University Press, 2020), 17.

51. Huang, 18.

52. Jinhua Dai, *After the Post–Cold War: The Future of Chinese History*, ed. Lisa Rofel (Durham, NC: Duke University Press, 2018), 4–5.

53. Suisheng Zhao, "Deng Xiaoping's Southern Tour: Elite Politics in Post-Tiananmen China," *Asian Survey* 33, no. 8 (August 1993): 746.

54. Steve Hess, "Nail-Houses, Land Rights, and Frames of Injustice on China's Protest Landscape," *Asian Survey* 50, no. 5 (October 2010): 910.

55. Freud, 243.

56. Freud, 249.

57. Freud, 251.

58. Freud, 246.

59. Other scholars have delved into the plausibility of Freud's claims in *Moses and Monotheism*. See Jan Assmann, "Monothéisme et Mémoire: Le Moïse de Freud et La Tradition Biblique," *Annales: Histoire, Sciences Sociales* 54, no. 5 (October 1999): 1011–26; Yosef Hayim Yerushalmi, *Freud's Moses: Judaism Terminable and Interminable* (New Haven, CT: Yale University Press, 1991).

60. There have been various hypotheses as to Freud's choice of topic in *Moses and Monotheism*. "*Moses and Monotheism* was in part Freud's effort to make this, his own 'essential nature' as a Jew, an essence that somehow persisted despite his alienation from the liturgical and ritual practices of Judaism, accessible to the 'science' of psychoanalysis." See Eric L. Santner, "Freud's 'Moses' and the Ethics of Nomotropic Desire," *October* 88 (1999): 14.

61. Cathy Caruth, *Unclaimed Experience: Trauma, Narrative and History* (Baltimore: Johns Hopkins University Press, 1996), 19.

62. Caruth, 15.

63. "It may happen that someone gets away from, apparently unharmed, the spot where he has suffered a shocking accident, for instance a train collision. In the course of the following weeks, however, he develops a series of grave psychical and motor symptoms, which one can ascribe only to his shock or whatever else happened at the time of the accident. He has developed a 'traumatic neurosis.' This appears quite incomprehensible and is therefore a novel fact. The time that elapsed between the accident and the first appearance of the symptoms is called the 'incubation period,' a transparent allusion to the pathology of infectious disease. As an afterthought we observe—in spite of the fundamental differences in the two cases, the problem of the traumatic neurosis and that of Jewish Monotheism—there is a correspondence in one point. It is the feature which one might term *latency*. There are the best grounds for thinking that in the history of the Jewish religion there is a long period—after the breaking away from the Moses religion—during which no trace is to be found of the monotheistic idea, the condemnation of ceremonial and the emphasis on the ethical side. Thus we are prepared for the possibility that the solution of our problem is to be sought in a special psychological situation." See *Moses and Monotheism*, 109–10.

64. For a recent study of how the theory of Abraham and Torok allows for the unearthing of missing bodies in cinema, see Ofer Eliaz, *Cinematic Cryptonymies: The Absent Body in Postwar Film* (Detroit: Wayne State University Press, 2018).

65. As Garrett Stewart writes, "If, beneath the shows of representation, the oscillating materiality of the cinematic mirage generates what can be entertained as modernism's exemplary filmic register, this is because, at a comparable depth, modernist writing also vibrates with the undulant undoing of continuous signification. Narrative cinema as film, literature as denaturalized language: these then are the modernist reductions that affiliate textualities beneath the contest of media." See *Between Film and Screen: Modernism's Photo Synthesis* (Chicago: University of Chicago Press, 2000), 266.

66. Apter, *Against World Literature*, 42–43.

67. Apter, 43–44.

68. A third national term aligning this translation is the United States, as it stands as both the symbol and the very real organizing center of postwar global capital development. However, I won't examine American film or literature

directly, but instead trace the symptomatology of silences that it casts on the texts of France and China. The Chinese and French texts, by contrast, are treated within their own national contexts before they are pulled together so that we can hear how the transnational affects rhyme in translation. In other words, in this book the United States does not speak for itself; I concentrate only on its transnational translation into French and Chinese circumstances. I focus on what the French and Chinese say about the United States and the way in which the United States is cryptically evoked through image, date, and detail.

69. Nicolas Abraham and Maria Torok, *The Wolf Man's Magic Word: A Cryptonymy* (Minneapolis: University of Minnesota Press, 2005), 81.

70. Abraham and Torok, 81.

71. Some of the other ways that transnational cinema becomes important to this book include the deterritorialization of "national" films in global circulation and their projection at international film festivals; the impact one movement of national cinema has on another (e.g., the influence of the French Nouvelle Vague on Chinese sixth-generation filmmakers); the co-production of a film by funding sources located in more than one nation, such as—just to give several examples by one director—the Chinese-French co-production of Lou Ye's (婁燁) 2006 film *Summer Palace* (頤和園; *Yihe yuan*), 2009 film *Spring Fever* (春風沈醉的夜晚; *Chunfeng chenzui de yewan*), or 2011 film *Love and Bruises* (花; *Hua*).

72. Deborah Shaw and Armida De La Garza, "Introducing Transnational Cinemas," *Transnational Cinemas* 1, no. 1 (January 1, 2010): 3, https://doi.org/10.1386/trac.1.1.3/2.

73. They write, "This proliferation of the term 'transnational' as a potentially empty, floating signifier . . . has led some scholars to question whether we can profitably use, or indeed need, the term at all." See Will Higbee and Song Hwee Lim, "Concepts of Transnational Cinema: Towards a Critical Transnationalism in Film Studies," *Transnational Cinemas* 1, no. 1 (January 1, 2010): 10, https://doi.org/10.1386/trac.1.1.7/1.

74. Higbee and Lim, 10.

75. Armida De La Garza, Ruth Doughty, and Deborah Shaw, "From Transnational Cinemas to Transnational Screens," *Transnational Screens* 10, no. 1 (January 2, 2019): i, https://doi.org/10.1080/25785273.2019.1660067.

76. Yet, the place of the national remains central to any real engagement with the transnational. As Song Hwee Lim explains of China in the inaugural issue of *Transnational Screens*, "What is noteworthy about the rise of China vis-à-vis cinema is that it has a decidedly transnational character. China's cinematic and other ambitions are backed by the state but their target is also the nation's chief rival—the US." Lim's insight here—that specific national circumstances might determine a cinema's transnationality—is salient both for this book and for other scholars of transnational cinema. See Song Hwee Lim, "Concepts of Transnational

Cinema Revisited," *Transnational Cinemas* 10, no. 1 (April 2019): 2, https://doi.org/10.1080/25785273.2019.1602334.

77. For further scholarship on Duras's *ciné-romans* and a broader discussion of her relationship with cinema, see Julie Beaulieu and Rosanna Maule, eds., *In the Dark Room: Marguerite Duras and Cinema* (Oxford: Peter Lang A. G., Internationaler Verlag der Wissenschaften, 2009).

78. Marguerite Duras, *Moderato cantabile* (Paris: Minuit, 1958), 22.

79. Nathalie Sarraute, *Tropismes* (Paris: Minuit, 1939).

80. Ran Chen, *A Private Life*, trans. John Howard-Gibbon (New York: Columbia University Press, 2004), 5.

81. For more discussion of this mirror sequence from *A Private Life*, see Lingzhen Wang, *Personal Matters: Women's Autobiographical Practice in Twentieth-Century China* (Stanford: Stanford University Press, 2004), 181–84.

82. For a more sustained discussion of Godardian essay films, see Rick Warner, *Godard and the Essay Film: A Form That Thinks* (Evanston, IL: Northwestern University Press, 2018).

83. As Garrett Stewart explains, "Just as the photograms that we register as continuous film images are in fact incremental textual imprints stripping over themselves from projected frame to frame, so too is the apparent ribbon of syntax a continual overlap of lexigrams and functional blanks." See Stewart, *Between Film and Screen*, 293.

84. Marie-Claire Ropars-Wuilleumier and Kimball Lockhart, "Film Reader of the Text," *Diacritics* 15, no. 1 (1985): 23, https://doi.org/10.2307/464628.

85. Stewart, *Between Film and Screen*, 311.

86. Stewart, 311.

87. As Varda says in a 1988 interview: "As for *cinécriture*, as I've said elsewhere, when you write a musical score, someone else can play it, it's a sign. When an architect draws up a detailed floor plan, anyone can build his house. As for me, there's no way I could write a scenario that someone else could shoot, since the scenario doesn't represent the writing of the film; it doesn't indicate the lighting, or the choice of lens or the speed of a tracking shot or the timing of the actor's lines or their expressions." See Jean Decock and Agnès Varda, "Interview with Varda on *The Vagabond*," in *Agnes Varda: Interviews*, ed. T. Jefferson Kline, repr. ed. (Jackson: University Press of Mississippi, 2015), 144.

88. Denise Riley, *Am I That Name?* (Minneapolis: University of Minnesota Press, 1988), 96.

89. Riley, 97.

90. And, of course, Riley is failing to account for the nonbiologically female.

91. In their introduction, Zhu and Xiao explain that for the book's conception of "feminisms" they privilege (after Dai Jinhua) the Chinese translation of *nüxing zhuyi* 女性主義 (womanism) as opposed to *nüquan zhuyi* 女權主義 (women's rights–isms). They argue that the former is broader and can encompass

the necessary plurality of Chinese feminisms. See Ping Zhu and Hui Faye Xiao, eds., *Feminisms with Chinese Characteristics* (Syracuse, NY: Syracuse University Press, 2021), 1.

92. Zhu and Xiao, 7.

93. Zhu and Xiao, 9.

94. Zhu and Xiao, 13.

95. Zhu and Xiao, 23.

96. Sara Ahmed, *Living a Feminist Life* (Durham, NC: Duke University Press, 2017), 65.

97. Lauren Berlant, *The Female Complaint: The Unfinished Business of Sentimentality in American Culture* (Durham, NC: Duke University Press, 2008), 5.

98. Lauren Berlant, *Cruel Optimism* (Durham, NC: Duke University Press, 2011), 27.

99. Jack Halberstam, *The Queer Art of Failure* (Durham, NC: Duke University Press, 2011), 2.

100. Sianne Ngai, *Our Aesthetic Categories: Zany, Cute, Interesting*, repr. ed. (Cambridge, MA: Harvard University Press, 2015), 29.

101. Amy Villarejo, *Lesbian Rule: Cultural Criticism and the Value of Desire* (Durham, NC: Duke University Press, 2003), 16. Following Deleuze, Villarejo also offers a useful description of the workings of affect vs. emotion in the cinema: "The close-up, as Deleuze notes, produces faciality as the surface for affectivity's disclosure and exploration, while melodrama is a privileged idiom for transcoding social conflict into emotional binarism."

102. It is with my affects—with melancholy, ambivalence, and exhaustion—that I make a fundamental break with the founding theorists of postmodernism and reveal my association with contemporary affect theorists. Eugenie Brinkema's book, *The Forms of the Affects*, begins "Is there any remaining doubt that we are now fully within the Episteme of the Affect? Must one even begin an argument anymore by refuting Fredric Jameson's infamous description of the 'waning of affect' in postmodernity?" See *The Forms of the Affects* (Durham, NC: Duke University Press 2014), xi. What constitutes the "beginning" of postmodernism is disputed; Linda Hutcheon claims it emerged out of "the political, social, and intellectual experience of the 1960s," while Fredric Jameson is more specific, arguing "the economic system and the cultural structure of feeling'—somehow crystallized in the great shock of the crises of 1973 (the oil crisis, the end of the international gold standard, for all intents and purposes the end of the great wave of 'wars of national liberation' and the beginning of the end of traditional communism)." Though, he also suggests what I believe to be true: that it began in the West economically after the Second World War and culturally in the 1960s. However, postmodernism couldn't begin in China until several years after the death of Mao in 1976: economically when it entered its current post-socialist phase in the 1980s, and culturally after the Tiananmen Square Incident in 1989.

As Wang Ning explains, China presents a multiplicity of temporalities: "Premodern, modern, postmodern, and even primitive. In a society such as this, which is subject to contingencies and uneven development, anything can happen at any time; so why not postmodernism? Moreover, postmodernism appears as a mutation, largely different from its original form(s) in the West. So Chinese postmodernity is a consequence of the encounter between Chinese and Western cultures; it encompasses a combination of both foreign and domestic elements." See Linda Hutcheon, *A Poetics of Postmodernism: History, Theory, Fiction* (New York: Routledge, 1988), 8; Fredric Jameson, *Postmodernism, or, the Cultural Logic of Late Capitalism* (Durham, NC: Duke University Press, 1992), xx–xi; Wang Ning, "The Mapping of Chinese Postmodernity," in *Postmodernism and China*, eds. Xudong Zhang and Arif Dirlik (Durham, NC: Duke University Press, 2000), 34–35. My work also takes up the notion that the movement of subjects through urban spaces allows a reading of affective responses to particular historical moments. As F. Hollis Griffin writes, "The representation of the urban is paradigmatic in that it underscores the extent to which modernity is an affective phenomenon in the United States: commerce puts bodies in new relations with one another, in the shadows of structures that place them amid capitalist democracy." See F. Hollis Griffin, *Feeling Normal: Sexuality and Media Criticism in the Digital Age* (Bloomington: Indiana University Press, 2017), 9.

103. Sigmund Freud, "Mourning and Melancholia" in *The Standard Edition of the Complete Psychological Works of Sigmund Freud*, 14:249.

104. Julia Kristeva, *Soleil noir: Dépression et mélancolie* (Paris: Gallimard, 1987), 233–34.

105. Xiaobing Tang, *Chinese Modern: The Heroic and the Quotidian* (Durham, NC: Duke University Press, 2000), 318.

106. Tang, 316.

107. Freud, 14:251.

108. Freud, 14:258.

109. Dai Jinhua, too, points to the years from 2001 to 2008 as signaling a change for China on the global stage: "We can confirm that after 9/11, after the financial tsunami and China's associated rise, the post–Cold War era ended." See Dai, *After the Post–Cold War*, 11.

110. For more on Haizi and an alternative analysis of Tang's use of his poetry in *Conjugation*, see Michael Berry, *A History of Pain: Trauma in Modern Chinese Literature and Film*, repr. ed. (New York: Columbia University Press, 2011), 336.

Chapter 1

1. Marguerite Duras, *The War: A Memoir*, trans. Brey, Barbara, 1st American ed. (New York: Pantheon, 1986), 8. I will be referring to this work using the title of Duras's untranslated text: *La Douleur* (Paris: Éditions P. O. L., 1985).

2. Wang Anyi, *Years of Sadness: Selected Autobiographical Writings of Wang Anyi*, ed. Lingzhen Wang, trans. Mary Ann O'Donnell (Ithaca, NY: Cornell University Press, 2011), 83.

3. An earlier version of this chapter has been published. See Erin Shevaugn Schlumpf, "Historical Melancholy, Feminine Allegory," *differences* 27, no. 3 (2016): 20–44, https://doi.org/10.1215/10407391-3696619.

4. Xiaobing Tang, *Chinese Modern: The Heroic and the Quotidian* (Durham, NC: Duke University Press, 2000), 316. Tang draws the two authors together under the heading of melancholy by first invoking Julia Kristeva's 1987 book *Black Sun: Depression and Melancholia*, in which Kristeva describes Duras's writing as melancholic, "a discourse of blunted pain," see *Soleil noir: Dépression et mélancholie* (Paris: Gallimard, 1987), 234.

5. Walter Benjamin, "Theses on the Philosophy of History" in *Illuminations: Essays and Reflections*, ed. Hannah Arendt, trans. Harry Zohn (New York: Schocken Books, 1969), 256–57.

6. In his reading of Wang Anyi, Ban Wang, likewise, considers her work as historiographic via a complex renegotiation of nostalgia for the pre-revolutionary commodity in post-socialist China. See *Illuminations from the Past: Trauma, Memory, and History in Modern China* (Stanford: Stanford University Press, 2004), 213.

7. Benjamin, "Paris," 40.

8. Benjamin, 110.

9. Trauma gives birth to history, but only in the unconscious repetition of this trauma, its uncanny return, does history truly take shape. The original facts of history, therefore, persist forever beyond reach; what materializes resembles the traumatic impetus, but has misplaced the details of the initial fact. Freud labels forgotten foundational trauma "*historical* truth": "It is specially worthy of note that every memory returning from the forgotten past does so with great force, produces an incomparably strong influence on the mass of mankind and puts forward an irresistible claim to be believed against which all logical objections remain powerless—very much like the *credo quia absurdum* (I believe because it is absurd). This strange characteristic can only be understood by comparison with the delusions in a psychotic case. It has long been recognized that delusions contain a piece of forgotten truth, which had at its return to put up with being distorted and misunderstood, and that the compulsive conviction appertaining to the delusion emanates from this core of truth and spreads to the errors that enshroud it. Such a kernel of truth—which we might call *historical* truth—must also be conceded to the doctrines of the various religions. They are, it is true, imbued with the character of psychotic symptoms, but as mass phenomena they have escaped the curse of isolation." See Sigmund Freud, *The Standard Edition of the Complete Psychological Works of Sigmund Freud*, vol. 23, *1937–1939: Moses and Monotheism; An Outline of Psychoanalysis, and Other Works*, ed. and trans. James Strachey (London: Hogarth Press, 1964), 136–37.

10. Michael Jennings, Introduction to Benjamin, in Walter Benjamin, *The Writer of Modern Life: Essays on Charles Baudelaire*, ed. Michael Jennings, trans. Howard Eiland, Edmund Jephcott, Rodney Livingstone, and Harry Zohn (Cambridge, MA: Harvard University Press, 2006), 14. Michael W. Jennings explains: "Benjamin champions Baudelaire precisely because his work claims a particular historical responsibility: in allowing itself to be marked by the ruptures and aporias of modern life, it reveals the brokenness and falseness of modern experience."

11. Rey Chow, "Walter Benjamin's Love Affair with Death," *New German Critique*, no. 48 (1989): 72, https://doi.org/10.2307/488233.

12. Chow, 72.

13. Chow, 84.

14. Benjamin qtd. in Chow, 86.

15. Chow, 85. Elissa Marder's *Dead Time: Temporal Disorders in the Wake of Modernity (Baudelaire and Flaubert)* (Stanford: Stanford University Press, 2002) also addresses Benjamin's quip about Baudelaire's whore poems by analyzing the function of women's speech in the few poems by Baudelaire in which it occurs: "This systematic muteness renders those rare moments in which women suddenly start speaking all the more striking. For when the woman does speak, it produces a shock. And, even more important, the 'shock' produced by the woman's voice becomes the very subject of the poem" (16).

16. "The nation: dream and reality of the 19th century. It seems to have reached its apogee and its limits with the 1929 crisis and the national-socialist apocalypse. We saw the pillars that constituted the nation collapse: economic homogeneity, historical tradition, linguistic unity. Waged in the name of national values, the Second World War brought an end to the national reality, replacing it with an illusion henceforth maintained for ideological or strictly political ends. Even if national and nationalist rebirths are to be hoped for or feared, the social and philosophical cohesiveness of the nation has reached its limits." See Julia Kristeva, *Les Nouvelles Maladies de l'âme* (Paris: Fayard, 1993), 297.

17. Kristeva, 303.

18. Alice Jardine, "Introduction to Julia Kristeva's 'Women's Time,'" *Signs* 7, no. 1 (1981): 5–12.

19. Kristeva, 298.

20. Emily Apter, "'Women's Time' in Theory," *differences* 21, no. 1 (May 1, 2010): 1–18, https://doi.org/10.1215/10407391-2009-013.

21. Emily Apter, "'Women's Time' in Theory," *differences* 21, no. 1 (May 1, 2010): 9, 16 https://doi.org/10.1215/10407391-2009-013.

22. "Duras gives up narrative conventions of literature after the mid-1950s. Cinema, together with theatre, provides the intertextual and intermedial context from which she takes inspiration when she abandons conventional storytelling. Madeleine Borgomano locates this shift with the novel *Le Square* (1955) in which Duras adopts a dialogue-based written style recalling that of theatre and film

scripts." See Rosanna Maule, "Introduction: Marguerite Duras, *la grande imagière*" in Julie Beaulieu and Rosanna Maule, eds., *In the Dark Room: Marguerite Duras and Cinema*, 1st new ed. (Oxford: Peter Lang A. G, Internationaler Verlag der Wissenschaften, 2009), 27.

23. Alwin Baum, "*Le Ravissement de l'autre*: Subjective Exile and Semiotic Subversion in Duras's *Écriture filmique*" in Beaulieu and Maule, 317–38.

24. As Jane Winston explains in her essay on Duras and her 1977 play *Eden cinéma*: "As far as her relation to feminism is concerned, it clearly has much more to do with concrete conditions of oppression than with essential *feminine* desire. In her view oppressed peoples, including women, are *constructed* as potential revolutionary agents by the concrete conditions of their oppression. Under capitalist (and colonial) patriarchy oppressed peoples and working class women are forced to waste their energies like *Eden*'s mother, trying to get by. As she sees it, oppressed peoples who, like Suzanne on the plain, have not been allowed *into the system at all* have a privileged relation to revolutionary agency. For this reason, she often portrays bourgeois women (and children) as the most likely purveyors of social change. . . . If they [bourgeois women] are proximate to desire and revolutionary disruption, then, that is because desiring is all that they have been permitted to do for two hundred years." See Jane Winston, "Marguerite Duras: Marxism, Feminism, Writing," *Theatre Journal* 47, no. 3 (1995): 365, https://doi.org/10.2307/3208892.

25. The *Manifeste des 121* was a letter signed by 121 French intellectuals calling for De Gaulle's government to acknowledge the Algerian War as a legitimate struggle for independence. The *Manifeste des 343* was a petition for the legalization of abortion spearheaded by Simone de Beauvoir and signed by French women who thereby publicly declared having had abortions.

26. Winston, "Marguerite Duras," 346. My emphasis.

27. Jane Winston, "Forever Feminine: Marguerite Duras and Her French Critics," *New Literary History* 24, no. 2 (1993): 469–70, https://doi.org/10.2307/469416.

28. This second definition of *xiaoshimin* comes from a 2001 interview with Wang Anyi conducted by Liu Jingdong. See Jincong Liu, "'Am I a Feminist?' An Interview with Wang Anyi," in *Feminisms with Chinese Characteristics*, eds. Ping Zhu and Hui Faye Xiao, trans. Ping Zhu (Syracuse, NY: Syracuse University Press, 2021), 211.

29. Anyi Wang, *The Song of Everlasting Sorrow: A Novel of Shanghai*, trans. Michael Berry and Susan Chan Egan (New York: Columbia University Press, 2008). This is a clarification only offered in Michael Berry and Susan Chan Egan's English translation of Wang's *Song*.

30. Wang Anyi 王安憶, Changhenge 長恨歌 (The Song of Everlasting Sorrow) Taibeishi: Maitian Chuban 台北市: 麥田出版 (Taipei: Chuban Press), 1996.

31. It might be noted that Michael Berry and Susan Chan Egan's published English translation of the novel also translates *chou* (愁) as "melancholy."

32. Ping Zhu, "Wang Anyi's New Shanghai: Gender and Labor in Fu Ping," in *Feminisms with Chinese Characteristics*, 221.

33. Zhu, 217.

34. Liu, "'Am I a Feminist?' An Interview with Wang Anyi," 211.

35. Zhu, "Wang Anyi's New Shanghai: Gender and Labor in Fu Ping," 229.

36. Zhu, 234.

37. Liu, "'Am I a Feminist?' An Interview with Wang Anyi," 206.

38. Liu, 212–13.

39. Liu, 213–14.

40. Marguerite Duras and Xavière Gauthier, *Les Parleuses* (Paris: Minuit, 1974), 76.

41. Duras and Gauthier, 58–59.

42. Marguerite Duras, *Moderato cantabile* (Paris: Minuit, 1958), 19.

43. Duras, 27.

44. Duras, 27.

45. Laure Adler, *Marguerite Duras* (Paris: Gallimard, 1998), 493.

46. Duras and Gauthier, *Les Parleuses*, 37. For more on *des blancs* in *Moderato*, see Trista Selous, "The Blanks" in *Critical Essays on Marguerite Duras*, ed. Bettina L. Knapp (New York: G. K. Hall, 1998), 48–87.

47. See, among others, Aliette Armel, *Marguerite Duras et l'autobiographie* (Pantin: Le Castor Astral, 1990); Martin Crowley, *Duras, Writing, and the Ethical: Making the Broken Whole* (Oxford: Clarendon Press, 2000). Andrew Slade, *Lyotard, Beckett, Duras, and the Postmodern Sublime* (New York: Peter Lang, 2007).

48. Duras and Gauthier, *Les Parleuses*, 161.

49. In her short essay on Marguerite Duras's oeuvre and postmodernism, Martine Antle writes: "How does one read the work of Duras in light of postmodern criticism? As we shall see, even if Duras's work does not fully make use of the processes of pastiche and irony typical of the postmodern text, it participates nevertheless in the ending of grand narratives and announces a profound crisis of subjectivity. In particular, Duras deconstructs the mechanisms of power—colonial power, fascism, or masculinity—through a radical requestioning of the social relations of domination." See Martine Antel, "Marguerite Duras," in *Postmodernism: The Key Figures*, eds. Hans Bertens and Joseph Natoli (Malden, MA: Wiley-Blackwell, 2002), 119.

50. However, Durassian exploration of feminine routine reaches its true apex in her films, especially *Nathalie Granger* (1974). This film is shot almost entirely in a domestic interior (of Duras's country house in Neauphle-le-Château) and features two women (Jeanne Moreau and Lucia Bose) discussing the problems posed by an absent child ("Nathalie") as they carry out domestic chores (including a notable long take of the back of Jeanne Moreau washing dishes).

51. Duras and Gauthier, *Les Parleuses*, 1.

52. Julia Kristeva, "The Pain of Sorrow in the Modern World: The Works of Marguerite Duras," trans. Katharine A. Jensen, *PMLA* 102, no. 2 (March 1987): 140.

53. "Our symbolic modes are emptied, petrified, nearly annihilated, as if they were overwhelmed or destroyed by an all too powerful force. At the edge of silence, the word *nothing* emerges, a prudish defense in the face of such incommensurable, internal and external, disorder. Never has a cataclysm been so apocalyptically exorbitant. Never has its representation been relegated to such inadequate symbolic modes. . . . A new rhetoric of the apocalypse-etymologically, *apocalypso* means demonstration, a visual uncovering (*dé-couvrement*), as opposed to *aletheia*, the philosophical unveiling of truth-became necessary to bring the vision of this monstrous nothing, this blinding and silencing monstrosity, into being." See Kristeva, 138–39.

54. Marguerite Duras, *Cahiers de la guerre et autres textes*, eds. Sophie Bogaert and Olivier Corpet (Paris: Folio, 2008), 10.

55. Kristeva, "The Pain of Sorrow in the Modern World," 144.

56. Wang Anyi, "A Woman Writer's Sense of Self" in *Years of Sadness*, 113.

57. Wang Anyi, 114.

58. Wang Anyi, 115.

59. Wang Anyi, 70. Wang writes, "My cohorts and I were a little over ten years old and the 'Four Clean-ups' Movement kept our parents busy. Some went into the factories while others went down to the villages. Those I in the villages might come home once a week or even only once every two weeks. As for factories, well, most were located at the city limits, at Dayangpu for example, far from the heart of the city where we lived. The trip required several bus changes so our parents left home before sunrise and only returned late at night."

60. Wang Anyi, 82. My emphasis.

61. Lingzhen Wang, *Personal Matters: Women's Autobiographical Practice in Twentieth-Century China* (Stanford: Stanford University Press, 2004), 20.

62. Duras, *Moderato cantabile*, 41.

63. Duras, 45.

64. Duras, 16.

65. Duras, 59.

66. Following Liberation, Albert Camus's 1947 *La Peste* provides a more conventional allegory of France under Occupation, by employing a long, extended metaphor: "The curious events that are the subject of this chronicle came to pass in 194–, at Oran" (11). These "curious events" are responses to the anachronistic resurgence of the bubonic plague in a French-Algerian city in the 1940s: a clear metaphor for the unimaginable and devastating power Hitler's Third Reich held in France during this same period. This evil, not believed endemic either to France or to the modern age, nonetheless triumphed and quickly reorganized the practice of everyday life. Camus's plague, likewise, wreaks havoc in Oran, taking the

lives of a growing number of inhabitants, as the city's leadership forbids people to leave. The novel shows how a group of individuals respond to unforeseen and consuming disaster: some live in denial, while others try to turn the events to their advantage, and only a few attempt to fight.

67. Claude Roy, "Madame Bovary Réécrite Par Bela Bartok," *Libération* 1, 1958.

68. Duras, *Moderato cantabile*, 129–30.

69. Duras, 135. Here, Anne's refusal to eat, her vomiting, and her general state of despondency align with Freud's description of melancholia: "The picture of a delusion of (mainly moral) inferiority is completed by sleeplessness and refusal to take nourishment, and—what is psychologically very remarkable—by an overcoming of the instinct which compels every living thing to cling to life." See "Mourning and Melancholia," in *The Standard Edition of the Complete Psychological Works of Sigmund Freud*, vol. 14, *1914–1916, On the History of the Psycho Analytic Movement, Papers on Metapsychology, and Other Works* (London: Hogarth Press, 1964), 246.

70. Duras, *Moderato cantabile*, 140.

71. Duras, 56–57.

72. Duras, 155.

73. I am evoking here the work of Abraham and Torok summarized in my book's introduction. Recall that the analysts theorize that the Wolf Man's suffering is unspeakable and can only be pronounced "provided it is disguised in the synonym of an alloseme, that is, as a *cryptonym.*" See Nicolas Abraham and Maria Torok, *The Wolf Man's Magic Word: A Cryptonymy* (Minneapolis: University of Minnesota Press, 2005), 81.

74. Siegfried Kracauer and Miriam Bratu Hansen, *Theory of Film*, new ed. (Princeton, NJ: Princeton University Press, 1997), 305.

75. Kracauer and Hansen, 306.

76. Wang 王, Changhenge 長恨歌 (The Song of Everlasting Sorrow), 34.

77. Wang 王, 35.

78. Genette on hypertextuality: "Therefore, it is this [type of transtextuality] that I rechristen henceforth *hypertextuality.* By this, I mean every relationship uniting a text B (which I will call *hypertext*) to an earlier text A (which I will call, of course, *hypotext*) on which it grafts itself in a manner other than that of commentary" (13). See Gérard Genette, *Palimpsestes: La Littérature du second dégré* (Paris: Seuil, 1982).

79. Chen Caizhi 陈才智, Zhongguo gudai shici zhongpin shang du congshu: Bai Juyi. Diyiban 中国古典诗词精品赏读丛书: 白居易, 第1版 (Collected Readings of Classical Chinese Poetry: Bai Juyi. Volume 1) Wuzhou: Wuzhou chuanbo chubanshe 五洲: 传播出版社 (Wuzhou: Communication Publishing House), 2017), 27.

80. Chen, Hong 陳鴻. "Changhenge Zhuan" 長恨歌傳 (An Account of The Song of Everlasting Sorrow). In *Gudai Wenyan Duanpian Xiaoshuo Xuan Zhu,*

Chuji 古代文言短篇　說選注, 初集 (Selected Short S-ories from Classical Chinese Literature, Early Works), ed. Baiquan Cheng 柏泉成 Shanghai guji chuban shi 上海古籍出版社 (Shanghai: Ancient Books Publishing House), 1983.

81. Wang 王, Changhenge 長恨歌, 48.

82. Paul W. Kroll, "Nostalgia and History in Mid-Ninth Century Verse: Cheng Yü's Poem on 'The Chin-Yang Gate,'" *T'oung Pao* 89, no. 4 (2003): 287.

83. Dai Jinhua and Judy T. H. Chen, "Imagined Nostalgia," *Boundary 2* 24, no. 3 (1997): 146–47.

84. Dai Jinhua and Chen, 148–49, 157.

85. Wang, *Illuminations from the Past*, 224.

86. Wang, 231.

87. Wang, 230.

88. Wang, 232.

89. Xudong Zhang, *Postsocialism and Cultural Politics: China in the Last Decade of the Twentieth Century* (Durham, NC: Duke University Press, 2008), 199.

90. Xudong Zhang, "Shanghai Image: Critical Iconography, Minor Literature, and the Un-Making of a Modern Chinese Mythology," *New Literary History* 33, no. 1 (Winter 2002): 143.

91. Wang, *Illuminations from the Past*, 102.

92. Wang 王, Changhenge 長恨歌, 19.

93. Wang 王, 22.

94. Wang 王, 22.

95. Stephen R. MacKinnon, "The Role of the Chinese and US Media," *Popular Protest and Political Culture in Modern China* (1992): 207.

96. MacKinnon, 206.

97. Sheldon Hsiao-Peng Lu, *China: Transnational Visuality, Global Postmodernity* (Stanford: Stanford University Press, 2001), 41.

98. Michael Berry, *A History of Pain: Trauma in Modern Chinese Literature and Film*, repr. ed. (New York: Columbia University Press, 2011), 301.

99. Berry, 6.

100. Wang 王, Changhenge 長恨歌, 42.

101. Hung Wu, "Tiananmen Square: A Political History of Monuments," *Representations* 35 (1991): 93.

102. Wang 王, Changhenge 長恨歌, 398.

103. Chen 陈, Zhongguo gudai shici zhongpin shang du congshu 中国古典诗词精品赏读丛书, 28.

104. Wang 王, Changhenge 長恨歌, 397.

105. Wang Anyi, *Years of Sadness*, 78.

106. Wang Anyi, 69–70.

107. Wang Anyi, 105.

108. Wang Anyi, 71.

109. Marguerite Duras, *L'Eden cinéma* (Paris: Folio, 1977), 16.

110. Marguerite Duras, *Un Barrage contre Le Pacifique* (Paris: French and European Publications, 1950), 285.

111. Duras, 122.

112. Duras, 188.

Chapter 2

1. Ross chronicles the coinciding expansion and contraction in French (domestic and imperial) spatial arrangements during these years: "Economists agree that the consolidation of a Fordist regime in France in the decade or so before 1968 . . . the peak decade, that is, of the thirty-year postwar economic boom—was an extraordinary voluntarist and thus wrenching experience. It took place, for instance, at the cost of a relentless dismantling of earlier spatial arrangements, particularly in Paris where the city underwent demolitions and renovations equivalent in scale to those Haussmann oversaw a hundred years earlier. And it transpired in the decade that oversaw the stumbling and final collapse of the French Empire, for the decisive battle of Dien Bien Phu in the spring of 1954, to the first major Algerian uprisings a few months later, to the referendum on African independence in 1958, to the granting of that independence in 1960, all the way. Through to the Evian Accords that officially announced the hard-won independence of Algeria in May 1962." See Kristin Ross, *Fast Cars, Clean Bodies: Decolonization and the Reordering of French Culture* (Cambridge, MA: MIT Press, 1996), 4, 6–7.

2. Ross, 4.

3. Ross, 4.

4. Dominique LeJeune, *La France Dans Des Trente Glorieuses 1945–1974* (Paris: Armand Colin, 2015), 108–9.

5. LeJeune, 112–13.

6. Jinhua Dai, *After the Post–Cold War: The Future of Chinese History*, ed. Lisa Rofel (Durham, NC: Duke University Press, 2018), 4–5.

7. "The *liumang* [hooligan] was celebrated in the work of Wang Shuo as a person who lives at the margin of urban society, plays around (*wan'r*), has sex, gets drunk and listens to rock music. However, under the forces of commercialization that swept over China after Deng Xiaoping's visit to the Southern special economic zones in the summer of 1992—after which a 'socialist market economy . . . quickly mushroomed'—both Wang Shuo's and rock music's appeal declined steadily, and with them the *liumang* generation faded away as well. Being marginal was no longer considered a desirable option. 'Plunging into the ocean' (*xiahai*), a popular metaphor for engaging in private business, and 'linking up with the tracks of the world' (*yu shijie jiegui*) became more popular lifestyle choices." See Joroen de Kloet, "Popular Music and Youth in Urban China: The

Dakou Generation," *China Quarterly*, no. 183, Culture in the Contemporary PRC (September 2005): 612.

8. For a socioeconomic history of the growing divide between China's urban and rural population, see Scott Rozelle and Natalie Hell, *Invisible China: How the Urban-Rural Divide Threatens China's Rise* Chicago: University of Chicago Press, 2020).

9. Dai, *After the Post–Cold War*, 4.

10. Dai, 6.

11. Dai, 5.

12. Sianne Ngai, *Our Aesthetic Categories: Zany, Cute, Interesting*, repr. ed. (Cambridge, MA: Harvard University Press, 2015), 29.

13. Ngai, 23.

14. Sianne Ngai, *Theory of the Gimmick: Aesthetic Judgment and Capitalist Form* (Cambridge, MA: Belknap Press of Harvard University Press, 2020), 23.

15. Rey Chow, *Sentimental Fabulations, Contemporary Chinese Films: Attachment in the Age of Global Visibility* (New York: Columbia University Press, 2007), 13.

16. Chow, 10.

17. Chow borrows from Gilles Deleuze's theorization of visibility: "Visibilities are not forms of objects, nor even forms that would show up under light, but rather forms of luminosity which are created by the light itself and allow a thing or object to exist only as a flash, sparkle, or shimmer." See Gilles Deleuze, *Foucault* (Minneapolis: University of Minnesota Press, 1988), 50, quoted in Chow, 11.

18. Chow, 17–18.

19. Chow, 19. My emphasis.

20. Chow, 23.

21. Elissa Marder, *The Mother in the Age of Mechanical Reproduction: Psychoanalysis, Photography, Deconstruction* (New York: Fordham University Press, 2012), 4.

22. Marder, 6.

23. In a footnote, Klein explains the relationship between part-objects and whole objects: "In dwelling on the infant's fundamental relation to the mother's breast and to the father's penis, and on the ensuing anxiety situations and defenses, I have in mind more than the relations to part-objects. In fact, these part-objects are from the beginning associated in the infant's mind with his mother and father. Day-to-day experiences with his parents, and the unconscious relation which develops to them as inner objects, come increasingly to cluster round these primary part-objects and add to their prominence in the child's unconscious." See Melanie Klein, "Oedipus Complex," in *Love, Guilt and Reparation: And Other Works 1921–1945* (New York: Free Press, 2002), 408.

24. Klein, *Love, Guilt and Reparation*, 408.

25. Klein, 287.

26. Jacqueline Rose, *The Jacqueline Rose Reader* (Durham, NC: Duke University Press, 2011), 63.

27. Rose, 66.

28. Richard Neupert, *A History of the French New Wave Cinema*, 2nd ed. (Madison: University of Wisconsin Press, 2007), 216.

29. Klein, "A Contribution to the Psychogenesis of Manic-Depressive States" (1935), in *Love, Guilt, and Reparation: And Other Works 1921–1945* (New York: Free Press, 2002), 269–70. My emphasis.

30. A longer meditation on the role of ambivalence in psychoanalytic theory goes beyond the constraints of this chapter. However, my reading of Klein synthesizes with much of the central arguments about ambivalence posited by Sigmund Freud and Jacques Lacan: " 'I love you to death' and 'I love you to pieces' are two everyday phrases that perfectly evoke the French psychoanalyst Jacques Lacan's statement from his twentieth seminar that 'analysis reminds us that one knows nothing of love without hate' (1999, p. 91). Perhaps ironically, but not surprisingly, someone who says 'I love you to death' is most often unaware of the hatred implied in such a statement, Ambivalence—or, *hainamoration* (hateloving), the term Lacan preferred—is the cornerstone of psychoanalysis for the very reason that psychoanalysis posits a subject who is fundamentally split by language. Far from being about 'mixed feelings,' as Freud explained the concept in his paper *Totem and Taboo*, ambivalence involved the conflict between two equally strong currents that are 'localised in the subject's mind in a way that they cannot come up against each other' (Freud, 1913, p. 35); when one current is conscious, the other is unconscious. *To have* an unconscious in these terms therefore, is at one and the same time to be ambivalent." See Stephanie Swales and Carol Owens, *Psychoanalysing Ambivalence with Freud and Lacan: On and Off the Couch* (New York: Routledge, 2019), xiv.

31. Marder, *The Mother in the Age of Mechanical Reproduction*, 248–49. My emphasis.

32. Marder, 229–30.

33. Marder, 231.

34. Marder, 235.

35. Garrett Stewart, *Between Film and Screen: Modernism's Photo Synthesis* (Chicago: University of Chicago Press, 2000), 5.

36. Stewart, 4.

37. Stewart, 8, 9, 214.

38. Jean Ma, *Melancholy Drift: Marking Time in Chinese Cinema* (Hong Kong: Hong Kong University Press, 2010), 60. Marder, *The Mother in the Age of Mechanical Reproduction*, 157.

39. Loïc Vadelorge, "Le Grand Paris Sous La Tutelle Des Aménageurs?," in *Une Autre Histoire Des "Trente Glorieuses,"* eds. Céline Pessis, Topçu Sezin, and Christophe Bonneuil (Paris: Découverte, 2013), 119.

40. Jean-Luc Godard and Jean Saint-Geours, *Débat sur la prostitution.* Excerpt from the television program *Zoom* (October 25, 1966).

41. "Godard has adopted a long series of metaphors to designate both the position of the filmmaker in relation to culture and the film industry, and the common workings of sexuality and money: consumerism (*Une femme mariée*), tourism (*Pierrot le fou*), prostitution (*Vivre sa vie, Deux ou trois choses que je sais d'elle*), and, now [with *Sauve qui peut (la vie)*] pornography. Pornography, however, is one of his most successful metaphors: the filmmaker as pornographer, sex and cinema (in our society) as pornographic. Like prostitution, pornography presents a configuration in which sexuality cannot be seen apart from selling it. But pornography as a metaphor has an important advantage over prostitution insofar as it cannot be romanticized. 'Filmmaker as prostitute' has an air of proud martyrdom about it that 'filmmaker as pornographer' does not. Prostitutes as individuals can be romanticized, as Godard has done repeatedly in his films, but, in pornography, as a business and as a fictional form, there are no martyrs or heroines." See Constance Penley, *The Future of an Illusion: Film, Feminism, and Psychoanalysis*, 2nd ed. (Minneapolis: University of Minnesota Press, 1989), 86.

42. Georg Simmel, *Georg Simmel on Individuality and Social Forms*, ed. Donald N. Levine (Chicago: University of Chicago Press, 1971), 122.

43. Simmel, 122.

44. Annie Fourcaut writes, "The population of the *Parisian* region increased by two million people between the census of 1954 and of 1968. . . . According to the famous image, every four minutes a provincial took off for Paris to find a job." See Annie Fourcaut, "Les premiers grands ensembles en région parisienne: Ne pas refaire la banlieue?," *French Historical Studies* 27, no. 1 (Winter 2004): 202.

45. Jeremy Carr, "The More Things Change: Godard in '67," *Film International* 15, no. 4 [82] (2017): 159: "It was, indeed, the role of women—these three specifically but also women in general—that largely informed *Two or Three Things I Know About Her* . . . a portrait of 'Her,' a portrait of the 'Paris region' and a portrait of Vlady's Juliette Jeanson, an emblematic figure of fashionable Parisian femininity."

46. Esso is the international name for ExxonMobil.

47. This is an instance of the free indirect discourse Deleuze makes use of in his cinema books. As Louis-Georges Schwartz writes, "Deleuze's theory of free indirect images revitalizes the study of cinematic subjectivity. Beyond the boundaries of film studies, Deleuzes's theory prepares us to think the ethical and political aspects in an implicit, unelaborated concept that informs contemporary modes of social control—the concert of 'life.'" Louis-Georges Schwartz, "Typewriter: Free Indirect Discourse in Deleuze's 'Cinema,'" *SubStance* 34, no. 3 (2005): 107.

48. This narration also reminds later viewers of Godard's later work, *Allemagne 90 neuf zero* (1991), which treats Berlin after the fall of the Wall.

49. Jean Ma, too, speaks of the relationship of contemporary Chinese-language cinema (specifically that of Hou Hsiao-hsien, Tsai Ming-liang, and

Wong Kar-wai) to uneven temporality and an unknown future: "In this regard contemporary Chinese cinema conveys something fundamental about what it is to exist in the turn of the twenty-first century—to find one's way in an attenuated present unanchored by the past, and before which a vastly different future looms as an unknown quantity. The impact of these directors resides in their mobilization of cinema's capacities to lend visible form to the irregular rhythms of historical transition, its cadences of hesitation, delay, interruption, return. The progressive march of modernity, their films suggest, is experienced at the ground level as an unpredictable drift, winding among past remains." See Jean Ma, *Melancholy Drift*, 7.

50. Corey Kai Nelson Schultz, *Moving Figures: Class and Feeling in the Films of Jia Zhangke* (Edinburgh: Edinburgh University Press, 2018), 2.

51. Michael Berry, *Xiao Wu, Platform, Unknown Pleasures: Jia Zhangke's "Hometown Trilogy"* (New York: Palgrave Macmillan, 2009), 12.

52. Shaoyi Sun and Xun Li, *Lights! Camera! Kaishi!: In-Depth Interviews with China's New Generation of Movie Directors* (Manchester: Eastbridge Books, 2008), 4–5.

53. Michael Berry, *Jia Zhangke's "Hometown Trilogy": Xiao Wu, Platform, Unknown Pleasures*, 2009 ed. (Basingstoke, UK: British Film Institute, 2009), 19.

54. Jason McGrath, "The Independent Cinema of Jia Zhangke: From Postsocialist Realism to Transnational Aesthetic," in *The Urban Generation: Chinese Cinema and Society at the Turn of the Twentieth-First Century*, ed. Zhen Zhang (Durham, NC: Duke University Press, 2007), 82.

55. Michael Berry, *Jia Zhangke on Jia Zhangke*, Sinotheory (Durham, NC: Duke University Press, 2022), 92.

56. Berry, 93.

57. Schultz, *Moving Figures*, 62.

58. Nick Stanley, "Can Art Education Become Reflective Praxis? Reflections on Theme Park Experience," *Visual Arts Research* 28, no. 2 (2002): 95.

59. Stanley, 97.

60. Stanley, 98.

61. See Dudley Andrew, "The Absent Subject of *The World*," *Journal of Chinese Cinemas* 12, no. 1 (2018): 59–73, https://doi.org/10.1080/17508061.20 17.1422896; Philippa Lovatt, "The Spectral Soundscapes of Postsocialist China in the Films of Jia Zhangke," *Screen* 53, no. 4 (Winter 2012): 418–35, https://doi.org/10.1093/screen/hjs034; David Richler, "Cinema, Realism, and the World According to Jia Zhangke," *Revue Canadienne d'Études Cinématographiques / Canadian Journal of Film Studies* 25, no. 2 (2016): 6–38.

62. Chow, *Sentimental Fabulations, Contemporary Chinese Films*, 178–79.

63. Andrew, "The Absent Subject of *The World*," 71.

64. Michelle E. Bloom, *Contemporary Sino-French Cinemas: Absent Fathers, Banned Books, and Red Balloons* (Honolulu: University of Hawaii Press, 2016), 178–79.

65. Schultz, *Moving Figures*, 82–83.

66. Dudley Andrew comments about this sequence: "Before and during their credits, films often signal the way they expect to be viewed. With this in mind, Jia Zhang-ke, a devotee of Bazin's aesthetic of discovery, might seem to privilege the probing camera over the displayed set in those initial shots. However, he immediately shows the need to account for both dimensions in grasping a subject as large as 'the world': the vertical dimension of depth, gradually emerging in time and the horizontal dimension of simultaneous extension. Both dimensions are present when the main title comes up in a signature shot: with the Eiffel Tower rising incongruously in the center of Beijing's dawn skyline, an old man enters in mid-plane from the left—a trash-gleaner, supported by a wooden stick and carrying a heavy sack. When he reaches the center of the frame, he pauses and turns, seeming to stare right at us just as the director's credit appears above the skyline; Jia Zhang-ke is winking at us!" See Andrew, "The Absent Subject of *The World*," 63.

67. Michelle Bloom provides further insight into this sequence from the film: "Qun then explains that she doubts her marital status because her husband left on a boat for France ten years earlier. She further offers that 'people from Wenzhou are attracted to going abroad.' Qun and her husband come from Wenzhou, which is situated in Zhejiang province in Southern China. She recounts that only six of his boatload arrived in France. However, a second shot of the photograph, taken a decade prior to Qun and Taisheng's flirtation, shows Qun's husband in front of Le Président. The photograph ironically shifts the periphery (Belleville, an immigrant, working-class neighborhood in northeastern Paris) toward the center by depicting Le Président, perhaps the most famous, upscale Chinese restaurant in Belleville, located steps from the Belleville metro stop. The neighborhood where the photograph is taken is not the affluent, touristy home of the Eiffel Tower. Situated outside of the city center, the location is nevertheless marked as Paris by the recognizable red 'Métropolitain' sign. The photograph, which portrays Qun's husband as well as the restaurant and metro signs, suggests that he was one of the lucky six, even if it does not adequately explain his long absence and the intervening silence." See Bloom, *Contemporary Sino-French Cinemas*, 182–83.

68. Jia Zhangke explains the origins of the film's Chinese title: "The first time I heard the term *jianghu ernü*, 'the sons and daughters of jianghu,' which is the Chinese title, was when I was shooting *I Wish I Knew* and interviewed the veteran actress Wei Wei. Wei Wei was the star of Fei Mu's masterpiece from the 1940s, *Spring in a Small Town* (*Xiaocheng zhi chun*, 1948). During our conversation, Wei Wei told me that during Fei Mu's later years he was actually planning to shoot a film called *Sons and Daughters of Jianghu*, which was later completed by Zhu Shilin. As soon as I heard that title, I was immediately drawn in because in traditional Chinese relationships the concept of jianghu was built on emotion, loyalty, and fraternity. So you can see that concept expressed throughout Chinese

film and literature, because so much is based on the logic and philosophy of jianghu. People's relationships with one another are built on *qing*, or 'emotion.' This
meant that all of these characters had rich emotional bonds and deep friendships.
So I have always liked this term 'sons and daughters of jianghu,' which like my
previous film *Mountains May Depart* also has a certain classical sensibility to it.
And both of them explore how these classical layers of meaning that had been
with us for so long are now gone." See Berry, *Jia Zhangke on Jia Zhangke*, 136.

69. Berry, *Jia Zhangke's "Hometown Trilogy,"* 152.

70. David Der-Wei Wang, *The Monster That Is History: History, Violence,
and Fictional Writing in Twentieth-Century China* (Berkeley: University of California Press, 2004), 279.

71. Ma, *Melancholy Drift*, 44. Though made in reference to Hou Hsiao-hsien's
A City of Sadness (1989), these comments by Jean Ma resonate with the films
under discussion here: "If history wounds men and women differently, then the
prospect of survival, witnessing, and healing is conditioned by women's exclusion
from the battlefields of historical struggle. The question of agency and passivity
therefore becomes complicated with the shift from the arena of history-making
to the realm of history-writing."

72. Laura Mulvey, "Some Thoughts on Theories of Fetishism in the Context
of Contemporary Culture," *October* 65 (1993): 13, https://doi.org/10.2307/778760.
My emphasis.

73. Mulvey, 13.

74. Deleuze would call the cut between these two images an irrational
cut, because it *"does not form part of either set, one of which has no more an end
than the other has a beginning*: false continuity is such an irrational cut. Thus,
in Godard, the interaction of two images engenders or traces a frontier which
belongs to neither one nor the other." See Gilles Deleuze, *Cinema 2: The Time
Image*, trans. Hugh Timlinson and Robert Galeta (Minneapolis: University of
Minnesota Press, 1989), 181.

75. Geneviève Sellier, "Women in the Nouvelle Vague: The Lost Continent?," in *Reclaiming the Archive: Feminism and Film History*, ed. Vicki Callahan
(Detroit: Wayne State University Press, 2010), 179. Of this new postwar generation
of male filmmakers, Sellier contends: "The Nouvelle Vague emerges as a revolt
of 'Young Turks' against the French 'tradition of quality,' that is, against a mass
culture that 'apes' intellectual culture on behalf of an innovative creative capacity
with no interest in academic rules. It sought instead the legitimacy of a singular
masculine point of view over the communal patriarchal authority that underlay
the cinema as mass culture."

76. Sellier, 180.

77. Sellier, 181.

78. Sellier, 182.

79. André Bazin, "Mort d'Humphrey Bogart," in *Qu'est-Ce Que Le Cinéma? III. Cinéma et Sociologie* (Paris: Éditions du cerf, 1961), 83.

80. For a more complete account of Sellier's argument, see Geneviève Sellier, *Masculine Singular: French New Wave Cinema*, trans. Kristin Ross (Durham, NC: Duke University Press, 2008).

81. Sellier, "Women in the Nouvelle Vague: The Lost Continent?," 182.

82. Kaja Silverman et al., *Speaking about Godard* (New York: New York University Press, 1998), 119.

83. Elisa Adami and Alex Fletcher, " 'To Think the Home in Terms of the Factory': Social Reproduction, Postproduction and Home Movies in Godard and Miéville," *Third Text* 31, no. 1 (2017): 79.

84. Silverman et al., *Speaking about Godard*, 120–21. Silverman goes on to say of Godard's role as author of the film: "Ever since the formation of the Dziga Vertov collective, he had been struggling to divest himself of authorship. 'In order to film in a politically just manner,' he wrote in a text from 1969, '[one must abandon] the notion of the author. . . . [This notion] is completely reactionary.' *Number Two* represents a limit-text in this respect. Godard claims to have 'invented' nothing in it. It was made, as he put it, 'under the influence of [Anne-Marie] Miéville.' The grandmother's long voice-over monologue was taken from Germaine Greer, and Godard for the most part coaxed the actors into creating their own lines. Even what you called the film's 'soft montage' indicates Godard's desire to avoid being the one to produce meaning. In the preface, he pushes this process one step further. First, he turns the 35 mm camera on himself, and in so doing renounces the most definitive attribute of traditional authorship: transcendence. He becomes embodied, localizable and visible. But that by itself would not be enough, since he is still exterior to the video monitor, which, much more emphatically than the workroom, signifies the 'textual frame.' He also shows himself with his video equipment, in what he calls his 'factory,' and is therefore associated with the enunciation. Consequently, he must put himself where his characters are: inside the video image."

85. Silverman et al., 135.

86. For a longer discussion on play (and, in particular, *jeux de mots*) in Godard and Miéville's film, see Stephen Forcer, "Word Games and Space Invaders: Form, Play and Philosophy in Jean-Luc Godard and Anne-Marie Miéville's Numéro Deux (1975)," *Studies in French Cinema* 5, no. 2 (2005): 87–97.

87. Jin Liu, "The Rhetoric of Local Languages as the Marginal: Chinese Underground and Independent Films by Jia Zhangke and Others," *Modern Chinese Literature and Culture* 18, no. 2 (2006): 196: "Jia Zhangke's first approved film, *Shijie* (*The World*, 2004), on migrants' failure to integrate into the seemingly easy-access global culture, continues his hybrid linguistic style of blending Shanxi Mandarin, Henan Mandarin, Wenzhou Wu, Putonghua Mandarin, and even Russian."

88. Ying Xiao, *China in the Mix: Cinema, Sound, and Popular Culture in the Age of Globalization* (Jackson: University Press of Mississippi, 2017), 120.

89. For an excellent discussion of *Platform* and its opening sequence, see also Qi Wang, *Memory, Subjectivity and Independent Chinese Cinema* (Edinburgh: Edinburgh University Press, 2014).

90. Jin Liu, "The Rhetoric of Local Languages as the Marginal: Chinese Underground and Independent Films by Jia Zhangke and Others," *Modern Chinese Literature and Culture* 18, no. 2 (2006): 176. Jin Liu points out that not one of the four protagonists in *Platform* speaks Fengyang Mandarin, and claims that this weakens and renders insincere Jia's portrayal of the provincial and working class.

91. Weijun Zheng et al., "Detraditionalisation and Attitudes to Sex Outside Marriage in China," *Culture, Health & Sexuality* 13, no. 5 (2011): 497–511, https://doi.org/10.1080/13691058.2011.563866.

92. Kin-Yan Szeto, "A Moist Heart: Love, Politics and China's Neoliberal Transition in the Films of Jia Zhangke," *Visual Anthropology* 22, no. 2–3 (March 30, 2009): 95.

93. Shuqin Cui, "Negotiating In-between: On New-Generation Filmmaking and Jia Zhangke's Films," *Modern Chinese Literature and Culture* 18, no. 2 (September 1, 2006): 107–8. She also says more broadly of the global and the local in transnational capitalism: "As the economy booms, China becomes increasingly enmeshed in the networks of transnational capitalism. The global/local interaction can best be viewed from a dialectical perspective: global capitalism both integrates with and contradicts postsocialist localities. China's affiliation with the world system accelerates its market-driven economy, but the central government retains its monopoly on power. Information technology and ecommodity circulation may offer connections to the global village, but the technological revolution distances Chinese people from their local origins and cultural traditions. As globalization weaves a web of relations among nations, it exacerbates difference and economic inequalities within the locality."

94. Qi Wang also writes about the synecdochic relationship between the surfaces of historically shaped city spaces and the faces of these city's inhabitants in the films of Jia Zhangke: "In his discussion of the cinema of Michelangelo Antonioni, Seymour Chatman offers an inspiring insight that the spaces and objects in the mise-en-scène have a metonymic rather than metaphoric relationship to the characters. . . . Not only is Chatman's observation of Antonioni applicable to the relationship between character and environment in the cinema of Jia Zhangke, it is also particularly inspiring for my current discussion of the wall as a revealing surface (or surfacing) of the characters' past. Etymologically, the word 'surface' originated from French in the early seventeenth century, referring to the 'out most boundary of anything' and the fine part just above the 'face.' Here it seems perfectly fitting that we attach to the wall, on top of its metonymical relationship to the character, a synecdochical quality in relation to history—the latter might

be defined as an amount of time and experience that has accumulated and forms a think and deeply structured interior right beneath the surface of the current moment." See Wang, *Memory, Subjectivity and Independent Chinese Cinema*, 106–7.

95. Zhangke Jia 賈樟柯, *The World*, Zeitgeist Films, 2006: the Chinese phrase is 看你往哪兒跑 (Kan ni wang nar pao).

Chapter 3

1. For a longer discussion of theories of exhaustion, see Anna K. Schaffner, *Exhaustion: A History* (New York: Columbia University Press, 2016).

2. Elena Gorfinkel, "Weariness, Waiting: Enduration and Art Cinema's Tired Bodies," *Discourse* 34, no. 2 (2012): 320.

3. Gilles Deleuze, "The Exhausted," trans. Anthony Uhlmann, *SubStance* 24, no. 3 (1995): 3, https://doi.org/10.2307/3685005.

4. Sigmund Freud, "Mourning and Melancholia," in *The Standard Edition of the Complete Psychological Works of Sigmund Freud*, vol. 14, *1914–1916, On the History of the Psycho Analytic Movement, Papers on Metapsychology, and Other Works* (London: Hogarth Press, 1964), 252.

5. Here, too, I will echo Elena Gorfinkel who underlines that the critique leveled by aesthetic exhaustion that she ascribes to certain works of global art cinema is primarily to be found elsewhere than plot: "Both films do far more in their *gestural and aesthetic economies* than in their *narratives* to critique the institution of work itself and its regimes of social utility, placing an emphasis on fatigue as a base-line symptom of survival, the constitutive condition of early twenty-first-century modernity." My emphasis. See Gorfinkel, "Weariness, Waiting," 342.

6. "À Nathalie Sarraute," *La Nuit Sur Un Plateau*, January 7, 1986.

7. "À Nathalie Sarraute."

8. "À Nathalie Sarraute."

9. Of course, other forms of feminist refusal are important to Mona's story; as Gorfinkel suggests of Varda's film, "We can discern an alternative feminist trajectory of nonwork and antiwork in which the labors of social reproduction are jettisoned in the interest of nonproductive time as well as nonreproductive time, of their wasted capital." See Gorfinkel, "Weariness, Waiting," 322.

10. Susan Hayward, "Beyond the Gaze and into *Femme-Filmécriture*: Agnès Varda's *Sans toit ni loi* (1985)," in *French Film: Texts and Contexts*, eds. Susan Hayward and Ginette Vincendeau, 2nd ed. (New York: Routledge, 2000), 270.

11. Hayward, "Beyond the Gaze and into *Femme-Filmécriture*," 276.

12. The characters in the protagonist's name (拗拗) corresponds to the romanization "Niuniu" or "Aoao," and the scholarship on Chen's novel has not settled on one name over the other. I will be using "Niuniu," because it is the romanization privileged in John Howard-Gibbon's English translation of the novel.

See Ran Chen, *A Private Life*, trans. John Howard-Gibbon (New York: Columbia University Press, 2004), 3.

13. Chen 陳, Siren shenghuo 私人生活 (A Private Life), 7.

14. Fiona Johnstone and Kristie Imber, "Introducing the Anti-Portrait," in *Anti-Portraiture: Challenging the Limits of the Portrait*, eds. Fiona Johnstone and Kirstie Imber (London: Bloomsbury Visual Arts, 2021), 15.

15. Gilles Deleuze and Felix Guattari, *A Thousand Plateaus: Capitalism and Schizophrenia*, trans. Brian Massumi (Minneapolis: University of Minnesota Press, 1987), 175.

16. Deleuze and Guattari, 171.

17. As I have written elsewhere, this argument holds for other literature of exhaustion from France following the Second World War and China following the Tiananmen Square Massacre. See Erin Shevaugn Schlumpf, "Exhaustion: In Defiance of Homogeneous Empty Time," *CR: The New Centennial Review* 21, no. 1 (2021): 237–69.

18. Benedict Anderson, *Imagined Communities: Reflections on the Origin and Spread of Nationalism*, rev. ed. (London: Verso, 2006), 25.

19. Anderson, 26.

20. Anderson, 35–36.

21. Harry Harootunian, "Remembering the Historical Present," *Critical Inquiry* 33, no. 3 (March 1, 2007): 486, https://doi.org/10.1086/513523.

22. Julia Kristeva, *Les Nouvelles maladies de l'âme* (Paris: Librairie Artheme Fayard, 1993), 18, 71.

23. "*The Planetarium* contains a number of clues identifying Beauvoir: Germaine Lemaire's association with a review called 'L'ère nouvelle' (The new era)—a transparent variant of *Les Temps modernes*—her collection of male disciples, and the mantilla she sports at one point. . . . But the key issue turns on aesthetics, and Germaine Lemaire is described as Madame Tussaud, the creator of waxwork figures, which have a superficial resemblance to living beings, but which in reality are as artificial as the fake stars in the painted sky of a planetarium. (The Planetarium and Mme Tussaud's are neighbours on London's Marylebone Road.) This artificiality is related to a second element in Nathalie's critique, namely Germaine Lemaire's preoccupation with her own celebrity, portrayed as a constant demand for adulation. This demand presupposes a hierarchal conception of human relations and is the very reverse of the psychology of tropism, which posits the existence of an entirely egalitarian underlying similarity between individuals, however different they otherwise appear to be." See Ann Jefferson, *Nathalie Sarraute: A Life Between* (Princeton, NJ: Princeton University Press, 2020), 237.

24. Nathalie Sarraute, "L'Ère du soupçon: Essais sur le roman," in *Oeuvres Complètes* (Paris: Gallimard, 1996), 1553–54.

25. Sarraute, 1554.

26. Sarraute, 1554.

27. See "Conversation et sous-conversation," in *L'Ère du soupçon*, Sarraute, 1587–1607.

28. Jean-Paul Sartre, "Préface à Portrait d'un Inconnu," in *Oeuvres Complète de Nathalie Sarraute* (Paris: Gallimard, 1996), 39.

29. Curiously, the other authors of so-called anti-novels named by Sartre include Vladimir Nabokov, Evelyn Waugh, and André Gide (at least as pertains to *Les Faux-monnayeurs*). See Sartre, 35.

30. Jefferson, *Nathalie Sarraute*, 223.

31. All but the last essay, "Ce que voient les oiseaux," had been previously published in either *Les Temps modernes* ("De Dostoïevski à Kafka" in 1947 and "L'Ère du soupçon" in 1950) or *La Nouvelle Nouvelle Revue française* (*NNRF*) ("Conversation et sous-conversation" in two parts in 1956), but it wasn't until all four essays appeared together that they provoked a significant critical response.

32. Emphasis in the original. See Stendhal, "Souvenirs d'égostisme," in *Oeuvres Intimes*, ed. Victor Del Litto, vol. 2 (Paris: Gallimard, 1981), 430.

33. Jefferson, *Nathalie Sarraute*, 194.

34. François Dosse, *History of Structuralism: The Sign Sets, 1967–Present*, trans. Deborah Glassman, vol. 2 (Minneapolis: University of Minnesota Press, 1998), 200.

35. Dosse, 2:204.

36. Dosse, 2:201.

37. Dosse, 2:204.

38. Roland Barthes, *Le Degré zéro de l'écriture* (Paris: Seuil, 1953), 11.

39. Barthes, 18.

40. Barthes, 48–49.

41. Sarraute, "L'Ère Du Soupçon: Essais Sur Le Roman," 1582.

42. Jefferson, *Nathalie Sarraute*, 147.

43. "The criterion of paternal nationality was a thinly veiled attempt to purge the profession of Jews, while allowing potential exception for assimilated 'Israelites' who had been established in France from several generations, a number of whom were distinguished lawyers." See Jefferson, 148.

44. Jefferson, 154.

45. This recalls Derrida's writing about Nicolas Abraham and Maria Torok's study of the Wolf Man: "Something like his proper name is what his cryptonyms kept secret. Cryptonomy is said first of his proper name." See Jacques Derrida, "Foreword: *Fors*: The English Words of Nicolas Abraham and Maria Torok," in *The Wolf Man's Magic Word: A Cryptonomy*, trans. Barbara Johnson (Minneapolis: University of Minnesota Press, 1986), xlv.

46. Sarraute, "L'Ère Du Soupçon: Essais Sur Le Roman," 1566.

47. Sarraute, 1557.

48. Sarraute, 1576–77.

49. Hannah Freed-Thall, "'Une Répugnante Complicité': Figuring History in *Le Planétarium*," *Contemporary French and Francophone Studies* 10, no. 2 (2006): 174, https://doi.org/10.1080/17409290600560260.

50. Sarraute, *Le Planétarium*, 7.

51. Sarraute, 8.

52. Sarraute, 9.

53. Sarraute, 11.

54. Sarraute, 11.

55. Sarraute, 12.

56. Sarraute, 15.

57. Sarraute, 16.

58. Sarraute, 16.

59. Sarraute, 19.

60. Freed-Thall, "'Une Répugnante Complicité,'" 177.

61. Sarraute, *Le Planétarium*, 26.

62. Sarraute, 26.

63. Sarraute, 28.

64. Sarraute, 35.

65. Alain Robbe-Grillet, *La Jalousie* (Paris: Minuit, 1957), 27.

66. Marguerite Duras, *Moderato cantabile* (Paris: Minuit, 1958), 22.

67. Sarraute, *Le Planétarium*, 35.

68. Sarraute, 35.

69. Sarraute, 35.

70. Sarraute, 186.

71. Sarraute, 188.

72. Jefferson, *Nathalie Sarraute*, 169.

73. Sarraute, *Le Planétarium*, 251.

74. Jefferson, *Nathalie Sarraute*, 369.

75. Monique Wittig, *The Straight Mind: And Other Essays* (Boston: Beacon Press, 1992), 32.

76. Jefferson, *Nathalie Sarraute*, 369.

77. Annabel L. Kim, *Unbecoming Language: Anti-Identitarian French Feminist Fictions* (Columbus: Ohio State University Press, 2018), 2.

78. Kim, 4.

79. Monique Wittig, "Le Lieu de l'action," *Digraphe* 32 (1984): 69.

80. Wittig, 70.

81. Wittig, 71.

82. Wittig, 71.

83. Wittig, 75.

84. Wittig, 75.

85. Lisa Rofel, *Desiring China: Experiments in Neoliberalism, Sexuality, and Public Culture* (Durham, NC: Duke University Press, 2007).

86. Rofel, 117.

87. Tze-Lan D. Sang, *The Emerging Lesbian Female Same-Sex Desire in Modern China*, Worlds of Desire: The Chicago Series on Sexuality, Gender, and Culture (Chicago: University of Chicago Press, 2003), 168, 174.

88. Sang, 203.

89. Sang follows this comment on Chen's longing for a genderless society with several important provisos: "But that positions her in an uneasy relation to the logic of fixed sex and gender choices in lesbian orientation. It also positions her in an uneasy relation to the logic of transgenderism." See Sang, 206.

90. Wendy Larson, "Women and the Discourse of Desire in Postrevolutionary China: The Awkward Postmodernism of Chen Ran," *Boundary 2* 24, no. 3 (1997): 215, https://doi.org/10.2307/303713.

91. Wendy Larson comments on the characters in Chen Ran's fiction: "The characters, especially the ubiquitous and seemingly autobiographical Ms. Dai Er, are challenged by a confusing and complex sexual identity, incomprehensible and unplumbable psychological sensations that threaten to overwhelm them, a murky but dispassionate past, and the inability to locate a real and conceptual homeland, although they still recall and ponder this concept." See Larson, 207.

92. Ran Chen, "Breaking Open," in *Red Is Not the Only Color: Contemporary Chinese Fiction on Love and Sex between Women, Collected Stories*, ed. Patricia Sieber, trans. Paola Zamperini (Lanham, MD: Rowman and Littlefield, 2001), 50.

93. Chen, 53.

94. Chen, 55.

95. Chen, 51.

96. Chen, 55.

97. Chen, 56.

98. Chen, 70.

99. Chen, 58.

100. Chen, 66–67.

101. Chen, 68.

102. Jinhua Dai, "Rewriting Women: Writing Gender and Cultural Space in the 1980s and 1990s," in *On China's Cultural Transformation*, ed. Keping Yu, vol. 5, *Issues in Contemporary Chinese Thought and Culture* (Leiden: Brill, 2016), 243.

103. Dai, 244.

104. Dai, 245.

105. Dai, 244.

106. Dai, 249.

107. Lingzhen Wang, *Personal Matters: Women's Autobiographical Practice in Twentieth-Century China* (Stanford: Stanford University Press, 2004), 176.

108. Lingzhen Wang points out: "The fact is that the state's construction of private space and self and the market demand for private self-narratives played a significant role in initiating and sustaining the production of women's

autobiographical fiction in the 1990s. At the same time, however, as recent scholarship on consumer culture has forcefully shown, although consumption constitutes the basis of everyday life and cultural activities in a commercialized society, the significations and effects produced by commodified fads . . . are diverse; different meanings are generated at different times, in different places, for different groups or individuals. The process of consumption is never merely one of passive reception; it involves specific negotiations, unpredictable associations, and unavoidable contradictions. . . . A unified social criticism might be hard to perceive in a commercialized society, but that does not mean that resistance has disappeared from everyday life." See Wang, 177–78.

109. Chen 陳, Siren Shenghuo 私人生活, 2.

110. Chen 陳, 3.

111. Chen 陳, 7.

112. Chen 陳, 8.

113. Chen 陳, 13.

114. Chen 陳, 20–21.

115. Chen 陳, 92.

116. Sang, *The Emerging Lesbian*, 210.

117. Chen 陳, Siren Shenghuo 私人生活, 118.

118. Chen 陳, 127.

119. Chen 陳, 165.

120. Chen 陳, 174. In John Howard-Gibbon's translation, "my hometown" (我的家鄉; *Wo de jiaxiang*) is replaced by "Tian'anmen." See Chen Ran, *A Private Life*, trans. John Howard-Gibbon (New York: Columbia University Press, 2004), 170.

121. Chen 陳, 186.

122. Chen 陳, 173.

123. Chen 陳, 188.

124. Chen 陳, 187.

125. Chen 陳, 192.

126. Li Zhang, *Anxious China: Inner Revolution and Politics of Psychotherapy* (Oakland: University of California Press, 2020), 4.

127. Zhang, 5.

128. Chen 陳, Siren Shenghuo 私人生活, 202.

129. As I have written elsewhere, in Ge Fei's 1992 novel, *The Idiot's Poems* (傻瓜的詩篇; *Shagua de shipian*), we also find ourselves with a "mentally ill" protagonist, Doctor Du Yu, in a psychiatric institution. The first chapter of the novella places us at the end of the story. We encounter Du Yu in his quasi-madness, a state to which he succumbs over the course of the novella. In my 2011 interview with Ge Fei, he explained that when we wrote *The Idiot's Poems* he thought of Lu Xun's famous 1918 allegorical short story, "A Madman's Diary" (*Kuangren Riji*), in which only a "madman" perceives his compatriots' cannibalism. In other words, Ge Fei told me, "Crazy people are not necessarily crazy; they simply don't follow the mainstream." See Schlumpf, "Exhaustion," 263–64.

130. Zhang, *Anxious China*, 22.

131. Mila Zuo, "Dull Sex in a Messy Square: Traumatic Boredom in Lou Ye's Summer Palace," *Women & Performance: A Journal of Feminist Theory* 29, no. 2 (2019): 112–13, https://doi.org/10.1080/0740770X.2019.1621606.

132. Zuo, 104.

133. Zuo, 105–6.

134. Chen陳, Siren Shenghuo 私人生活, 212.

135. Chen陳, 212.

136. Chen陳, 209.

137. Chen 陳, 210.

138. Chen 陳, 214.

139. Chen 陳, 68.

140. Chen 陳, 70.

141. Chen 陳, 75. My emphasis.

142. Agnès Varda and Pierre Uytterhoeven, "Agnès Varda from 5 to 7," in *Agnès Varda: Interviews*, ed. and trans. T. Jefferson Kline (Jackson: University Press of Mississippi, 2014), 4.

143. Agnès Varda and Jean Darrigol, "Agnès Varda: Playing with Tarot Cards," in *Agnès Varda: Interviews*, ed. and trans. T. Jefferson Kline (Jackson: University Press of Mississippi, 2014), 150–51.

144. Sandy Flitterman-Lewis, *To Desire Differently*, rev. ed. (New York: Columbia University Press, 1996), 227.

145. Barbara Quart and Agnès Varda, "Agnès Varda: A Conversation," in *Agnès Varda: Interviews*, ed. T. Jefferson Kline (Jackson: University Press of Mississippi, 2014), 127.

146. Hayward, "Beyond the Gaze and into *Femme-Filmécriture*: Agnès Varda's *Sans toit ni loi* (1985)," 276.

147. Agnès Varda and Françoise Wera, "Interview with Agnès Varda," in *Agnès Varda: Interviews*, ed. and trans. T. Jefferson Kline (Jackson: University Press of Mississippi, 2014), 124.

148. Quart and Varda, "Agnès Varda: A Conversation," 129.

149. Quart and Varda, 129.

150. Flitterman-Lewis, *To Desire Differently*, 245.

151. Flitterman-Lewis, 245.

Conclusion

1. Kristin Ross, *May '68 and Its Afterlives* (Chicago: University of Chicago Press, 2004), 3–4.

2. Chris Reynolds, *Memories of May '68: France's Convenient Consensus* (Cardiff: University of Wales Press, 2011), 2.

3. Reynolds, 2.

4. Daniel Cohn-Bendit, *Forget 68: Entretiens avec Stéphane Paoli et Jean Viard* (La Tour d'Aigues: L'Aube, 2009), 10.

5. Ross, *May '68 and Its Afterlives*, 25–26.

6. "During the 2007 electoral campaign, the questions were principally concentrated on an axis: left, right, center. . . . Wasn't there the possibility that a right-wing party—which today calls itself centrist—might move to the left? Posing the problem in 'anti-68' terms permits a recognition by the extreme right—by definition anti-68, for it compares '68 to national destruction—to the right inextricably anti-68, to the innermost UDF [Union for French Democracy]—in other words the clerical bourgeoisie, even the European and the Giscardian—that '68 represents a total fiasco." See Cohn-Bendit, *Forget 68: Entretiens avec Stéphane Paoli et Jean Viard*, 38.

7. Antoine de Baecque, *Godard* (Paris: Grasset, 2010), 380.

8. Jacques Rancière, *La fable cinématographique* (Paris: Points, 2016), 193.

9. I have previously written on Godard and Guo Xiaolu. See Erin Shevaugn Schlumpf, "Intermediality, Translation, Comparative Literature, and World Literature," *CLCWeb: Comparative Literature and Culture* 13, no. 3 (2011).

10. Nicolas Crousse and Guo Xiaolu (郭小橹), "Xiaolu Guo répond à Godard," *Le Soir*, October 15, 2009.

11. Kate Merkel-Hess, "Introduction: China in 2008: Reflections on a Year of Great Significance," in *China in 2008: A Year of Great Significance*, eds. Jeffrey N. Wasserstrom et al. (Lanham, MD: Rowman and Littlefield, 2009), 10.

12. "The utility of the Olympics to the Chinese authorities was illustrated by the manner in which the Games were used to distract from and silence criticism of the shoddy construction and deep-rooted corruption revealed in the aftermath of May's devastating earthquake in Sichuan province." Pallavi Aiyar, "China's Olympic Run," in *China in 2008*, 207.

13. Jinhua Dai, *After the Post–Cold War: The Future of Chinese History*, ed. Lisa Rofel (Durham: Duke University Press, 2018), 15.

14. Dai, 14–15.

15. Geremie Barmé, "China's Flat Earth: History and 8 August 2008," *China Quarterly* 197 (March 2009): 64.

16. "Entitled 'The Beautiful Olympics' (*meilide Aolinpike*; 美麗的奧林匹克), the show was divided into two 'acts' of roughly equal length, each containing a number of vignettes. The first act, 'Brilliant civilization' (*canlan wenming*; 燦爛文明), employed three of the 'four great inventions' (*si da faming*; 四大發明) of the pre-modern era as an organizing theme. The second act, 'Glorious age' (*huihuang shidai*; 輝煌時代), reflected the country's present and hopes for the future." See Barmé, 69–70.

17. Barmé, 70–71.

18. Barmé, 71.

19. Haiyan Lee, "It's Right to Party, En Masse," in *China in 2008*, 176–77.

20. Xiaolu Guo, "Writer Xiaolu Guo: Fragments of My Life," *The Independent*, May 10, 2008.

21. Guo.

22. Xiaolu Guo, *A Concise Chinese-English Dictionary for Lovers* (London: Vintage, 2007), 9.

23. Guo, 13.

24. Guo, 325.

25. Ha Jin, *The Writer as Migrant* (Chicago: University of Chicago Press, 2008), 31–32.

26. Jin, 59–60.

27. Guo, *A Concise Chinese-English Dictionary for Lovers*, 195.

28. Guo, 196.

29. Roland Barthes, *Mythologies: The Complete Edition, in a New Translation*, trans. Richard Howard and Annette Lavers (New York: Hill and Wang, 2013), 119.

Bibliography

"À Nathalie Sarraute." *La Nuit Sur Un Plateau*, January 7, 1986.

Abraham, Nicolas, and Maria Torok. *The Wolf Man's Magic Word: A Cryptonymy*. Minneapolis: University of Minnesota Press, 2005.

Adami, Elisa, and Alex Fletcher. " 'To Think the Home in Terms of the Factory': Social Reproduction, Postproduction and Home Movies in Godard and Miéville." *Third Text* 31, no. 1 (2017): 79.

Adler, Laure. *Marguerite Duras*. Paris: Gallimard, 1998.

Agamben, Giorgio. *Remnants of Auschwitz: The Witness and the Archive*. Translated by Daniel Heller-Roazen. Rev. ed. New York: Zone Books, 2002.

Ahmed, Sara. *Living a Feminist Life*. Durham, NC: Duke University Press, 2017.

Aiyar, Pallavi. "China's Olympic Run." In *China in 2008: A Year of Great Significance*, edited by Kate Merkely-Hess, Kenneth L. Pomerance, and Jeffrey N. Wasserstrom. Lanham, MD: Rowman and Littlefield, 2009.

Anderson, Benedict. *Imagined Communities: Reflections on the Origin and Spread of Nationalism*. London: Verso, 2006.

Andrew, Dudley. "The Absent Subject of The World." *Journal of Chinese Cinemas* 12, no. 1 (2018): 59–73. https://doi.org/10.1080/17508061.2017.1422896.

Apter, Emily. *Against World Literature: On the Politics of Untranslatability*. London: Verso, 2013.

———. " 'Women's Time' in Theory." *Differences* 21, no. 1 (May 1, 2010): 1–18. https://doi.org/10.1215/10407391-2009-013.

Armel, Aliette. *Marguerite Duras et l'autobiographie*. Pantin: Le Castor Astral, 1990.

Assmann, Jan. "Monothéisme et Mémoire: Le Moïse de Freud et La Tradition Biblique." *Annales: Histoire, Sciences Sociales* 54e Année, no. 5 (October 1999): 1011–26.

Baecque, Antoine de. *Godard*. Paris: Grasset, 2010.

Barmé, Geremie. "China's Flat Earth: History and 8 August 2008." *China Quarterly* 197 (March 2009).

Barthes, Roland. *Le Degré zéro de l'écriture*. Paris: Seuil, 1953.

———. *Mythologies: The Complete Edition, in a New Translation.* Translated by Richard Howard and Annette Lavers. 2nd ed. Hill and Wang, 2013.

Bazin, André. "Mort d'Humphrey Bogart." In *Qu'est-Ce Que Le Cinéma? III. Cinéma et Sociologie.* Paris: Éditions du cerf, 1961.

Beaulieu, Julie, and Rosanna Maule, eds. *In the Dark Room: Marguerite Duras and Cinema.* 1st new ed. Oxford: Peter Lang A. G., Internationaler Verlag der Wissenschaften, 2009.

Benjamin, Walter. *Illuminations: Essays and Reflections.* Edited by Hannah Arendt. Translated by Harry Zohn. New York: Schocken Books, 1969.

———. *The Writer of Modern Life: Essays on Charles Baudelaire.* Edited by Michael W. Jennings. Translated by Howard Eiland, Edmund Jephcott, Rodney Livingstone, and Harry Zohn. N. ed. Cambridge, MA: Belknap Press of Harvard University Press, 2006.

Berlant, Lauren. *Cruel Optimism.* Durham, NC: Duke University Press, 2011.

———. *The Female Complaint: The Unfinished Business of Sentimentality in American Culture.* Durham, NC: Duke University Press, 2008.

Berry, Michael. *A History of Pain: Trauma in Modern Chinese Literature and Film.* Repr. ed. New York: Columbia University Press, 2011.

———. *Jia Zhangke on Jia Zhangke.* Sinotheory. Durham, NC: Duke University Press, 2022.

———. *Jia Zhangke's "Hometown Trilogy": Xiao Wu, Platform, Unknown Pleasures.* 2009 ed. Basingstoke, UK: British Film Institute, 2009.

Bertens, Hans, and Joseph Natoli, eds. *Postmodernism: The Key Figures.* Malden, MA: Wiley-Blackwell, 2002.

Bloom, Michelle E. *Contemporary Sino-French Cinemas: Absent Fathers, Banned Books, and Red Balloons.* Honolulu: University of Hawaii Press, 2016.

Braester, Yomi. *Witness Against History: Literature, Film, and Public Discourse in Twentieth-Century China.* Stanford: Stanford University Press, 2003.

Brinkema, Eugenie. *The Forms of the Affects.* Durham, NC: Duke University Press, 2014.

Burrin, Philippe. *La France à l'heure Allemande: 1940–1944.* Paris: Seuil, 1997.

Carr, Jeremy. "The More Things Change: Godard in '67." *Film International* 15, no. 4 [82] (2017): 158–63.

Caruth, Cathy. *Unclaimed Experience: Trauma, Narrative and History.* Baltimore: Johns Hopkins University Press, 1996.

Chen, Ran. *A Private Life.* Translated by John Howard-Gibbon. New York: Columbia University Press, 2004.

———. "Breaking Open." In *Red Is Not the Only Color: Contemporary Chinese Fiction on Love and Sex between Women, Collected Stories,* edited by Patricia Sieber, translated by Paola Zamperini, 49–71. Lanham, MD: Rowman and Littlefield, 2001.

Chen, Ran 陳染. Siren Shenghuo 私人生活 (A Private Life). Shanghai: Baihuazhou Wenyi Chubanshe 上海: 百花洲文藝出版社 (Shanghai: Baihuazhou Art and Literature Press), 2015.

Chen, Hong 陳鴻. "Changhenge Zhuan" 長恨歌傳 (An Account of The Song of Everlasting Sorrow). In *Gudai Wenyan Duanpian Xiaoshuo Xuan Zhu, Chuji* 古代文言短篇小說選注, 初集 (Selected Short Stories from Classical Chinese Literature, Early Works), edited by Baiquan Cheng 柏泉成. Shanghai guji chuban shi 上海古籍出版社 (Shanghai: Ancient Books Publishing House), 1983.

Chen, Caizhi 陈才智. Zhongguo gudai shici zhongpin shang du congshu: Bai Juyi. Diyiban. 中国古典诗词精品赏读丛书: 白居易. 第1版. (Collected Readings of Classical Chinese Poetry: Bai Juyi. Volume 1.) Wuzhou: chuanbo chubanshe 五洲: 传播出版社 (Wuzhou: Communication Publishing House), 2017.

Chow, Rey. *Sentimental Fabulations, Contemporary Chinese Films: Attachment in the Age of Global Visibility*. New York: Columbia University Press, 2007.

———. "Walter Benjamin's Love Affair with Death." *New German Critique*, no. 48 (1989): 63–86. https://doi.org/10.2307/488233.

Clements, Jonathan, and T. David Mason. "Tiananmen Square Thirteen Years after: The Prospects for Civil Unrest in China." *Asian Affairs* 29, no. 3 (Fall 2002).

Cohn-Bendit, Daniel. *Forget 68: Entretiens avec Stéphane Paoli et Jean Viard*. La Tour d'Aigues: L'Aube, 2009.

Crowley, Martin. *Duras, Writing, and the Ethical: Making the Broken Whole*. Oxford: New York: Clarendon Press, 2000.

Cui, Shuqin. "Negotiating In-between: On New-Generation Filmmaking and Jia Zhangke's Films." *Modern Chinese Literature and Culture* 18, no. 2 (September 1, 2006): 98–130.

Dai, Jinhua. *After the Post–Cold War: The Future of Chinese History*. Edited by Lisa Rofel. Durham, NC: Duke University Press, 2018.

———. *Cinema and Desire: Feminist Marxism and Cultural Politics in the Work of Dai Jinhua*. Edited by Jing Wang and Tani E. Barlow. 1st printing ed. London: Verso, 2002.

———. "Rewriting Women: Writing Gender and Cultural Space in the 1980s and 1990s." In *On China's Cultural Transformation*, edited by Keping Yu, vol. 5, *Issues in Contemporary Chinese Thought and Culture*. Leiden: Brill, 2016.

Dai Jinhua, and Judy T. H. Chen. "Imagined Nostalgia." *Boundary 2*, no. 3 (1997): 143.

Decock, Jean, and Agnès Varda. "Interview with Varda on the Vagabond." In *Agnes Varda: Interviews*, edited by T. Jefferson Kline. Repr. ed. Jackson: University Press of Mississippi, 2015.

Deleuze, Gilles. "The Exhausted." Translated by Anthony Uhlmann. *SubStance* 24, no. 3 (1995): 3–28. https://doi.org/10.2307/3685005.

———. *The Time-Image*. Translated by Robert Galeta and Hugh Tomlinson. Minneapolis: University of Minnesota Press, 1989.

Deleuze, Gilles, and Felix Guattari. *A Thousand Plateaus: Capitalism and Schizophrenia*. Translated by Brian Massumi. Minneapolis: University of Minnesota Press, 1987.

Derrida, Jacques. "Foreword: Fors: The English Words of Nicolas Abraham and Maria Torok." In *The Wolf Man's Magic Word: A Cryptonomy*, translated by Barbara Johnson. Minneapolis: University of Minnesota Press, 1986.

———. *Specters of Marx: The State of the Debt, the Work of Mourning and the New International*. 1st pub. Routledge Classics. New York: Routledge, 2006.

Doran, Sabine. *The Culture of Yellow: Or the Visual Politics of Late Modernity*. New York: Bloomsbury Academic, 2013.

Dosse, François. *History of Structuralism: The Sign Sets, 1967–Present*. Translated by Deborah Glassman. Vol. 2 of 2. Minneapolis: University of Minnesota Press, 1998.

Duras, Margarite. *Cahiers de la guerre et autres textes*. Edited by Sophie Bogaert and Olivier Corpet. Paris: Folio, 2008.

———. *L'Eden cinéma*. Paris: Folio, 1977.

———. *Moderato cantabile*. Paris: Minuit, 1958.

———. *The War: A Memoir*. Translated by Barbara Brey. 1st American ed. New York: Pantheon, 1986.

———. *Un Barrage contre Le Pacifique*. Paris: French and European Publications, 1950.

Duras, Marguerite, and Xavière Gauthier. *Les Parleuses*. Paris: Minuit, 1974.

———. *Woman to Woman*. Translated by Katharine A. Jensen. Lincoln: University of Nebraska Press, 2004.

Eliaz, Ofer. *Cinematic Cryptonymies: The Absent Body in Postwar Film*. Detroit: Wayne State University Press, 2018.

Felman, Shoshana, and Dori Laub. *Testimony: Crises of Witnessing in Literature, Psychoanalysis, and History*. New York: Routledge, 1991.

Flitterman-Lewis, Sandy. *To Desire Differently*. Rev. ed. New York: Columbia University Press, 1996.

Forcer, Stephen. "Word Games and Space Invaders: Form, Play and Philosophy in Jean-Luc Godard and Anne-Marie Miéville's Numéro Deux (1975)." *Studies in French Cinema* 5, no. 2 (2005): 87–97.

Foucault, Michel. *The Birth of Biopolitics: Lectures at the Collège de France, 1978–1979*. 1st Edition. New York: Picador, 2010.

Freed-Thall, Hannah. "'Une Répugnante Complicité': Figuring History in *Le Planétarium*." *Contemporary French and Francophone Studies* 10, no. 2 (2006): 173–81. https://doi.org/10.1080/17409290600560260.

Freud, Sigmund. *The Standard Edition of the Complete Psychological Works of Sigmund Freud Volume XIV (1914–1916): On the History of the Psycho*

Analytic Movement, Papers on Metapsychology, and Other Works. London: Hogarth Press, 1964.

———. *The Standard Edition of the Complete Psychological Works of Sigmund Freud Volume XXIII (1937–39): Moses and Monotheism, An Outline of Psychoanalysis, and Other Works.* Edited and translated by James Strachey. London: Hogarth Press, 1964.

Garza, Armida De La, Ruth Doughty, and Deborah Shaw. "From Transnational Cinemas to Transnational Screens." *Transnational Screens* 10, no. 1 (January 2, 2019): i–vi. https://doi.org/10.1080/25785273.2019.1660067.

Gorfinkel, Elena. "Weariness, Waiting: Enduration and Art Cinema's Tired Bodies." *Discourse* 34, no. 2 (2012): 311–47.

Griffin, F. Hollis. *Feeling Normal: Sexuality and Media Criticism in the Digital Age.* Bloomington: Indiana University Press, 2017.

Guo, Xiaolu. *A Concise Chinese-English Dictionary for Lovers.* London: Vintage, 2007.

———. "Writer Xiaolu Guo: Fragments of My Life." *The Independent*, May 10, 2008.

Halberstam, Jack. *The Queer Art of Failure.* Durham, NC: Duke University Press, 2011.

Harootunian, Harry. "Remembering the Historical Present." *Critical Inquiry* 33, no. 3 (March 1, 2007): 471–94. https://doi.org/10.1086/513523.

Harvey, David. *A Brief History of Neoliberalism.* Oxford: Oxford University Press, 2007.

Hayward, Susan. "Beyond the Gaze and into Femme-Filmécriture: Agnès Varda's Sans Toi Ni Loi (1985)." In *French Film: Texts and Contexts*, edited by Susan Hayward and Ginette Vincendeau, 2nd ed., 269–80. New York: Routledge, 2000.

Hess, Steve. "Nail-Houses, Land Rights, and Frames of Injustice on China's Protest Landscape." *Asian Survey* 50, no. 5 (October 2010).

Higbee, Will, and Song Hwee Lim. "Concepts of Transnational Cinema: Towards a Critical Transnationalism in Film Studies." *Transnational Cinemas* 1, no. 1 (January 1, 2010): 7–21. https://doi.org/10.1386/trac.1.1.7/1.

Hillenbrand, Margaret. *Negative Exposures: Knowing What Not to Know in Contemporary China.* Durham, NC: Duke University Press, 2020.

Huang, Erin Y. *Urban Horror: Neoliberal Post-Socialism and the Limits of Visibility.* Durham, NC: Duke University Press, 2020.

Hutcheon, Linda. *A Poetics of Postmodernism: History, Theory, Fiction.* New York: Routledge, 1988.

Jardine, Alice. "Introduction to Julia Kristeva's 'Women's Time.'" *Signs* 7, no. 1 (1981): 5–12.

Jefferson, Ann. *Nathalie Sarraute: A Life Between.* Princeton, NJ: Princeton University Press, 2020.

Jia, Zhangke 贾樟柯. *The World.* 2004; New York: Zeitgeist Films, 2006.

Jin, Ha. *The Writer as Migrant*. Chicago: University of Chicago Press, 2008.

Johnstone, Fiona, and Kristie Imber. "Introducing the Anti-Portrait." In *Anti-Portraiture: Challenging the Limits of the Portrait*, edited by Fiona Johnstone and Kirstie Imber. London: Bloomsbury Visual Arts, 2021.

Kim, Annabel L. *Unbecoming Language: Anti-Identitarian French Feminist Fictions*. Columbus: Ohio State University Press, 2018.

Klein, Melanie. *Love, Guilt and Reparation: And Other Works 1921–1945*. New York: Free Press, 2002.

———. "Oedipus Complex." In *Love, Guilt and Reparation: And Other Works 1921–1945*. New York: Free Press, 2002.

Kloet, Joroen de. "Popular Music and Youth in Urban China: The Dakou Generation." *China Quarterly*, no. 183, Culture in the Contemporary PRC (September 2005).

Knapp, Bettina L., ed. *Critical Essays on Marguerite Duras*. New York: London: G. K. Hall, 1998.

Kracauer, Siegfried, and Miriam Bratu Hansen. *Theory of Film*. New ed. Princeton, NJ: Princeton University Press, 1997.

Kristeva, Julia. *Les Nouvelles maladies de l'âme*. Paris: Fayard, 1993.

Kroll, Paul W. "Nostalgia and History in Mid-Ninth-Century Verse: Cheng Yü's Poem on 'The Chin-Yang Gate.'" *T'oung Pao* 89, no. 4 (2003): 286–366.

Larson, Wendy. "Women and the Discourse of Desire in Postrevolutionary China: The Awkward Postmodernism of Chen Ran." *Boundary 2* 24, no. 3 (1997): 201–23. https://doi.org/10.2307/303713.

Lee, Haiyan. "It's Right to Party, En Masse." In *China in 2008: A Year of Great Significance*, edited by Kate Merkely-Hess, Kenneth L. Pomerance, and Jeffrey N. Wasserstrom. Lanham, MD: Rowman and Littlefield, 2009.

LeJeune, Dominique. *La France Des Trente Glorieuses 1945–1974*. Paris: Armand Colin, 2015.

Li, Shuangyi. *Proust, China and Intertextual Engagement: Translation and Transcultural Dialogue*. Singapore: Palgrave Macmillan, 2017.

———. *Travel, Translation and Transmedia Aesthetics: Franco-Chinese Literature and Visual Arts in a Global Age*, 2021 ed. Singapore: Palgrave Macmillan, 2022.

Liu, Alan P. L. "Symbols of Repression at Tiananmen Square, April–June 1989." *Political Psychology* 13, no. 1 (March 1992).

Liu, Jin. "The Rhetoric of Local Languages as the Marginal: Chinese Underground and Independent Films by Jia Zhangke and Others." *Modern Chinese Literature and Culture* 18, no. 2 (2006): 163–205.

Liu, Jindong. "'Am I a Feminist?' An Interview with Wang Anyi." In *Feminisms with Chinese Characteristics*, edited by Ping Zhu and Hui Faye Xiao, translated by Ping Zhu, 205–15. Syracuse, NY: Syracuse University Press, 2021.

Lovatt, Philippa. "The Spectral Soundscapes of Postsocialist China in the Films of Jia Zhangke." *Screen* 53, no. 4 (Winter 2012): 418–35. https://doi.org/10.1093/screen/hjs034.

Lu, Sheldon Hsiao-Peng. *China: Transnational Visuality, Global Postmodernity*. Palo Alto: Stanford University Press, 2001.

Ma, Jean. *Melancholy Drift: Marking Time in Chinese Cinema*. Hong Kong: Hong Kong University Press, 2010.

MacKinnon, Stephen R. "The Role of the Chinese and US Media." *Popular Protest and Political Culture in Modern China*, 1992, 206–14.

Marder, Elissa. *The Mother in the Age of Mechanical Reproduction: Psychoanalysis, Photography, Deconstruction*. New York: Fordham University Press, 2012.

McGrath, Jason. "The Independent Cinema of Jia Zhangke: From Postsocialist Realism to Transnational Aesthetic." In *The Urban Generation: Chinese Cinema and Society at the Turn of the Twentieth-First Century*, edited by Zhen Zhang. Durham, NC: Duke University Press, 2007.

Merkely-Hess, Kate. "Introduction: China in 2008: Reflections on a Year of Great Significance." In *China in 2008: A Year of Great Significance*, edited by Jeffrey N. Wasserstrom, Kenneth L. Pomerance, and Kate Merkely-Hess. Lanham, MD: Rowman and Littlefield, 2009.

Mulvey, Laura. "Some Thoughts on Theories of Fetishism in the Context of Contemporary Culture." *October* 65 (1993): 3–20. https://doi.org/10.2307/778760.

Nathan, Andrew J. "The Tiananmen Papers." *Foreign Affairs* 80, no. 1 (February 2001).

Neupert, Richard. *A History of the French New Wave Cinema*. 2nd ed. Madison: University of Wisconsin Press, 2007.

Ngai, Sianne. *Our Aesthetic Categories: Zany, Cute, Interesting*. Repr. ed. Cambridge, MA: Harvard University Press, 2015.

———. *Theory of the Gimmick: Aesthetic Judgment and Capitalist Form*. Cambridge, MA: Belknap Press of Harvard University Press, 2020.

Penley, Constance. *The Future of an Illusion: Film, Feminism, and Psychoanalysis*. 2nd ed. Minneapolis: University of Minnesota Press, 1989.

Quart, Barbara, and Agnès Varda. "Agnès Varda: A Conversation." In *Agnès Varda: Interviews*, edited by T. Jefferson Kline. Jackson: University Press of Mississippi, 2014.

Rancière, Jacques. *La Fable cinématographique*. Paris: Points, 2016.

Reynolds, Chris. *Memories of May '68: France's Convenient Consensus*. Cardiff: University of Wales Press, 2011.

Richler, David. "Cinema, Realism, and the World According to Jia Zhangke." *Revue Canadienne d'Études Cinématographiques / Canadian Journal of Film Studies* 25, no. 2 (2016): 6–38.

Riley, Denise. *Am I That Name?* Minneapolis: University of Minnesota Press, 1988.

Robbe-Grillet, Alain. *La Jalousie*. Paris: Minuit, 1957.

Rofel, Lisa. *Desiring China: Experiments in Neoliberalism, Sexuality, and Public Culture*. Durham, NC: Duke University Press, 2007.

Ropars-Wuilleumier, Marie-Claire, and Kimball Lockhart. "Film Reader of the Text." *Diacritics* 15, no. 1 (1985): 16. https://doi.org/10.2307/464628.

Rose, Jacqueline. *The Jacqueline Rose Reader*. Durham, NC: Duke University Press, 2011.

Ross, Kristin. *Fast Cars, Clean Bodies: Decolonization and the Reordering of French Culture*. Cambridge, MA: MIT Press, 1996.

———. *May '68 and Its Afterlives*. Chicago: University of Chicago Press, 2004.

Rousso, Henry. *Le Syndrome de Vichy de 1944 à nos jours*. 2nd ed. Paris: Seuil, 1990.

Roy, Claude. "Madame Bovary Réécrite Par Bela Bartok." *Libération* 1, 1958.

Rozelle, Scott, and Natalie Hell. *Invisible China: How the Urban-Rural Divide Threatens China's Rise*. Chicago: University of Chicago Press, 2020.

Sang, Tze-Lan D. *The Emerging Lesbian: Female Same-Sex Desire in Modern China*. Worlds of Desire: The Chicago Series on Sexuality, Gender, and Culture. Chicago: University of Chicago Press, 2003. https://press.uchicago.edu/ucp/books/book/chicago/E/bo3625634.html.

Santner, Eric L. "Freud's 'Moses' and the Ethics of Nomotropic Desire." *October* 88, 1999.

Sarraute, Nathalie. *Le Planétarium*. Paris: Gallimard, 1959.

———. "L'Ère du soupçon: Essais Sur Le Roman." In *Oeuvres Complètes de Nathalie Sarraute*. Paris: Gallimard, 1996.

———. *Tropismes*. Paris: Minuit, 1939.

Sartre, Jean-Paul. "Préface à Portrait d'un inconnu." In *Oeuvres Complète de Nathalie Sarraute*. Paris: Gallimard, 1996.

Schaffner, Anna K. *Exhaustion: A History*. New York: Columbia University Press, 2016.

Schlumpf, Erin Shevaugn. "Exhaustion: In Defiance of Homogeneous Empty Time." *CR: The New Centennial Review* 21, no. 1 (2021): 237–69.

———. "Historical Melancholy, Feminine Allegory." *differences* 27, no. 3 (2016): 20–44. https://doi.org/10.1215/10407391-3696619.

———. "Intermediality, Translation, Comparative Literature, and World Literature." *CLCWeb: Comparative Literature and Culture* 13, no. 3 (2011).

Schultz, Corey Kai Nelson. *Moving Figures: Class and Feeling in the Films of Jia Zhangke*. Edinburgh: Edinburgh University Press, 2018.

Schwartz, Louis-Georges. "Typewriter: Free Indirect Discourse in Deleuze's 'Cinema.'" *SubStance* 34, no. 3 (2005): 107–35.

Sellier, Geneviève. *Masculine Singular: French New Wave Cinema*. Translated by Kristin Ross. Durham, NC: Duke University Press, 2008.

———. "Women in the Nouvelle Vague: The Lost Continent?" In *Reclaiming the Archive: Feminism and Film History*, edited by Vicki Callahan. Detroit: Wayne State University Press, 2010.

Shaw, Deborah, and Armida De La Garza. "Introducing Transnational Cinemas." *Transnational Cinemas* 1, no. 1 (January 1, 2010): 3–6. https://doi.org/10.1386/trac.1.1.3/2.

Silverman, Kaja, Harun Farocki, and Constance Penley. *Speaking about Godard*. New York: New York University Press, 1998.

Simmel, Georg. *Georg Simmel on Individuality and Social Forms*. Edited by Donald N. Levine. Chicago: University of Chicago Press, 1971.

Slade, Andrew. *Lyotard, Beckett, Duras, and the Postmodern Sublime*. New York: Peter Lang, 2007.

Song Hwee Lim. "Concepts of Transnational Cinema Revisited." *Transnational Cinemas* 10, no. 1 (April 2019): 1–12. https://doi.org/10.1080/25785273.2019.1602334.

Stanley, Nick. "Can Art Education Become Reflective Praxis? Reflections on Theme Park Experience." *Visual Arts Research* 28, no. 2 (2002): 94–101.

Stendhal, Gustav. "Souvenirs d'égostisme." In *Oevures Intimes*, edited by Victor Del Litto, vol. 2. Paris: Gallimard, 1981.

Stewart, Garrett. *Between Film and Screen: Modernism's Photo Synthesis*. Chicago: University of Chicago Press, 2000.

Suleiman, Susan Rubin. *Crises of Memory and the Second World War*. Cambridge: Harvard University Press, 2006.

Sun, Shaoyi, and Xun Li. *Lights! Camera! Kaishi!: In-Depth Interviews with China's New Generation of Movie Directors*. Manchester: Eastbridge Books, 2008.

Swales, Stephanie, and Carol Owens. *Psychoanalysing Ambivalence with Freud and Lacan: On and Off the Couch*. New York: Routledge, 2019.

Szeto, Kin-Yan. "A Moist Heart: Love, Politics and China's Neoliberal Transition in the Films of Jia Zhangke." *Visual Anthropology* 22, no. 2–3 (March 30, 2009): 95–107. https://doi.org/10.1080/08949460802623515.

Tang, Xiaobing. *Chinese Modern: The Heroic and the Quotidian*. Durham, NC: Duke University Press, 2000.

———. *Chinese Modern: The Heroic and the Quotidian*. Durham, NC: Duke University Press, 2000.

Vadelorge, Loïc. "Le Grand Paris Sous La Tutelle Des Aménageurs?" In *Une Autre Histoire Des "Trente Glorieuses,"* edited by Céline Pessis, Topçu Sezin, and Christophe Bonneuil. Paris: Éditions la Découverte, 2013.

Varda, Agnès, and Jean Darrigol. "Agnès Varda: Playing with Tarot Cards." In *Agnès Varda: Interviews*, edited and translated by T. Jefferson Kline. Jackson: University Press of Mississippi, 2014.

Varda, Agnès, and Pierre Uytterhoeven. "Agnès Varda from 5 to 7." In *Agnès Varda*, 3–16.

Varda, Agnès, and Françoise Wera. "Interview with Agnès Varda." In *Agnès Varda*, 118–25.

Villarejo, Amy. *Lesbian Rule: Cultural Criticism and the Value of Desire*. Durham, NC: Duke University Press, 2003.

Wallerstein, Immanuel. *The Capitalist World-Economy*. Cambridge: Cambridge University Press, 1979.

Wang, Anyi 王安憶. Changhenge 長恨歌 (The Song of Everlasting Sorry). Taibeishi: Maitian Chuban 台北市: 麥田出版 (Taipei: Chuban Press), 1996.

————. *The Song of Everlasting Sorrow: A Novel of Shanghai.* Translated by Michael Berry and Susan Chan Egan. New York: Columbia University Press, 2008.

————. *Years of Sadness: Selected Autobiographical Writings of Wang Anyi.* Edited by Lingzhen Wang. Translated by Mary Ann O'Donnell. Ithaca, NY: Cornell University, Cornell East Asia Series, 2011.

Wang, Ban. *Illuminations from the Past: Trauma, Memory, and History in Modern China.* Stanford: Stanford University Press, 2004.

Wang, David Der-Wei. *The Monster That Is History: History, Violence, and Fictional Writing in Twentieth-Century China.* Berkeley: University of California Press, 2004.

Wang, Lingzhen. *Personal Matters: Women's Autobiographical Practice in Twentieth-Century China.* Stanford: Stanford University Press, 2004.

Wang, Qi. *Memory, Subjectivity and Independent Chinese Cinema.* Edinburgh: Edinburgh University Press, 2014.

Warner, Rick. *Godard and the Essay Film: A Form That Thinks.* Evanston, IL: Northwestern University Press, 2018.

Weijun Zheng, Xudong Zhou, Chi Zhou, Wei Liu, Lu Li, and Therese Hesketh. "Detraditionalisation and Attitudes to Sex Outside Marriage in China." *Culture, Health & Sexuality* 13, no. 5 (2011): 497. https://doi.org/10.1080/13691058.2011.563866.

Winston, Jane. "Forever Feminine: Marguerite Duras and Her French Critics." *New Literary History* 24, no. 2 (1993): 467–82. https://doi.org/10.2307/469416.

————. "Marguerite Duras: Marxism, Feminism, Writing." *Theatre Journal* 47, no. 3 (1995): 345–65. https://doi.org/10.2307/3208892.

Wittig, Monique. "Le Lieu de l'action." *Digraphe* 32 (1984): 69–75.

————. *The Straight Mind: And Other Essays.* Boston: Beacon Press, 1992.

Wu, Hung. "Tiananmen Square: A Political History of Monuments." *Representations* 35 (1991): 84–117.

Xavier, Subha. *The Migrant Text: Making and Marketing a Global French Literature.* Montreal: McGill–Queen's University Press, 2016.

Xiao, Ying. *China in the Mix: Cinema, Sound, and Popular Culture in the Age of Globalization.* Jackson: University Press of Mississippi, 2017.

Yang, Yuqing. "Cross-Cultural Transactions in the Film Adaptation of Wolf Totem." *Journal of Chinese Cinemas* 14, no. 3 (November 2020): 242–58. https://doi.org/10.1080/17508061.2020.1839245.

Yerushalmi, Yosef Hayim. *Freud's Moses: Judaism Terminable and Interminable.* New Haven, CT: Yale University Press, 1991.

Zhang, Li. *Anxious China: Inner Revolution and Politics of Psychotherapy.* Oakland: University of California Press, 2020.

Zhang, X. "Shanghai Image: Critical Iconography, Minor Literature, and the Un-Making of a Modern Chinese Mythology." *New Literary History*, 2002.

Zhang, Xudong. *Postsocialism and Cultural Politics: China in the Last Decade of the Twentieth Century*. Illustrated ed. Durham, NC: Duke University Press, 2008.

Zhang, Xudong, and Arif Dirlik, eds. *Postmodernism and China*. Durham, NC: Duke University Press, 2000.

Zhang, Yingde. "La Francophonie Chinoise d'aujourd'hui et l'héritage Du Général Tcheng Ki-Tong." In *Traits Chinois/Lignes Francophones*, edited by Rosalind Silvester and Guillaume Thouroude. Quebec: University of Montreal Press, 2012.

Zhao, Suisheng. "Deng Xiaoping's Southern Tour: Elite Politics in Post-Tiananmen China." *Asian Survey* 33, no. 8 (August 1993).

Zhen, Zhang, ed. *The Urban Generation: Chinese Cinema and Society at the Turn of the Twenty-First Century*. Durham, NC: Duke University Press, 2007.

Zhu, Ping. "Wang Anyi's New Shanghai: Gender and Labor in Fu Ping." In *Feminisms with Chinese Characteristics*, edited by Ping Zhu and Hui Faye Xiao, 216–42. Syracuse, NY: Syracuse University Press, 2021.

Zhu, Ping, and Hui Faye Xiao, eds. *Feminisms with Chinese Characteristics*. Syracuse, NY: Syracuse University Press, 2021.

Zuo, Mila. "Dull Sex in a Messy Square: Traumatic Boredom in Lou Ye's Summer Palace." *Women & Performance: A Journal of Feminist Theory* 29, no. 2 (2019): 103–24. https://doi.org/10.1080/0740770X.2019.1621606.

Index

9 798855 802146